U.S. Immigration and Migration
Primary Sources

U.S. Immigration and Migration Primary Sources

James L. Outman

Lawrence W. Baker,
Project Editor

U.X.L
A part of Gale, Cengage Learning

GALE
CENGAGE Learning

Detroit • New York • San Francisco • New Haven, Conn • Waterville, Maine • London

GALE
CENGAGE Learning

U.S. Immigration and Migration: Primary Sources

James L. Outman

Project Editor
Lawrence W. Baker

Editorial
Sarah Hermsen, Diane Sawinski

Permissions
Shalice Shah-Caldwell

Imaging and Multimedia
Dean Dauphinais, Lezlie Light, Mike Logusz

Product Design
Pamela A. E. Galbreath, Kate Scheible

Composition
Evi Seoud

Mansfacturing
Rita Wimberley

LIBRARY OF CONGRESS CATALOGING-IN-PUBLICATION DATA

U.S. immigration and migration. Primary sources / [compiled by] James L. Outman ; Lawrence W. Baker, editor.

p. cm. — ([U.S. immigration and migration reference library])

Includes bibliographical references and index.

ISBN 0-7876-7669-1 (hardcover : alk. paper)

1. United States—Emigration and immigration—History—Sources—Juvenile literature. I. Title: US immigration and migration. Primary sources. II. Outman, James L., 1946–. III. Baker, Lawrence W. IV. Series.

JV6460.U5 2004
325.73—dc22

2004003553

Printed in the United States of America
5 6 7 8 9 10 14 13 12 11 10 09 08

Contents

Reader's Guide

The U.S. Constitution, signed in 1789, gave Congress the right to create laws involving immigration and citizenship. When the first Congress assembled, it created a loose idea of what it meant to be a citizen of the United States: all "free white persons" who had lived in the country for a couple of years were eligible. But the concept of citizenship was still vague. The naturalization process—the set of rules for becoming a citizen—was initially quite simple. The young nation actively sought immigrants to bring their professional skills and labor and to take part in expanding the borders of the nation from the Atlantic Ocean to the Pacific Ocean. There were initially no immigration agencies or border patrols—no passports or green cards. But not everyone was allowed to become a citizen or afforded the same rights. Issues of race for non-whites and Hispanics as well as a historical preference for the northwestern European immigrants led to inequalities and discrimination from the start.

Legislations and policies have continually added to or changed the original vague requirements, rights, and responsibilities of citizenship and immigration. Through the Fourteenth and Fifteenth Amendments after the American Civil War (1861–65), the concept of the "free white persons" eligible to become citizens was amended to include African Americans. Women's citizenship generally was dependent on their husband or father's citizenship until 1920. Until 1943, most Asians were not included in the definition of someone who could become a citizen.

American sentiment toward immigrants has always gone back and forth between positive and negative for a number of reasons. During good economic times when labor is needed, immigrants usually receive better treatment than during economic downturns when people fear the competition for employment. When mass migrations from particular areas begin, there is often hostility in the United States toward the latest group to arrive. They are often perceived as different and as a threat to "American values," leaning more toward Western European traditions. Immigration has almost always been at the center of political controversy in the United States. In fact, the first anti-immigrant government policies began to arise within only a few years of the signing of the Constitution.

Immigration restrictions brought about by nativist (favoring the interests of people who are native-born to a country, though generally not concerning Native Americans, as opposed to its immigrants), racist, or anti-immigrant attitudes have had a very major impact on the U.S. population, dictating who entered the country and in what numbers. The Chinese, for example, were virtually stopped from immigrating by the Chinese Exclusion Act of 1882 until it was repealed in 1943. Many families were separated for decades because of the severity of U.S. restrictions. Immigration from many other countries was significantly reduced by the immigration quota (assigned proportions) systems of 1921 and 1924.

Most immigrants, since the first English settlers landed at Jamestown, have had to pay tremendous dues to settle in North America. There has been a long-held pattern in which the latest arrivals have often been forced to take on the lowest-paying and most undesirable jobs. However, many historians of immigration point out that the brightest and most promising professional prospects of the nations of the world have immigrated to the United States. A daring spirit and the ability to overcome obstacles have always been, and continue to be today, qualities common to the immigrants coming into the nation.

The United States differs from many other countries of the world in having a population made up of people descended from all of the world's nations. Immigration controversy continues to confront the United States in the early twenty-first century, posing difficult questions from concerns about regulating entry and controlling undocumented immigration, to providing public services and a decent education to recently arrived immigrants. In the early years of the twenty-first century, the U.S. Marines intercepted refugees from the civil uprising in Haiti and sent them back to their country, where they feared for their lives. When does the United States provide refuge and what makes the nation deny others who are in need? These concerns are not likely to be resolved in the near future. The value of studying the historical and cultural background of immigration and migration in the nation goes well beyond understanding these difficult issues.

Why study immigration and migration?

As a chronicle of the American people's roots, the history of immigration and migration provides a very intimate approach to the nation's past. Immigration history is strongly centered on the people of the United States rather than the presidential administrations or the wars the nation has fought. Learning about the waves of immigration and migration that populated the continent and seeing the American culture as the mix of many cultures is central to understanding the rich diversity of the United States and appreciating it as a multicultural nation.

U.S. Immigration and Migration: Primary Sources tells the story of U.S. immigration and migration in the words of the people who lived and shaped it. Eighteen documents provide a wide range of perspectives on this period of history. Included are excerpts from French immigrant Hector St. John de Crèvecoeur's 1782 *Letters from an American Farmer,* in which he describes the advantages of being an American; the Chinese Exclusion Act of 1882, which banned Chinese immigrants; *My Antonia,* novelist Willa Cather's depiction of the difficulties experienced by European immigrants in the United States; President Harry S. Truman's veto of the Immigration and Nationality Act of 1952; and *The Death of the West*, conservative commentator Patrick J. Buchanan's laments over the rise in U.S. immigration. Document-specific glossaries provide context to unfamiliar terms on the pages on which they appear.

Each excerpt presented in *U.S. Immigration and Migration: Primary Sources* includes the following additional material:

- An **introduction** places the document and its author in a historical context.
- **"Things to remember while reading ..."** offers readers important background information and directs them to central ideas in the text.
- **"What happened next ..."** provides an account of subsequent events, both in immigration and migration and in the life of the author.
- **"Did you know ..."** provides significant and interesting facts about the document, the author, or the events discussed.
- **"For more information"** lists sources for further reading on the author, the topic, or the document.

U.S. Immigration and Migration: Primary Sources also features sidebars containing interesting facts about people and events related to immigration and migration, over forty photographs, a "U.S. Immigration and Migration Timeline" that lists significant dates and events associated with immigration and migration, and an index.

U.S. Immigration and Migration Reference Library

U.S. Immigration and Migration: Primary Sources is only one component of the three-part U.S. Immigration and Migration Reference Library. The other two titles in this set are:

- *U.S. Immigration and Migration: Almanac* (two volumes) presents a comprehensive overview of the groups of people who have immigrated to the United States from the nations of Africa, Europe, Asia, and Latin America, as well as those who migrated within the country to unexplored lands or to newly industrialized cities. Its seventeen chapters include information on groups or clusters of groups of immigrants from other nations and cultures: Pre-Columbian; Spanish; English; Scotch and Scotch-Irish; French and Dutch; Africans; German; Irish; Scandinavian; Chinese, Japanese, and Filipino; Jewish; Italian and Greek; Eastern European; Arab; Asian Indian, Korean, and Southeast Asian; Mexican; and other Latino and Caribbean groups. Internal migration is also covered, including westward expansion, forced migration, and industrialization and urbanization. The *Almanac* also contains more than 150 black-and-white photographs and maps, "Fact Focus" and "Words to Know" boxes, a "Research and Activity Ideas" section, a timeline, and an index.

- *U.S. Immigration and Migration: Biographies* (two volumes) presents the life stories of fifty individuals who either played key roles in the governmental and societal influences on U.S. immigration and migration or are immigrants who became successful in the United States. Profiled are well-known figures such as German-born physicist Albert Einstein; Scottish-born industrialist Andrew Carnegie; Czech-born Madeleine Albright, the first female U.S. secretary of state; and English-born comedic actor Charlie Chaplin. In addition, lesser-known individuals are featured, such as Kalpana Chawla, the first female astronaut from India; Mexican-born Antonia Hernández, a lawyer and activist for Latino causes; and folk singer Woody Guthrie, whose songs focused on the plight of victims of the Great Depression and the Dust Bowl of the 1930s—migrants who left the Midwest in search of a better life in the West. *Biographies* also contains nearly 130 black-and-white photographs, a timeline, and an index.

- A cumulative index of all three titles in the U.S. Immigration and Migration Reference Library is also available.

Acknowledgments

Thanks to copyeditor and indexer Theresa Murray, proofreader Amy Marcaccio Keyzer, and typesetter Jake Di Vita of the Graphix Group for their fine work. Additional thanks to Julie Burwinkel, media director at Ursuline Academy, Cincinnati, Ohio, and Janet Sarratt, library media specialist at

John E. Ewing Middle School, Gaffney, South Carolina, for their help during the early stages of the project.

Test permissions

Following is a list of the copyright holders who have granted us permission to reproduce excerpts from primary source documents in *U.S. Immigration and Migration: Primary Sources*. Every effort has been made to trace copyright; if omissions have been made, please contact us.

- Buchanan, Patrick J. From an introduction to *The Death of the West: How Dying Populations and Immigrant Invasions Imperil Our Country and Civilization*. Thomas Dunne Books, 2002. Copyright © 2002 by Patrick J. Buchanan. Reprinted by permission of St. Martin's Press, LLC.

- Davis, Marilyn P. From *Mexican Voices, American Dreams: An Oral History of Mexican Immigration to the United States*. Henry Holt and Company, 1990. Copyright © 1990 by Marilyn P. Davis. Reproduced by permission of Henry Holt and Company, LLC.

Comments and suggestions

We welcome your comments on *U.S. Immigration and Migration: Primary Sources* as well as your suggestions for topics to be featured in future editions. Please write to: Editor, *U.S. Immigration and Migration: Primary Sources*, U•X•L, 27500 Drake Road, Farmington Hills, Michigan, 48331-3535; call toll-free: 800-877-4253; fax to 248-414-5043; or send e-mail via http:// www.gale.com.

U.S. Immigration and Migration Timeline

c. 13,000 B.C.E. The first immigrants arrive on the North American continent and gradually migrate in groups throughout North and South America. Neither the timing of the first migrations nor their origins are known.

c. 400 C.E. The Anasazi culture emerges in the Four Corners region of present-day Arizona, New Mexico, Utah, and Colorado. The Anasazi, thought to be the ancestors of the Pueblo, Zuni, and Hopi Indians, were known for their basketry and pottery as well as their elaborate mansions built into high cliff walls.

c. 700 People of the moundbuilding Mississippian culture build the city of Cahokia near present-day East St.

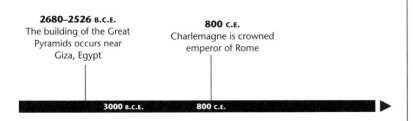

2680–2526 B.C.E.
The building of the Great
Pyramids occurs near
Giza, Egypt

800 C.E.
Charlemagne is crowned
emperor of Rome

3000 B.C.E.   800 C.E.

Louis, Illinois, about five square miles wide, and containing about a hundred mounds situated around central plazas.

1000   Norse explorer Leif Eriksson sets out from Greenland and apparently sails to Vinland, in present-day Newfoundland, Canada.

1492   Navigator Christopher Columbus arrives in the Caribbean while searching for a route to Asia on an expedition for the kingdom of Spain. He returns to Hispaniola (the island which today is home to Haiti and the Dominican Republic) with settlers the following year.

1565   Spanish explorers and settlers establish Saint Augustine, Florida, the oldest permanent European settlement in the United States.

1607   The Jamestown settlers from England arrive in Virginia and establish a colony.

1618–1725   From five to seven thousand Huguenots flee the persecution in France and sail to America to settle in the British colonies.

1619   A Dutch warship brings twenty African slaves to Jamestown, Virginia, the first Africans to arrive in the British colonies.

1620   The Pilgrims and other British colonists aboard the *Mayflower* land in Plymouth Harbor to found a new British colony.

1624   The first wave of Dutch immigrants to New Netherlands arrives in what is now New York. Most settle at Fort Orange, where the city of Albany now stands.

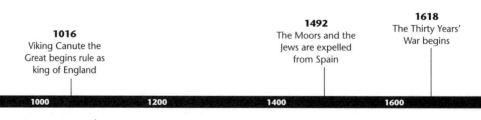

1016
Viking Canute the
Great begins rule as
king of England

1492
The Moors and the
Jews are expelled
from Spain

1618
The Thirty Years'
War begins

1000   1200   1400   1600

1630–40 In the Great Migration from England to New England, about twenty thousand men, women, and children, many of them Puritans, migrate.

1649 An Act Concerning Religion (The Maryland Toleration Act) is issued, allowing the English colony of Maryland to be a refuge for English Catholics who were often persecuted for their beliefs during the English civil war. The act sets the stage for future religious freedoms.

1718 The vast territory of Louisiana becomes a province of France; the European population of the colony numbers about four hundred.

1769 Two Spanish expeditions—one by land and one by sea—leave Mexico to colonize Alta California, the present-day state of California.

1782 French immigrant Hector St. John de Crèvecoeur writes *Letters from an American Farmer,* in which he discusses the advantages of being an American.

1784 The Treaty of Fort Stanwix is enacted; the United States agrees to give Native Americans control of the western territory in an attempt to protect native lands from further takeovers by Europeans. However, European settlers ignore the act and it is never enforced by either the British or the U.S. government.

1790 Congress passes an act providing that "free white persons" who have lived in the United States for at least two years can be naturalized (become citizens) in any U.S. court. Along with non-white males, this also excludes indentured servants, slaves, children, and most women, all of whom are considered dependents.

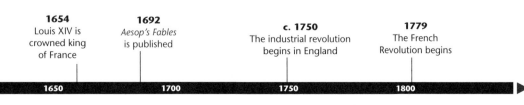

1654
Louis XIV is
crowned king
of France

1692
Aesop's Fables
is published

c. 1750
The industrial revolution
begins in England

1779
The French
Revolution begins

1650   1700   1750   1800

1804 Meriwether Lewis and William Clark set out on their overland trip across the continent to the Pacific Ocean, forging a path never before explored by European Americans.

1808 Congress prohibits the importation of slaves into the United States, but the slave trade continues until the end of the American Civil War in 1865.

1815–45 About one million Irish Catholics immigrate to the United States.

1825 A group of Norwegians immigrate to the United States, eventually settling in Illinois, where they begin the Fox River settlement. This serves as the base camp for future Norwegian immigrants to the United States.

1830s Many tribes from the Northeast and Southeast are forcibly moved to Indian Territory (present-day Oklahoma and Kansas). Southern tribes to be removed include the Cherokee, Chickasaw, Choctaw, Creek, Seminole, and others. In the North, the Delaware, Miami, Ottawa, Peoria, Potawatomi, Sauk and Fox, Seneca, and Wyandot tribes are removed. The government is not prepared to provide supplies for so many Indians along the trails and in new homes, causing great suffering and death for the Native Americans.

1830s The mass migration of Germans to the United States begins.

1836 The Mexican province of Texas declares its independence from Mexico. Texas will become a state in 1845.

1836–60 The Jewish population of the United States grows from fewer than 15,000 to about 160,000. Most of the

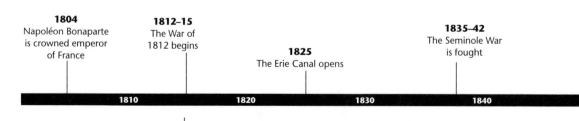

1804
Napoléon Bonaparte
is crowned emperor
of France

1812–15
The War of
1812 begins

1825
The Erie Canal opens

1835–42
The Seminole War
is fought

1810   1820   1830   1840

Jewish immigrants during this period are from Germany.

1841 The first wagon trains cross the continent on the Oregon Trail.

1845 The potato crop in Ireland is hit with a mysterious disease, beginning the Irish potato famine. By the winter of 1847, tens of thousands of people are dying of starvation or related diseases. An estimated one to one and a half million Irish Catholics leave Ireland for the United States over the next few years.

1848 After the Mexican-American War, the United States acquires the Mexican provinces of New Mexico, Arizona, California, and parts of Nevada, Colorado, and Utah. Between 80,000 and 100,000 Mexicans suddenly find themselves living in the United States. Those who choose to stay in their homes automatically become citizens of the United States.

1848 Gold is discovered in the foothills of northern California's Sierra Nevada Mountains. In the next few years, hundreds of thousands of people from all over the United States and around the world migrate to California hoping to strike it rich.

1848–1914 An estimated 400,000 Czechs immigrate to the United States from Austria-Hungary.

1850s Anti-immigrant associations, such as the American Party (also known as the Know-Nothing Party), the Order of United Americans, and the Order of the Star-Spangled Banner, are on the rise. Their primary targets are Catholics, primarily Irish Americans and German Americans.

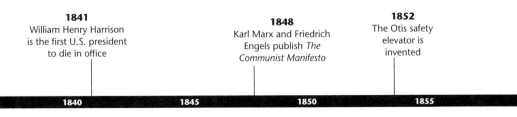

1841
William Henry Harrison is the first U.S. president to die in office

1848
Karl Marx and Friedrich Engels publish *The Communist Manifesto*

1852
The Otis safety elevator is invented

1840   1845   1850   1855

1851–1929 More than 1.2 million Swedish immigrants enter the United States.

1855 Castle Island, operated by the State of New York, becomes the first central immigrant-processing center in the United States.

1855 The anti-immigration Know-Nothing Party reveals its platform. A year later, former president Millard Fillmore is this party's candidate in the presidential election; he loses.

1862 Congress passes the Homestead Act to encourage people to settle west of the Mississippi River. Under this act, a person can gain ownership of 160 acres simply by living on the land and cultivating it for five years.

1864–69 Thousands of Chinese laborers work on the first transcontinental railroad in the United States, cutting a path through treacherous mountains.

1866–1914 More than 600,000 Norwegians immigrate to the United States.

1867–1914 About 1.8 Hungarians immigrate to the United States.

1868 The Fourteenth Amendment of the Constitution provides citizenship rights to African Americans.

1869 The first transcontinental railroad in the United States is completed.

1869 John A. Johnson, a U.S. businessman from Norway, writes *Concerning Emigration,* in which he gives immigration suggestions to the natives back home.

1870 The Fifteenth Amendment gives African American citizens the right to vote.

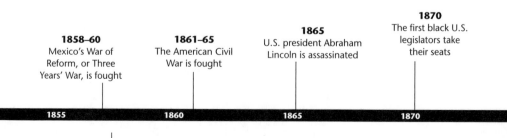

1858–60
Mexico's War of Reform, or Three Years' War, is fought

1861–65
The American Civil War is fought

1865
U.S. president Abraham Lincoln is assassinated

1870
The first black U.S. legislators take their seats

1855   1860   1865   1870

1870 Polish serfs are given their freedom and begin to emigrate. Up to two million Poles will immigrate to the United States between 1870 and 1914.

1870–1920 About 340,000 Finns immigrate to the United States.

1880–1920 About 35 million people, mainly from southern and eastern Europe, arrive on U.S. shores.

1880–1920 About 4 million people leave Italy for the United States, making Italians the single largest European national group of this era of mass migration to move to America.

1880–1924 About 95,000 Arabs immigrate to the United States, most from the area known as Greater Syria—present-day Syria, Lebanon, Jordan, Palestine, and Israel.

1881–1914 About 2 million Eastern European Jews arrive in the United States.

1882 The Chinese Exclusion Act prohibits the naturalization of Chinese immigrants for ten years and prohibits Chinese laborers from entering the country. For the Chinese already in the country, it denies hope of gaining citizenship and for many Chinese men it meant that their wives or families would not be able to join them. The act, the first major restriction on immigration in the United States, is extended twice and becomes permanent in 1902.

1885–1924 About 200,000 Japanese people immigrate to Hawaii.

1890 The Superintendent of the United States Census issues a statement that the American frontier has closed—that is, it has become populated and is therefore no longer a frontier.

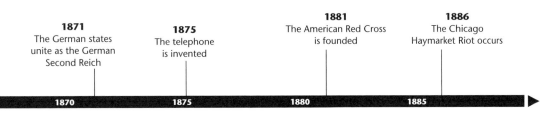

1871
The German states
unite as the German
Second Reich

1875
The telephone
is invented

1881
The American Red Cross
is founded

1886
The Chicago
Haymarket Riot occurs

1870   1875   1880   1885

1891 The Immigration and Naturalization Service (INS) is created as the department that administers federal laws relating to admitting, excluding, or deporting aliens and to naturalizing the foreign-born who are in the United States legally. It remains in operation until 2003.

1892 The federal government takes over the process of screening incoming immigrants at the Port of New York and creates an immigration reception center at Ellis Island, one mile southwest of Manhattan. Before it closes in 1954, more than 16 million immigrants will pass through Ellis Island.

1898 In his article "Concerning the Jews," well known writer Mark Twain tries to explain why prejudice against Jews exists.

1900 In this one year, one-tenth of Denmark's total population immigrates to the United States.

1907 The Dillingham Commission, set up by Congress to investigate immigration, produces a forty-two-volume report. The commission claims that its studies show that people from southern and eastern Europe have a higher potential for criminal activity, are more likely to end up poor and sick, and are less intelligent than other Americans. The report warns that the waves of immigration threaten the "American" way of life.

1907 As anti-Asian immigrant sentiment rises in the United States, Congress works out the "Gentlemen's Agreement" with Japan, in which the United States agrees not to ban all Japanese immigration as long as Japan promises not to issue passports to Japanese laborers for travel to the continental United States.

1891
The escalator is invented

1898
The Spanish-American War is fought

1904
The movie camera is created

1910
The Mexican Revolution begins

1890   1895   1900   1905

1910   To enforce the Chinese Exclusion Act, an immigration station is built at Angel Island in the San Francisco Bay. Any Chinese people arriving in San Francisco go through an initial inspection upon arrival; many are then sent to Angel Island for further processing and thousands are held there for long periods of time.

1910–1920 Between 500,000 and 1,000,000 African Americans migrate from the southern United States to the cities of the North.

1912   Jane Addams's publishes *Twenty Years at Hull-House,* in which she writes of her experiences as owner of a house primarily designed to help immigrants trying to adjust to a completely different way of life.

1913   California passes the Alien Land Laws, which prohibit Chinese and Japanese people from owning land in the state.

1917   Congress creates the "Asiatic barred zone," which excludes immigration from most of Asia, including China, India, and Japan, regardless of literacy.

1918   Willa Cather publishes her novel *My Antonia,* in which she relates the difficulties experienced by European immigrants in the United States in the late nineteenth century.

1920s–30s More than 40,000 Russians come to the United States in the first few years after the Russian Revolution of 1917. Many Russians go into exile in other European cities. In the 1930s, those in exile in Europe begin fleeing the rising Nazi movement. More than a million people who had been born in Russia but were living elsewhere in Europe immigrate to the United States in the 1930s.

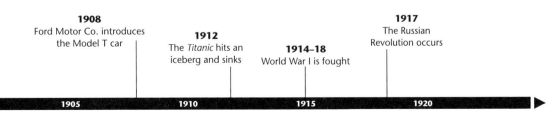

1908
Ford Motor Co. introduces the Model T car

1912
The *Titanic* hits an iceberg and sinks

1914–18
World War I is fought

1917
The Russian Revolution occurs

1905   1910   1915   1920

1921 Congress passes the Emergency Quota Act, which stipulates that each nation has an annual quota (proportion) of immigrants it may send to the United States, which is equal to 3 percent of that country's total population in the United States in 1910. Because the majority of the U.S. population was from northwestern Europe in 1910, this method favors northwestern Europeans over other immigrants.

1921 In *Ozawa v. United States,* the U.S. Supreme Court rules against an upstanding twenty-year Chinese immigrant resident of the United States who had applied to become a U.S. citizen on the grounds that he was not "white."

1924 Congress passes the Immigration Act of 1924 (National Origins Act), which restricts the number of immigrants even beyond the Emergency Quota Act of 1921. Under the new act, immigration is decreased to a total equaling 2 percent of the population in 1890. Under this act, each country may only send 2 percent of its 1890 population in the United States per year. The new act skews the permitted immigration even further in favor of Western Europe, with the United Kingdom, Germany, and Ireland receiving more than two-thirds of the annual maximum quota. This legislation ends the era of mass migrations to the United States.

1924 The Oriental Exclusion Act prohibits most Asian immigration, including the wives and children of U.S. citizens of Chinese ancestry.

1924 Congress creates the Border Patrol, a uniformed law enforcement agency of the Immigration Bureau in charge of fighting smuggling and illegal immigration.

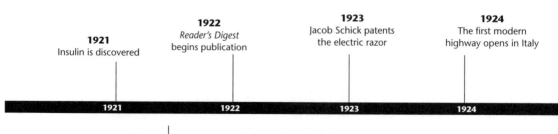

1921
Insulin is discovered

1922
Reader's Digest begins publication

1923
Jacob Schick patents the electric razor

1924
The first modern highway opens in Italy

| 1921 | 1922 | 1923 | 1924 |

1925   One out of every four Greek men between the ages of fifteen and forty-five have immigrated to the United States.

1934   The Tydings-McDuffie Act sets the date and some of the terms of independence for the Philippines on July 4, 1946. Since the United States had acquired the Philippines from Spain in 1898, Filipinos had entered the United States as nationals (people who live in a country legally, are loyal to the country and protected by it, but are not citizens). The act takes away status of Filipinos as U.S. nationals, reclassifying them as aliens, and restricts Filipino immigration by establishing an annual immigration quota of 50.

1942   The United States, heavily involved in World War II, needs laborers at home and turns to Mexico. The U.S. and Mexican governments reach an agreement called the Mexican Farm Labor Supply Program, or the *bracero* program. The program permits Mexicans to enter the country to work under contract as farm and railroad laborers. The program continues for twenty-two years and brings 4.8 million Mexicans to work on U.S. farms and in businesses.

1942   During World War II, President Franklin D. Roosevelt signs Executive Order 9066, which dictates the removal and internment of Japanese Americans. More than 112,000 Japanese Americans living along the Pacific coast are taken from their homes and placed in ten internment camps for the duration of the war.

1943   Congress repeals the Chinese exclusion acts. Immigration from China resumes. Most of the new immigrants are females, the wives of Chinese men who have been in the United States for decades.

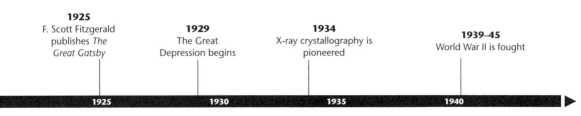

1925
F. Scott Fitzgerald publishes *The Great Gatsby*

1929
The Great Depression begins

1934
X-ray crystallography is pioneered

1939–45
World War II is fought

1925   1930   1935   1940

1945   As World War II ends, more than 40,000 refugees from Europe flee to the United States. Because the quota system does not provide for them, they are admitted under presidential directive.

1945   The War Brides Act allows foreign-born spouses and adopted children of personnel of the U.S. armed forces to enter the United States. The act brings in many Japanese, Chinese, and Korean women, among other groups.

1948   The first U.S. refugee policy, the Displaced Persons Act, enables nearly 410,000 European refugees to enter the United States after World War II.

1950   The Internal Security Act forces all communists to register with the government and denies admission to any foreigner who is a communist or who might engage in subversive activities.

1952   Congress overrides President Harry S. Truman's veto of the Immigration and Nationality Act, which upholds the quota system set in 1921–24 but removes race as a bar to immigration and naturalization and removes discrimination between sexes. The act gives preference to immigrants with special skills needed in the United States, provides for more rigorous screening of immigrants in order to eliminate people considered to be subversive (particularly communists and homosexuals), and allows broader grounds for the deportation of criminal aliens.

1954   As jobs in the United States become harder to find, Mexican workers are viewed as unwanted competition by many. Under Operation Wetback, a special government force locates undocumented workers and forces them to return to Mexico. In one year alone,

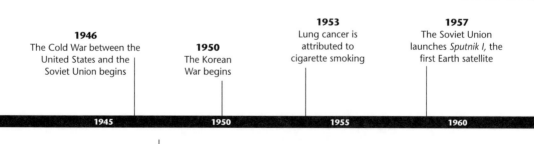

1946
The Cold War between the United States and the Soviet Union begins

1950
The Korean War begins

1953
Lung cancer is attributed to cigarette smoking

1957
The Soviet Union launches *Sputnik I,* the first Earth satellite

1945   1950   1955   1960

about one million people of Mexican descent are deported.

1959   The Cuban Revolution initiates a mass migration from Cuba to the United States—more than one million Cubans will immigrate after this year.

1960–80 The Filipino population in the United States more than quadruples, from 176,130 to 781,894.

1960s   Between 4 and 5 million African Americans have migrated from the South to the North since the turn of the century.

1965   In a new spirit of immigration reform, Congress repeals the national-origins quotas and gives each Eastern Hemisphere nation an annual quota of 20,000, excluding immediate family members of U.S. citizens. The Eastern Hemisphere receives 170,000 places for immigrants and the Western Hemisphere 120,000. (In 1978, Congress creates a worldwide immigration system by combining the two hemispheres.)

1966–80 About 14,000 Dominicans per year enter the United States, most seeking employment they cannot find at home.

1972–81 Sailboats carrying Haitians begin to arrive on the shores of Florida. More than 55,000 Haitian "boat people"—and perhaps more than 100,000—arrive in this wave.

1975   Saigon, the South Vietnamese capital, falls to the communist North on April 30; at least 65,000 South Vietnamese immediately flee the country.

1975–81 About 123,600 Laotian refugees enter the United States.

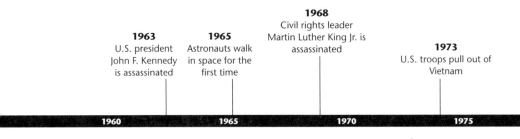

1968
Civil rights leader
Martin Luther King Jr. is
assassinated

1963
U.S. president
John F. Kennedy
is assassinated

1965
Astronauts walk
in space for the
first time

1973
U.S. troops pull out of
Vietnam

1960   1965   1970   1975

1979 In the aftermath of the Vietnam War, the Orderly Departure Program (ODP) is established to provide a safe alternative for Vietnamese people who are fleeing the country in large numbers, often risking their lives in overcrowded old boats. Under the ODP, refugees are allowed to leave Vietnam directly for resettlement in one of two dozen countries, including the United States. There are about 165,000 admissions to the United States under the ODP by 1989, and new arrivals continue into the 1990s.

1980 More than 125,000 Cubans flee to the United States during the Mariel Boat Lift.

1980–86 Tens of thousands of Cambodian refugees enter the United States annually.

1981–2000 The United States accepts 531,310 Vietnamese refugees.

1982 In *Plyler v. Doe,* the U.S. Supreme Court rules that the children of illegal immigrants have the same rights as everyone else, especially the right to an education.

1986 The Immigration Reform and Control Act (IRCA) provides amnesty (pardon to a group of people) to more than 3 million undocumented immigrants who had entered the United States before 1982, allowing them to become legal residents. The measure outlaws the knowing employment of undocumented immigrants and makes it more difficult for undocumented immigrants to receive public assistance.

1988 Congress passes the Amerasian Homecoming Act, which brings thousands of children—most are the offspring of American servicemen and Asian mothers—to the United States.

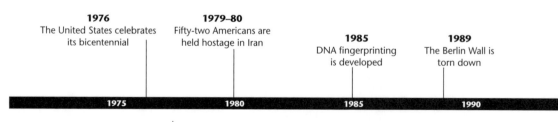

1976
The United States celebrates its bicentennial

1979–80
Fifty-two Americans are held hostage in Iran

1985
DNA fingerprinting is developed

1989
The Berlin Wall is torn down

1975   1980   1985   1990

1990   *Mexican Voices, American Dreams: An Oral History of Mexican Immigration to the United States* is published.

1991–93 Some 43,000 Haitians try to reach the United States by boat. Many of their boats are intercepted by U.S. officials and those emigrants are taken to Guantánamo Bay, a U.S. naval base in Cuba.

1994   In an effort to stop undocumented workers from illegally crossing the border, the government adopts Operation Gatekeeper, an extensive border patrol system at Imperial Beach at the border between Mexico and southern California. The number of border agents is increased and new hi-tech equipment is put to use, costing billions of dollars over the next few years. Illegal immigration moves further inland where the climate is more severe, proving to be deadly in some cases.

1994   The United States enters a Wet Feet–Dry Feet agreement with Cuba under which, if fleeing Cubans trying to reach the United States are caught at sea, U.S. authorities will send them back to Cuba. If the Cubans make it to U.S. shores, they will be admitted to the country.

1994   California citizens vote in favor of Proposition 187, a law designed to stop immigrants without visas from receiving public benefits from the state; a judge later blocks the state from putting the proposition into effect.

1996   Congress passes the Illegal Immigration Reform and Immigrant Responsibility Act (IIRIRA). The IIRIRA creates a huge increase in funding for border patrol personnel and equipment. This act creates harsher penalties for illegal immigration, restricts welfare benefits

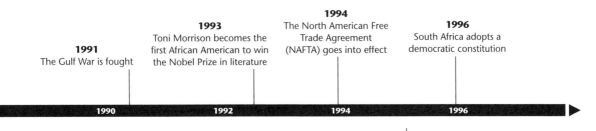

1991
The Gulf War is fought

1993
Toni Morrison becomes the first African American to win the Nobel Prize in literature

1994
The North American Free Trade Agreement (NAFTA) goes into effect

1996
South Africa adopts a democratic constitution

1990   1992   1994   1996

to recent immigrants, and makes the deportation process easier for U.S. administrators. The IIRIRA also tries to make it harder for foreign terrorists to enter the United States.

1996   The bombing of the Oklahoma Federal Building at the hands of a terrorist (a U.S. citizen) in 1995 raises new fears about terrorism. The Anti-terrorism Act is passed, making deportation automatic if an immigrant commits a deportable felony (a grave crime), even if the immigrant has been in the United States since early childhood. By 2003, 500,000 people had been deported under the terms of this act.

1997   The Border Patrol initiates Operation Rio Grande, strengthening the Texas-Mexico border with more agents to deter people from crossing.

1998   California passes Proposition 227, a referendum that bans bilingual classroom education and English as a second language (ESL) program, replacing them with a one-year intensive English immersion program.

2000   The Immigration and Naturalization Service estimates the number of undocumented immigrants in the country at about 7 million, up from the estimate of 5.8 million in 1996. About 70 percent of the undocumented immigrants are from Mexico.

2001   Congress passes the USA PATRIOT Act ("Uniting and Strengthening America by Providing Appropriate Tools Required to Intercept and Obstruct Terrorism"). The bill calls for increased border patrol and tightened provisions for screening and restricting immigrants. It grants sweeping new powers to federal police agencies and permits indefinite detention of

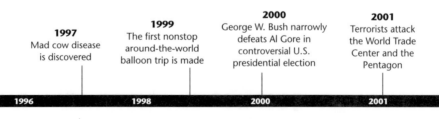

1997
Mad cow disease is discovered

1999
The first nonstop around-the-world balloon trip is made

2000
George W. Bush narrowly defeats Al Gore in controversial U.S. presidential election

2001
Terrorists attack the World Trade Center and the Pentagon

1996   1998   2000   2001

immigrants and aliens in the country for minor immigration status violations.

2001　Within weeks of the September 11 terrorist attacks on New York and Washington, D.C., approximately 1,200 immigrants are arrested by federal government agents as part of an anti-terrorist campaign. Most are from Saudi Arabia, Egypt, and Pakistan. Many are held without charges and without access to attorneys or their families. Many are deported. None are charged with terrorism.

2002　The Homeland Security Department requires the annual registration of temporary male immigrants from twenty-four predominantly Arab or Muslim countries as well as North Korea. People from the following countries are required to register: Afghanistan, Algeria, Bahrain, Eritrea, Iran, Iraq, Lebanon, Libya, Morocco, North Korea, Oman, Pakistan, Qatar, Saudi Arabia, Somalia, Sudan, Syria, Tunisia, United Arab Emirates, and Yemen. The following year, five more countries are added to the list: Bangladesh, Egypt, Indonesia, Jordan, and Kuwait. Of the 83,519 people who register with immigration officials in 2002, 13,799 are put in deportation proceedings. Others complain of terrifying or humiliating interrogations and harsh conditions. Immigrant and civil liberties groups protest the policy.

2002　Conservative talk-show host and former presidential candidate Patrick J. Buchanan publishes *The Death of the West: How Dying Populations and Immigrant Invasions Imperil Our Country and Civilization,* in which he warns that immigration and low birth rates would result in white people being a minority in the United States, where they once constituted an overwhelming majority.

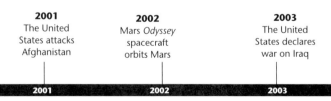

2001
The United States attacks Afghanistan

2002
Mars *Odyssey* spacecraft orbits Mars

2003
The United States declares war on Iraq

2001　　　　　2002　　　　　2003

U.S. Immigration and Migration
Primary Sources

Lord Baltimore

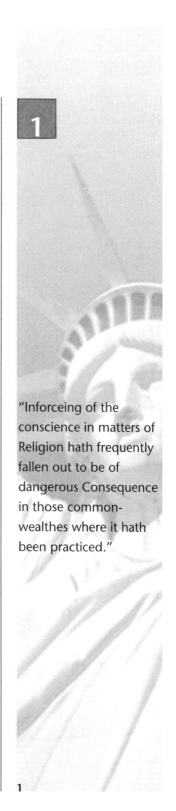

An Act Concerning Religion (The Maryland Toleration Act)
Issued in 1649; reprinted on *AMDOCS:*
Documents for the Study of American History (Web site)

A seventeenth-century Maryland law
sets the stage for future religious freedoms

In 1649, in the English colony of Maryland, a law was issued by Cecilius Calvert, Lord Baron of Baltimore (1605–1675; known as Lord Baltimore), the governor of the colony, banning criticism of various forms of Christianity and allowing people to practice their Christian religion freely. It was the first law establishing freedom of religion (or at least, Christianity) in North America. The law, the Maryland Toleration Act, helped set the stage for the freedom of religion that would mark the independent United States 140 years later. The act was issued at a time when England was in the midst of a civil war in which religion was a central issue. The act made Maryland a refuge for English Catholics who were often persecuted for their beliefs during the English civil war (1638–60).

The 1600s were a time of religious and political turmoil in England and throughout Europe, and consequently in England's North American colonies. The religious unrest had begun in Wittenberg, Germany, in 1517, when a German priest named Martin Luther (1483–1546) posted on a church door a list of ninety-five objections to various teachings and practices of the Roman Catholic religion. Luther insisted that the Roman

> "Inforceing of the conscience in matters of Religion hath frequently fallen out to be of dangerous Consequence in those commonwealthes where it hath been practiced."

Martin Luther, leader of changes in the Roman Catholic Church, called the Reformation. *New York Public Library.*

Catholic Church should be reformed, and the movement he launched is called the Reformation. Eighteen years later, in 1535, the king of England, Henry VIII (1491–1547; reigned 1509–47), declared that he, and not the pope, would be head of the Christian church in England. The English king had a different motivation: he had asked Pope Paul III (1468–1549), leader of the Roman Catholic Church, to grant him a divorce so that he could leave his wife and marry another woman who might be able to give him a son and an heir to his throne. The pope refused to grant the divorce, in part because it violated church teaching and in part because without another heir, the throne of England stood to come under Spanish control. Henry VIII's first wife was Catherine of Aragon (1485–1536), his older brother's widow and the daughter of King Ferdinand V (1452–1516) and Queen Isabella (1451–1504) of Spain.

The two events—Luther's religious challenge to the teachings of the Catholic Church and King Henry VIII's establishment of the new Church of England—demonstrated how closely linked religion and politics were in the sixteenth century. Kings depended on the pope to give his blessing to their political power, and the pope depended on kings to enforce adherence to the one and only permitted religion. This system, which had been in place for hundreds of years, was destroyed by both Luther and Henry VIII. Within a few years, other theologians and rulers joined the dispute. A variety of religious theorists published their own objections and alternatives to Catholic teachings, and attracted followers who preferred to worship outside the regular church. Rulers chose sides in the dispute between Luther and the pope, resulting in wars over religious preferences.

In England, the struggle over whether the Roman Catholic Church should be the official religion of the country carried on for over 150 years during the reigns of the next five monarchs: King Edward VI (1537–1553; reigned 1547–53); Queen Mary I (1516–1558; reigned 1553–58); Queen Elizabeth I (1533–1603; reigned 1558–1603); King James I (1566–1625, reigned 1603–25); and King Charles I (1600–1649; reigned 1625–49). Their reigns were marked by continuing controversy and violence over whether the Church of England should remain separated from the Roman Catholic Church or whether England's official religion should revert to Roman Catholicism. Queen Mary and King Charles, both of whom were Catholics, were in fact each executed. On top of the argument about the official religion were the teachings of several different theologians. Some wanted to establish new, separate churches. Some wanted to reform the Church of England to rid it of influences left over from the Roman Catholic religion.

The religious disputes in England were also reflected in England's colonies along the Atlantic coast of North America. Early English immigrants in the colony of Virginia (named after Queen Elizabeth, who never married and was known as the Virgin Queen) were primarily pursuing wealth. But followers of various Protestant religious leaders emigrated for a different reason: They seized on the opportunity to establish settlements in North America where they could worship according to their religious convictions without interference by authorities in England. The best known of these religious groups in North America were the Pilgrims, who established a settlement at Plymouth in 1620, called the Massachusetts Bay Colony. The Pilgrims were so-called Separatists, meaning they wanted to establish a church separate from the Church of England rather than reform it. A larger group of religiously motivated settlers in the Massachusetts Bay Colony were the Puritans, who established the town of Salem in 1628. (Two years later, a larger group of Puritans founded another town, Boston, also in the Massachusetts Bay Colony.) Although these early settlers are sometimes described as seeking religious freedom, this did not mean freedom for everyone. The Puritans, in particular, were intent on having an official church—the Church of England—that was "purified" of Roman Catholic influence.

Four years after the Puritans established their outpost in Salem, a Catholic aristocrat in England, Lord Baltimore, received a charter, or permission, from King Charles to establish a colony in North America, to be called Maryland in

Lord Baltimore.

honor of the King's wife, Queen Henrietta Maria. (At the time, the king of England claimed control over a broad stretch of North America along the Atlantic coast; in turn, he granted charters to companies or individuals, as in the case of his friend Lord Baltimore, to organize settlements.) Lord Baltimore founded Maryland as a safe haven for Catholics who were persecuted by Puritans in New England and Church of England settlers in the colony of Virginia. But Protestants in other colonies, who strongly disapproved of establishing a Catholic colony in North America, moved into Maryland, soon leaving Catholics as a minority representing only a quarter of the population. As a result, Lord Baltimore felt compelled to persuade the colonial assembly to pass a law in 1649 that allowed Christians of all persuasions to practice their religious beliefs in peace.

At about the same time, a religious civil war had broken out in England, pitting the Puritans, who had gained control over Parliament, against the Catholic King Charles I. The king was overthrown and executed in 1649. The Puritans abolished the monarchy and established a commonwealth, a form of government based on the common good of the citizens rather than the rule of a monarch. For the next twenty years, a civil war raged in England, pitting the Puritans against Catholics and loyalists of the monarchy.

Although the English civil war seemed to be about religion, it also took in two different views of the nature of government. King Charles I had believed that whatever powers the Parliament held were, in essence, a gift of the king. Members of Parliament, on the other hand, felt just the opposite: that the real authority in the country should rest with the elected members of Parliament, who might then grant the king some authority. In the decade before, armed conflict broke out between forces loyal to King Charles I and forces loyal to the Puritan-controlled Parliament, the two sides had argued continually over the king's power to levy, or charge, taxes, and the Parliament's unwillingness to raises taxes as a tool to limit the power of the king.

Things to remember while reading An Act Concerning Religion:

- The notion of "freedom of religion" contained in the act did not mean residents of the colony were entirely free; it meant that various forms of the Christian faith were permitted to coexist. People caught criticizing religion in general, or specific beliefs of religious sects (such as the importance of the mother of Jesus, which was a central belief of the Catholic religion) were subject to being fined, imprisoned, or whipped in public.

King Charles I. *Library of Congress.*

- The act was designed in part to calm passions over religion. It prohibited people in Maryland from calling one another names that were based on religious conflicts and that might be viewed as leading to conflict, names like "roundhead," "idolator" (worshiper of idols, or statues), or even "Brownian" (a follower of English theologian Robert Browne) or "Lutheran," a follower of Martin Luther. Such terms carried much more emotional weight at the time than they do in the twenty-first century.

- The text of An Act Concerning Religion reflects the conventions of the mid-seventeenth century, when there was no universal agreement on how to spell words.

Descriptions of Religious Groups Mentioned in the Act

The Act Concerning Religion of 1649 barred people in Maryland from calling one another names that would be offensive and result in religious strife. Many of the names are largely unfamiliar in the twenty-first century, since they refer to religious leaders and small groups that either took on different names or ceased to exist. Among the groups referred to in the act were:

- **Anabaptists:** People who followed the teachings of Ulrich Zwingli (1484–1531) of Zurich, Switzerland. Zwingli questioned many church teachings and practices (including the ban on letting Catholic priests marry) and eventually led a large number of believers in Switzerland and Germany.

- **Antinomians:** From two Greek words meaning "against" (anti) and "nomos" (laws), the term Antinomian was applied to Protestants who believed that following strict laws laid down by the Catholic Church was not necessary to gain "grace," or the favor of God.

- **Barrowists:** Followers of the teachings of Henry Barrow (c. 1550–1593), who advocated separating from the Church of England and establishing a new church, free of influence of the Catholic Church.

- **Brownists:** Followers of English theologian Robert Browne (c. 1550–1633), who advocated establishing a new church in which religious authority would rest within members of each local church or congregation, rather than in the priesthood. Browne is often cited as a primary founder of the Protestant church called Congregationalists.

- **Calvinists:** Followers of John Calvin (1509–1564), a French priest living in Geneva, Switzerland, who came about twenty years after Luther and challenged Catholic teachings about the relationship between God and man. Calvin taught that whether a person would meet the approval of God (referred to as the "grace" of God) was determined before birth, and that an individual's actions in life would not make a difference. Calvin was an important religious leader of the Puritans,

An Act Concerning Religion

Forasmuch as in a well governed and Christian Common Wealth matters concerning Religion and the honor of God ought in who wanted to "purify" the Church of England of Catholic influences.

- **Jesuits** and **Jesuit papists:** Catholic priests who are trained by and belong to an order called the Society of Jesus, formed in Paris in 1534. (All Catholic priests belong to one of several organizations, or orders, that accept all Catholic traditions and teachings but may choose to emphasize some over others. Other orders may have to give account of themselves to high-ranking officials in the Catholic Church, but the vicar-general, the leader of the Jesuit order, answers only to the pope.) Jesuits were particularly active in efforts to counter the influence of Reformation—the movement to reform the Catholic Church and even to establish other churches—that started with Martin Luther, among others, in 1517. The term "papist" means a Roman Catholic; it refers to the leadership of the pope (*papa* in Latin) and is usually used in an uncomplimentary way.

- **Lutherans:** Followers of Martin Luther who had sparked the challenge to the authority of the Catholic Church in 1517. Luther believed that the Bible, rather than church authorities, was the source of truth about the Christian religion.

- **Presbyterians:** Followers of the teachings of Calvin in Scotland (and later in England) who put the religious authority in the hands of elders, or presbyters. A presbyter, or elder, was the highest rank among the church members, unlike the rankings of priests in both the Catholic Church and the Church of England. The term presbyter came from the organization of the Christian church in the first years after the death of Jesus of Nazareth.

- **Roundheads:** Between 1642 and 1660, Puritans in England battled Catholics loyal to King Charles I for political power in a civil war. The Puritans favored short haircuts, and were nicknamed Roundheads, as opposed to the king's supporters who favored long-haired wigs and were called Cavaliers.

the first place to bee taken, into serious consideracion and endeavoured to bee settled, Be it therefore ordered and enacted by the Right Honourable Cecilius Lord Baron of Baltemore absolute Lord and Proprietary of this Province with the advise and consent of this Generall Assembly:

That whatsoever person or persons within this Province and the Islands thereunto belonging shall from henceforth blaspheme God,

Reproachfull: Disapproving.

Heires: Heirs; people designated to receive the property and holdings of a person upon his or her death.

Aforesaid: Previously mentioned.

Holy Apostles: The twelve close followers of Jesus Christ.

Evangelists: Those who preach the Gospel.

Levyed: Levied; charged.

Chattells: Items of property not connected to land, such as furniture.

Banished: Removed.

Denominate: Designate; name.

Traffiqueing: Trafficking; trading or dealing in merchandise; sometimes associated with illegal goods.

Comerceing: Commercing; doing business.

Heritick: Heretic; one who preaches a religious message that does not conform to the established religion.

Scismatick: Schismatic; one who participates in the formal division of or separation from a church or religious body.

Idolator: One who worships idols, such as statues.

Jesuite: Jesuit; a Catholic priest who is trained by and belongs to an order called the Society of Jesus.

Separatist: One who wanted to establish a church separate from the Church of England rather than reform it.

*that is Curse him, or deny our Saviour Jesus Christ to bee the sonne of God, or shall deny the holy Trinity the father sonne and holy Ghost, or the Godhead of any of the said Three persons of the Trinity or the Unity of the Godhead, or shall use or utter any **reproachfull** Speeches, words or language concerning the said Holy Trinity, or any of the said three persons thereof, shalbe [shall be] punished with death and confiscation or forfeiture of all his or her lands and goods to the Lord Proprietary and his **heires.***

*And bee it also Enacted by the Authority and with the advise and assent **aforesaid**, That whatsoever person or persons shall from henceforth use or utter any reproachfull words or Speeches concerning the blessed Virgin Mary the Mother of our Saviour or the **holy Apostles** or **Evangelists** or any of them shall in such case for the first offence forfeit to the said Lord Proprietary and his heirs Lords and Proprietaries of this Province the summe of five pound Sterling or the value thereof to be **Levyed** on the goods and **chattells** of every such person soe offending, but in case such Offender or Offenders, shall not then have goods and chattells sufficient for the satisfyeing of such forfeiture, or that the same bee not otherwise speedily satisfyed that then such Offender or Offenders shalbe publiquely whipt and bee imprisoned during the pleasure of the Lord Proprietary or the Lieutenant or cheife [chief] Governor of this Province for the time being. And that every such Offender or Offenders for every second offence shall forfeit tenne pound sterling or the value thereof to bee levyed as aforesaid, or in case such offender or Offenders shall not then have goods and chattells within this Province sufficient for that purpose then to bee publiquely and severely whipt and imprisoned as before is expressed. And that every person or persons before mentioned offending herein the third time, shall for such third Offence forfeit all his lands and Goods and bee for ever **banished** and expelled out of this Province.*

*And be it also further Enacted by the same authority advise and assent that whatsoever person or persons shall from henceforth upon any occasion of Offence or otherwise in a reproachful manner or Way declare call or **denominate** any person or persons whatsoever inhabiting, residing, **traffiqueing** trading or **comerceing** within this Province or within any the Ports, Harbors, Creeks or Havens to the same belonging an **heritick, Scismatick, Idolator,** puritan, Independant, Prespiterian, popish prest [priest], **Jesuite,** Jesuited papist, Lutheran, Calvenist, Anabaptist, Brownist, Antinomian, Barrowist, Roundhead [see box for discussion of many of these groups], **Separatist,** or any other name or terme in a reproachfull* manner relating to matter of Religion shall for every such Offence forfeit and loose the somme of tenne shillings sterling or the value thereof to bee levyed on the goods and chattells of every such Offender and Offenders, the one half thereof to be forfeited and paid unto the person and persons of whom such reproachfull words are or shalbe spoken or uttered, and the other half thereof to the Lord Proprietary and his heires Lords and Proprietaries of this Province. But if such person or persons who shall at any time utter or speake any such reproachfull words or Language shall not have Goods or Chattells sufficient and **overt** within this Province to bee taken to satisfie the penalty aforesaid or that the same bee not otherwise speedily satisfyed, that then the person or persons soe offending shalbe publickly whipt, and shall suffer imprisonment without **baile or maineprise** untill hee, shee or they respectively shall satisfy the party soe offended or greived by such reproachfull Language by asking him or her respectively forgivenes publiquely for such his Offence before the Magistrate of cheife Officer or Officers of the Towne or place where such Offence shalbe given.

And be it further likewise Enacted by the Authority and consent aforesaid That every person and persons within this Province that shall at any time hereafter **prophane** the Sabbath or Lords day called Sunday by frequent swearing, drunkennes or by any uncivill or disorderly recreacion [recreation], or by working on that day when absolute necessity doth not require it shall for every such first offence forfeit **2s.6d sterling** or the value thereof, and for the second offence **5s** sterling or the value thereof, and for the third offence and soe for every time he shall offend in like manner afterwards 10s sterling or the value thereof. And in case such offender and offenders shall not have sufficient goods or chattells within this Province to satisfy any of the said Penalties respectively hereby imposed for prophaning the Sabbath or Lords day called Sunday as aforesaid, That in Every such case the partie soe offending shall for the first and second offence in that kinde be imprisoned till hee or shee shall publickly in open Court before the cheife Commander Judge or Magistrate, of that County Towne or precinct where such offence shalbe committed acknowledg the Scandall and offence he hath in that respect given against God and the good and civill Governement of this Province, And for the third offence and for every time after shall also bee publickly whipt.

And whereas the inforceing of the conscience in matters of Religion hath frequently fallen out to be of dangerous Consequence in those commonwealthes where it hath been practised, And for the

Overt: Open; public.

Baile or maineprise: Bail; generally money paid for the temporary release of a prisoner until his or her trial.

Prophane: Profane; treat something that is sacred with abuse or irreverence.

2s6d: Two pounds, six pence; English units of currency, comparable to, respectively, the dollar and penny in the United States.

Sterling: A synonym for an English pound.

5s: Five shillings; the shilling is a subdivision of the British pound; under a discontinued scheme of currency, there were twenty shillings in a pound.

*more quiett and peaceable governement of this Province, and the better to preserve mutuall Love and amity amongst the Inhabitants thereof, Be it Therefore also by the Lord Proprietary with the advise and consent of this Assembly **Ordeyned** and enacted (except as in this present Act is before Declared and sett forth that noe person or persons whatsoever within this Province, or the Islands, Ports, Harbors, Creekes, or havens thereunto belonging professing to beleive in Jesus Christ, shall from henceforth bee any waies [ways] troubled, **Molested or discountenanced** for or in respect of his or her religion nor in the free exercise thereof within this Province or the Islands thereunto belonging nor any way compelled to the beleife or exercise of any other Religion against his or her consent, soe as they be not unfaithfull to the Lord Proprietary, or molest or conspire against the civill Governement established or to bee established in this Province under him or his heires. And that all and every person and persons that shall presume Contrary to this Act and the true intent and meaning thereof directly or indirectly either in person or estate willfully to wrong disturbe trouble or molest any person whatsoever within this Province professing to beleive in Jesus Christ for or in respect of his or her religion or the free exercise thereof within this Province other than is provided for in this Act that such person or persons soe offending, shalbe compelled to pay treble [triple] damages to the party soe wronged or molested, and for every such offence shall also forfeit 20s sterling in money or the value thereof, half thereof for the use of the Lord Proprietary, and his heires Lords and Proprietaries of this Province, and the other half for the use of the party soe wronged or molested as aforesaid, Or if the partie soe offending as aforesaid shall refuse or bee unable to **recompense** the party soe wronged, or to satisfy such fyne [fine] or forfeiture, then such Offender shalbe severely punished by publick whipping and imprisonment during the pleasure of the Lord Proprietary, or his Lieutenant or cheife Governor of this Province for the tyme being without baile or maineprise.*

*And bee it further alsoe Enacted by the authority and consent aforesaid That the Sheriff or other Officer or Officers from time to time to bee appointed and authorized for that purpose, of the County Towne or precinct where every particular offence in this present Act conteyned [contained] shall happen at any time to bee committed and whereupon there is hereby a forfeiture fyne or penalty imposed shall from time to time **distraine** and seise [seize] the goods and estate of every such person soe offending as aforesaid against this present Act or any part thereof, and sell the same*

Ordeyned: Ordained; established by decree or law.

Molested or discountenanced: Persecuted or looked upon with disfavor, as a means of discouraging an act or person.

Recompense: Pay or compensate.

Distraine: Distrain; vigorously force to fulfill an obligation.

or any part thereof for the full satisfaccion of such forfeiture, fine, or penalty as aforesaid, Restoring unto the partie soe offending the Remainder or **overplus** *of the said goods or estate after such satisfaccion soe made as aforesaid.*

The freemen have assented.

What happened next ...

In England, the civil war ended with the eventual defeat of the Puritan-controlled Parliament and restoration of the monarchy in Charles II (1630–1685; reigned 1660–85), the eldest son of Charles I. Upon the death of Charles II, his brother, James II (1633–1701; reigned 1685–88), who had converted to Catholicism, became king. Although the Puritans did not maintain control of the British government, the Catholic Church was not reestablished as the official church of the country. James did, however, try to install Catholics in high positions. Protestant nobles upset by James welcomed Dutch prince William of Orange (William III; 1650–1702; reigned 1689–1702), and his English wife Mary (1662–1694), as king and queen of England. In a bloodless revolution called the Glorious Revolution of 1688, James was forced to abdicate, or give up the throne, to William and Mary.

In England's colonies, religious intolerance diminished in line with events in England. Although some colonies maintained official religions for many years—in some cases, even after the colonies became independent states after the Declaration of Independence in 1776—the right to practice religion freely was guaranteed by the first Amendment to the U.S. Constitution adopted in 1789. Two years later, the states ratified the first ten amendments to the Constitution, called the Bill of Rights. The first amendment begins with the words: "Congress shall make no law respecting an establishment of religion, or prohibiting the free exercise thereof...." The principles of the Maryland Toleration Act had become a part of the basic law of the United States.

Although the law guaranteed the freedom to practice any religion—or none at all—this was not an end to religious intolerance. In the 1840s, significant numbers of Roman Catholics from Ireland and Germany began immigrating to the United States. The reaction was the Know Nothing movement, a group of secretive organizations opposed to the free immigration of Catholics. A similar anti-Catholic reaction occurred from 1915 to 1924, when a large number of Italian immigrants, almost all of them Catholic, arrived. As late as 1960, the Catholicism of U.S. senator John F. Kennedy (1917–1963) of Massachusetts, the presidential candidate of the Democratic Party, was considered a possible negative factor. In fact, Kennedy narrowly beat his Republican opponent, Vice President Richard Nixon (1913–1994), and became the first Catholic to serve as president of the United States.

Did you know ...

- Freedom of religion was not the only distinguishing characteristic of colonial Maryland. Part of the colony's royal charter, or license, granted in 1632 to Lord Baltimore called for laws governing the colony to be "of and with the advise, assent, and approbation of the free-men of the said Province, or the greater part of them, or of their delegates or deputies." Other colonies also had provisions for representative government, but in other cases those entitled to vote constituted a relatively small group of men among a much larger population. In Maryland, all free men (that is, men who were not slaves or indentured servants, people who agreed to work for a period of time in exchange for passage) were entitled to a vote. In 1648, a woman, Margaret Brent (1600–1671), tried to vote, but was denied. Women in Maryland were not entitled to vote until 1920, after the passage of the Nineteenth Amendment to the Constitution.

- At the same time the Maryland Toleration Act was passed, in the Puritan colony of Massachusetts, blasphemy, a statement showing contempt for God, was punishable by death. The general laws of Massachusetts of 1649 stated: "If any person within this Jurisdiction whether Christian or Pagan shall wittingly and willingly presume to BLASPHEME the holy Name of God, Father, Son or Holy-Ghost, with direct, expresse, presumptuous, or high-handed blasphemy, either by wilfull or obstinate denying the true God, or his Creation, or Government of the world: or shall curse God in like manner, or reproach the holy Religion of God as if it were but a politick device to keep ignorant men in awe; or shal utter any other kinde of Blasphemy of the like nature & degree they shall be put to death."

For More Information

Books

Andrews, Matthew Page. *The Founding of Maryland.* New York and London: D. Appleton-Century, 1933.

Fisher, Louis. *Religious Liberty in America: Political Safeguards.* Lawrence: University Press of Kansas, 2002.

Hamburger, Philip. *Separation of Church and State.* Cambridge, MA: Harvard University Press, 2002.

Ives, J. Moss. *The Ark and the Dove; the Beginning of Civil and Religious Liberties in America.* New York: Cooper Square Publishers, 1969.

Let Freedom Ring: The Words That Shaped Our America. New York: Sterling Publishing, 2001.

McGreevy, John T. *Catholicism and American Freedom: A History.* New York: W. W. Norton, 2003.

Periodicals

Schwarz, Frederic D. "1649 Three Hundred and Fifty Years Ago." *American Heritage* (April 1999): p. 138.

Slavicek, Louise Chipley. "Religious Freedom in Colonial America." *Cobblestone* (January 2000): p. 10.

Web sites

"Lauues and Libertyes of Massachusetts (1648)." *Legal History and Philosophy.* Reprinted from the copy of the 1648 edition in The Henry E. Huntington Library, a special edition of The Legal Classics Library, Division of Gryphon Editions, Birmingham, 1982. http://www.commonlaw.com/Mass.html (accessed on January 16, 2004).

"An Act Concerning Religion, April 21, 1649: An Interpretation and Tribute to the Citizen Legislators of Maryland." *AMDOCS: Documents for the Study of American History.* http://www.ku.edu/carrie/docs/texts/maryland.htm (accessed on January 15, 2004).

"The Catholic Encyclopedia: Ulrich Zwingli." *New Advent.* http://www.newadvent.org/cathen/15772a.htm (accessed on January 16, 2004).

2

Hector St. John de Crèvecoeur

Excerpt from Letters from an American Farmer
Written in 1782

A French immigrant writes about the advantages of being an American

> "The American is a new man, who acts upon new principles; he must therefore entertain new ideas, and form new opinions. From involuntary idleness, servile dependence, penury and useless labour, he has passed to toils of a very different nature, rewarded by ample subsistence. — This is an American."

In 1782, a French immigrant to North America, Hector St. John de Crèvecoeur (1735–1813), published a series of es-says titled *Letters from an American Farmer.* It was one of the first presentations of the idea that settlers in the newly inde-pendent United States would constitute a new nationality based on a shared dream of freedom and equality. The Amer-ican, he declared, would be distinct from the various Euro-pean nationalities from which Americans had originated. De Crèvecoeur had no way of knowing when he wrote his essay in 1782 just how complex the question of American nation-ality would become. But his idea, written midway between the Declaration of Independence (1776) and the adoption of the Constitution of the United States (1788)—milestone documents that established the United States as a nation—laid out an ideal that became popular in the American imag-ination, even if it fell far short of the reality of a nation of immigrants.

Most people in America can trace their ancestry to some other place. In some cases, citizens were born on an-other continent and came to the United States as immigrants, or they are the children of immigrants. In other cases, their last name—O'Reilly, Schmidt, Ferraro, or Li, for example—suggests that a long-forgotten ancestor emigrated from Ireland, Germany, Italy, or China to the United States.

Almost from the beginning, residents of the United States had two ideas about their nationality. On the one hand, they were Americans, citizens of a new republic who had overthrown the rule of a king and governed themselves by voting for the people who served in a type of government called a democracy. (A republic is a government without a king, based on the popular will of the people; a democracy is a government chosen by the citizens through the process of voting.) On the other hand, they remembered their ancestors from another place, and in some sense thought of themselves as English or Italian or Chinese but living in North America, even if they personally had never visited their ancestors' country. Indeed, the leaders of the American revolution against British rule in 1776 gave as one reason for demanding independence their belief that their political rights *as Englishmen* had been violated by King George III (1738–1820; reigned 1760–1820) of England.

Hector St. John de Crèvecoeur.

Michel-Guillaume Jean de Crèvecoeur, better known as Hector St. John de Crèvecoeur, was a native of Normandy, in France, who had come to the United States in 1765. He lived in New Jersey and wrote a series of essays titled *Letters from an American Farmer.* They were among the first essays to suggest that coming to North America to seek a fortune under the freedom of a new democracy made residents of the United States somehow different than people still living in Europe.

The essential traits of this new nationality, de Crèvecoeur wrote, were a belief in the equality of all men, and a desire to go about their business without undue interference from the government or from an organized church. For de Crèvecoeur, the essential nature of Americans was their common political beliefs.

Things to remember while reading an excerpt from *Letters from an American Farmer:*

- The author, in viewing the new nationality called Americans, left out one important group: Africans. The slaves who tilled the fields of America—not just only in the South, but also in the North when de Crèvecoeur wrote—had not come voluntarily and did not participate in the joys and benefits of a newfound freedom. To the contrary, they suffered generations of slavery, toiling without compensation or hope of freedom, watching their children or even their spouses sold away like cattle. The inability of Africans to participate in de Crèvecoeur's vision was for hundreds of years a living contradiction to his theory.

- De Crèvecoeur also ignored the existence of Native Americans, who had inhabited North America and established well-organized societies long before any Europeans ventured across the ocean. Instead, he pretended that Europeans discovered a new and empty continent where they could conduct a new experiment in a society comprised of people who had dreamed of freedom from European customs and prejudices, even if it meant pushing the native inhabitants off their land by violence.

- The author thought in 1782 that Europeans from many backgrounds would come together to form new families whose common nationality was American. "I could point out to you a family whose grandfather was an Englishman, whose wife was Dutch, whose son married a French woman, and whose present four sons have now four wives of different nations," he wrote in *Letters from an American Farmer.* The reality was somewhat different. For most of American history, immigrants have remained attached to their original national identity, tending to marry people of the same nationality and remaining in touch with communities of people of the same original nationality.

LETTERS

FROM AN

AMERICAN FARMER;

DESCRIBING

CERTAIN PROVINCIAL SITUATIONS,
MANNERS, AND CUSTOMS,

NOT GENERALLY KNOWN;

AND CONVEYING

SOME IDEA OF THE LATE AND PRESENT
INTERIOR CIRCUMSTANCES

OF THE

BRITISH COLONIES

IN

NORTH AMERICA.

WRITTEN FOR THE INFORMATION OF A FRIEND
IN ENGLAND,

By J. HECTOR ST. JOHN,
A FARMER IN PENNSYLVANIA.

LONDON,
PRINTED FOR THOMAS DAVIES IN RUSSEL STREET COVENT-
GARDEN, AND LOCKYER DAVIS IN HOLBORN.
M DCC LXXXII.

• De Crèvecoeur's account of immigration to the United States before 1782 was idealized. Some Europeans had come to the United States as indentured servants, individuals who were obligated to work for little or no pay for a set period, usually seven years, in exchange for their passage. These Americans were not participating in new visions of freedom; they were, for a period, essentially slaves who did not have the freedom to strike out into the American frontier to make their fortunes. Women also had few political rights in the United States.

- For most of the nineteenth century, de Crèvecoeur's essays were ignored. After being first published in London in 1782, the essays were published once in Philadelphia in 1793. After that, there is no record of a reprinting until 1904. The fact these essays were published in 1904 is significant because this was a period when waves of Europeans were immigrating. De Crèvecoeur's book contributed to the notion of Americans as a new nationality just at a time when some Americans worried that immigrants from southern and eastern Europe might dilute the nature of the American character. Although it was written in the eighteenth century, the real significance of *Letters from an American Farmer* lay in the early twentieth century.

Excerpt from Letters from an American Farmer

Letter III. What Is an American.

*I wish I could be acquainted with the feelings and thoughts which must agitate the heart and present themselves to the mind of an enlightened Englishman, when he first lands on this continent. He must greatly rejoice that he lived at a time to see this fair country discovered and settled; he must necessarily feel a share of national pride, when he views the chain of settlements which **embellishes** these extended shores. When he says to himself, this is the work of my countrymen, who, when **convulsed by factions**, afflicted by a variety of miseries and wants, restless and impatient, took **refuge** here. They brought along with them their national genius, to which they principally owe what liberty they enjoy, and what **substance** they possess. Here he sees the industry of his native country displayed in a new manner, and traces in their works the **embryos** of all the arts, sciences, and **ingenuity** which flourish in Europe. Here he beholds fair cities, substantial villages, extensive fields, an immense country filled with decent houses, good roads, orchards, meadows, and bridges, where an hundred years ago all was wild, woody and*

Embellishes: Makes more beautiful; enhances.

Convulsed by factions: In government, upset by groups of people with differing views.

Refuge: A safe place.

Substance: Property or wealth.

Embryos: Very beginnings.

Ingenuity: Inventiveness and inventions.

uncultivated! What a **train** of pleasing ideas this fair spectacle must suggest; it is a prospect which must inspire a good citizen with the most heartfelt pleasure. The difficulty consists in the manner of viewing so extensive a scene. He is arrived on a new continent; a modern society offers itself to his **contemplation,** different from what he had **hitherto** seen. It is not composed, as in Europe, of great lords who possess everything and of a herd of people who have nothing. Here are no **aristocratical** families, no **courts,** no kings, no bishops, no **ecclesiastical** dominion, no invisible power giving to a few a very visible one; no great manufacturers employing thousands, no great refinements of luxury. The rich and the poor are not so far removed from each other as they are in Europe. Some few towns excepted, we are all **tillers of the earth,** from Nova Scotia to West Florida. We are a people of cultivators, scattered over an immense territory communicating with each other by means of good roads and navigable rivers, united by the silken bands of mild government, all respecting the laws, without dreading their power, because they are equitable. We are all animated with the spirit of an industry which is **unfettered** and unrestrained, because each person works for himself. If he travels through our rural districts he views not the **hostile castle,** and the **haughty mansion,** contrasted with the clay-built hut and miserable cabin, where cattle and men help to keep each other warm, and dwell in meanness, smoke, and **indigence.** A pleasing uniformity of decent competence appears throughout our habitations. The meanest of our log-houses is a dry and comfortable habitation. Lawyer or merchant are the fairest titles our towns afford; that of a farmer is the only **appellation** of the rural inhabitants of our country. It must take some time **ere** he can reconcile himself to our dictionary, which is but short in words of dignity, and names of honour. There, on a Sunday, he sees a congregation of respectable farmers and their wives, all clad in neat **homespun,** well mounted, or riding in their own humble waggons. There is not among them an **esquire,** saving the **unlettered magistrate.** There he sees a **parson** as simple as his flock, a farmer who does not **riot** on the labour of others. We have no princes, for whom we toil, starve, and bleed: we are the most perfect society now existing in the world. Here man is free; as he ought to be; nor is this pleasing equality so transitory as many others are. Many ages will not see the shores of our great lakes replenished with inland nations, nor the unknown bounds of North America entirely peopled. Who can tell how far it extends? Who can tell the millions of men whom it will feed and contain? For no European foot has as yet travelled half the extent of this mighty continent!

Uncultivated: Unplanted.

Train: Sequence.

Contemplation: Thought.

Hitherto: Previously.

Aristocratical: Legally superior to most people.

Courts: The people and functions surrounding royalty.

Ecclesiastical: Related to the church.

Tillers of the earth: Farmers.

Unfettered: Free.

Hostile castle: A king's residence, often regarded as unfriendly by commoners.

Haughty mansion: The house of a rich person who considers himself or herself to be superior to ordinary people.

Indigence: Without money.

Appellation: Name.

Ere: Before.

Homespun: Homemade cloth.

Esquire: The title of one who is more learned, or richer than, an ordinary person.

Unlettered magistrate: A local official who is not highly educated in the law.

Parson: A local clergyman.

Riot: Engage in unrestrained celebration.

The next wish of this traveller will be to know **whence** came all these people? They are a mixture of English, Scotch, Irish, French, Dutch, Germans, and Swedes. From this **promiscuous breed**, that race now called Americans have arisen. The eastern provinces must indeed be excepted, as being the unmixed descendants of Englishmen. I have heard many wish that they had been more intermixed also: for my part, I am no wisher, and think it much better as it has happened. They exhibit a most **conspicuous** figure in this great and **variegated** picture; they too enter for a great share in the pleasing perspective displayed in these thirteen provinces. I know it is fashionable to reflect on them, but I respect them for what they have done; for the accuracy and wisdom with which they have settled their territory; for the decency of their manners; for their early love of letters; their ancient college, the first in this hemisphere; for their industry; which to me who am but a farmer, is the criterion of everything. There never was a people, situated as they are, who with **so ungrateful a soil** have done more in so short a time. Do you think that the **monarchical ingredients** which are more prevalent in other governments, have purged them from all foul stains? Their histories assert the contrary.

In this great American **asylum**, the poor of Europe have by some means met together, and in consequence of various causes; to what purpose should they ask one another what countrymen they are? Alas, two thirds of them had no country. Can a **wretch** who wanders about, who works and starves, whose life is a continual scene of sore affliction or pinching **penury**; can that man call England or any other kingdom his country? A country that had no bread for him, whose fields **procured** him no harvest, who met with nothing but the frowns of the rich, the severity of the laws, with jails and punishments; who owned not a single foot of the extensive surface of this planet? No! Urged by a variety of motives, here they came. Every thing has tended to **regenerate** them; new laws, a new mode of living, a new social system; here they are become men: in Europe they were as so many useless plants, wanting **vegitative mould**, and refreshing showers; they withered, and were mowed down by want, hunger, and war; but now by the power of transplantation, like all other plants they have taken root and flourished! Formerly they were not numbered in any **civil lists** of their country, except in those of the poor; here they rank as citizens. By what invisible power has this surprising **metamorphosis** been performed? By that of the laws and that of their industry. The laws, the **indulgent** laws, protect them as they arrive, stamping on them the sym-

Whence: From what place.

Promiscuous breed: An assortment of people not restricted to a single type or class.

Conspicuous: Obvious.

Variegated: Of different colors.

So ungrateful a soil: Earth that is hard to farm.

Monarchical ingredients: Characteristics of a monarchy.

Asylum: Shelter.

Wretch: A poor, miserable person.

Penury: Severe poverty.

Procured: Obtained.

Regenerate: Reform.

Vegitative [vegetative] mould: Soft, crumbling earth suitable for plant growth.

Civil lists: Official government lists, such as lists of voters.

Metamorphosis: Dramatic transformation.

Indulgent: Tolerant.

bol of adoption; they receive ample rewards for their labours; these accumulated rewards procure them lands; those lands confer on them the title of freemen, and to that title every benefit is affixed which men can possibly require. This is the great operation daily performed by our laws. From whence proceed these laws? From our government. Whence the government? It is derived from the original genius and strong desire of the people ratified and confirmed by the crown. This is the great chain which links us all....

What attachment can a poor European emigrant have for a country where he had nothing? The knowledge of the language, the love of a few kindred as poor as himself, were the only cords that tied him: his country is now that which gives him land, bread, protection, and consequence: **Ubi panis ibi patria,** is the motto of all emigrants. What then is the American, this new man? He is either an European, or the descendant of an European, hence that strange mixture of blood, which you will find in no other country. I could point out to you a family whose grandfather was an Englishman, whose wife was Dutch, whose son married a French woman, and whose present four sons have now four wives of different nations. He *is* an American, who leaving behind him all his ancient prejudices and manners, receives new ones from the new mode of life he has embraced, the new government he obeys, and the new rank he holds. He becomes an American by being received in the broad lap of our great **Alma Mater.** Here individuals of all nations are melted into a new race of men, whose labours and posterity will one day cause great changes in the world. Americans are the western pilgrims, who are carrying along with them that great mass of arts, sciences, **vigour,** and industry which began long since in the east; they will finish the great circle. The Americans were once scattered all over Europe; here they are **incorporated** into one of the finest systems of population which has ever appeared, and which will hereafter become distinct by the power of the different climates they inhabit. The American ought therefore to love this country much better than that wherein either he or his forefathers were born. Here the rewards of his industry follow with equal steps the progress of his labour; his labour is founded on the basis of nature, self-interest; can it want a stronger **allurement**? Wives and children, who before in vain demanded of him a morsel of bread, now, fat and **frolicsome,** gladly help their father to clear those fields whence **exuberant** crops are to arise to feed and to clothe them all; without any part being claimed, either by a **despotic** prince, a rich **abbot,** or a mighty **lord.** Here religion demands but little of him; a small volun-

Ubi panis ibi patria: Latin phrase meaning "Where there is bread (food) there is my country."

Alma Mater: Latin phrase meaning "fostering mother."

Vigour: Energy and enthusiasm.

Incorporated: Brought together as a body.

Allurement: Attraction.

Frolicsome: Inclined to play.

Exuberant: Abundant.

Despotic: Dictatorial.

Abbot: A church official.

Lord: A landowner who in Europe was likely to be an aristocrat with the formal title "Lord" preceding his name.

tary salary to the minister, and gratitude to God; can he refuse these? The American is a new man, who acts upon new principles; he must therefore entertain new ideas, and form new opinions. From involuntary idleness, **servile** dependence, penury, and useless labour, he has passed to toils of a very different nature, rewarded by ample **subsistence.** —This is an American….

After a foreigner from any part of Europe is arrived, and become a citizen; let him devoutly listen to the voice of **our great parent**, which says to him, "Welcome to my shores, distressed European; bless the hour in which thou didst see my **verdant fields**, my fair navigable rivers, and my green mountains!—If thou wilt work, I have bread for thee; if thou wilt be honest, sober, and industrious, I have greater rewards to confer on thee—ease and independence. I will give thee fields to feed and cloath thee; a comfortable fireside to sit by, and tell thy children by what means thou hast prospered; and a decent bed to **repose** on. I shall endow thee beside with the **immunities of a freeman.** If thou wilt carefully educate thy children, teach them gratitude to God, and reverence to that government that **philanthropic** government, which has collected here so many men and made them happy. I will also provide for thy **progeny**; and to every good man this ought to be the most holy, the most Powerful, the most earnest wish he can possibly form, as well as the most consolatory prospect when he dies. Go thou and work and till; thou shalt prosper, provided thou be just, grateful and industrious."

What happened next …

Initially, laws of the United States were in accord with de Crèvecoeur's vision. People from any nationality were free to become citizens after living in the country for a period of years, with one notable exception: to become a citizen, a person had to be "free and white," according to the nation's first naturalization law passed in 1790. (Naturalization is the process by which an immigrant achieves the rights of a citizen, notably the right to vote in elections.) Even after people whose skin was regarded as "black" achieved equal rights, people from Asian ancestors continued to be denied the right to become citizens. The Chinese Exclusion Act of 1882 (see chapter 8), for example, banned immigration of Chinese people to the United States for ten years, a period later extended until 1944. Chinese were also excluded from being naturalized.

Although de Crèvecoeur wrote of a society in which there were no great distinctions between rich and poor, as in Europe, over the course of the next century enormous distinctions developed between rich business owners and poor workers or small farmers. By the beginning of the twentieth century, when *Letters from an American Farmer* was republished for the first time since 1793, the social and economic conditions of the United States had changed dramatically. Huge factories had risen in cities, employing thousands of European immigrants for wages barely high enough on which to live. On the other end of the economic scale, men like John D. Rockefeller (1839–1937) and Andrew Carnegie (1835–1919) had built huge fortunes in oil and steel respectively. Their wealth was so vast that they were nicknamed the "Robber Barons," using an ancient title of European aristocrats to convey a sense that in the United States, the old ideal of equality had been replaced by the reality of a huge gap between the wealthy and their workers—a sharp contrast to the picture painted by de Crèvecoeur. Nevertheless, the idealistic portrait of a country populated by hard-working independent farmers was a powerful myth, one kept alive in part by twentieth-century reproductions of the essays of de Crèvecoeur.

The idea of an American "melting pot" has not always been favored in the United States. Throughout the nineteenth centuries, there were movements that objected to the immigration of people from outside northern Europe. The Know-Nothing Party, for example, ran presidential candidates in 1848 and 1852, advocating an end to the immigration of Roman Catholics from Ireland and other people who did not fit the mold of a Protestant, white, northern-European population. The Workingman's Party of California became a strong, though short-lived, influence in 1878 and 1879 in reaction against immigration by Chinese. In more modern times, political movements have tried to control the character of American society by insisting that all public school classes be taught in English, a position widely understood to be aimed at Spanish-speaking immigrants from Mexico and Central America.

Did you know ...

• The idea that American society is a "melting pot" started gaining popularity in the early twentieth century. The term referred to a process in which the habits and characteristics of immigrants from many different countries merge together and become a new nationality. The phrase "melting pot" dates from a play by that title written by a Jewish immigrant, Israel Zangwill (1864–1926). The play was first produced in Washington, D.C., in 1904.

• De Crèvecoeur himself did not become an American, about which he wrote. After living in New Jersey, he was appointed the French consul (representative) in New York City. He later returned to Europe, where he died in 1813.

Israel Zangwill, creator of the phrase "melting pot."
Hulton-Deutsch Collection/Corbis-Bettman.

For More Information

Books

De Crèvecoeur, Hector St. John. *Letters from an American Farmer.* London: J. M. Dent and Sons Ltd, 1782. Multiple reprints.

Glazer, Nathan, and Daniel P. Moynihan. *Beyond the Melting Pot: The Negroes, Puerto Ricans, Jews, Italians, and Irish of New York City.* 2nd ed. Cambridge, MA: MIT Press, 1970.

O'Neill, Teresa, ed. *Immigration: Opposing Viewpoints.* San Diego, CA: Greenhaven Press, 1992.

Zangwell, Israel. *The Melting-Pot: Drama in Four Acts.* New York: Macmillan, 1909. Reprint, Arno Press, 1975.

Periodicals

Wortham, Anne. "The Melting Pot—Are We There Yet?" *World and I* (September 2001): p. 261.

Web Sites

Woodlief, Ann M. "Negotiating Nature/Wilderness: Crèvecoeur and American Identity in Letters from an American Farmer." *English Department, Virginia Commonwealth University.* http://www.vcu.edu/engweb/crev.htm (accessed on January 26, 2004).

Treaty of Fort Stanwix

Enacted in 1784

Reprinted on *Oneida Indian Nation* (Web site)

The United States agrees to give Native Americans control of the western territory

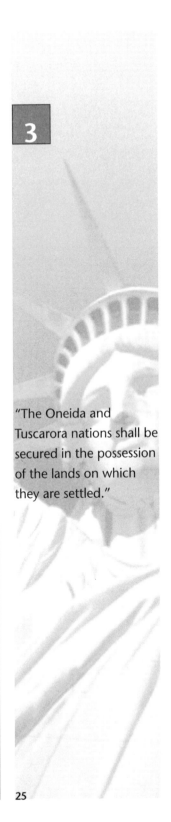

3

The flow of European emigrants to the United States that started in the early seventeenth century created constant pressure to acquire more land for farming in areas occupied by Native Americans. A long series of treaties, or formal agreements, were negotiated by the Native Americans on one side and the British or American governments on the other in an effort to avoid conflict. The Treaty of Fort Stanwix in 1784 is one example of an American promise to protect native lands from further takeovers by Europeans. Likewise, it also stands as an example of yet another treaty that was ignored by European settlers and never enforced by either the British or the U.S. government. For the arriving Europeans, the paper meant nothing compared with the opportunity to own land. Pushing out Native Americans was viewed as simply a necessary part of European migration to North America.

From 1754 to 1763, the British and the British colonists fought a war against France—the French and Indian War (1754–63; known in Europe as the Seven Years' War)—allied with several tribes of Native Americans, for domination over North America. The territory involved in the war includ-

"The Oneida and Tuscarora nations shall be secured in the possession of the lands on which they are settled."

ed much of present-day Ohio as well as northern New York and western Pennsylvania. The British colonists won the conflict, but their victory led to many new problems. The British, having paid the cost of fighting the war, turned to the British colonialists to help repay those costs. But since the colonialists did not have representatives in Parliament, the new taxes raised a storm of protest. "Taxation without representation!" the settlers complained, and eventually their discontent sparked the move for American independence, in 1776.

The British victory over the French also created a new set of problems for the British. Native Americans who had been allied with the French fell under British rule, even though British troops did not firmly control the disputed territory. White settlers, starting with the British and continuing under the government of the independent United States, repeatedly negotiated peace treaties with the Native Americans. The general form of the treaties was similar: the government (British or American) promised to keep new settlers east of a line specified in the treaty, giving the Native Americans control of the territory to the west.

These treaties, of which the Treaty of Fort Stanwix signed in 1784 is an example, are remembered by Native Americans as demonstrations that Europeans could not be trusted to keep their promises, even when the promises were put in writing. None of the treaties had any meaningful impact on slowing the flow of Europeans moving westward in search of new land to settle.

European migration to North America, starting in the early seventeenth century, was not just a question of peaceful Europeans coming under attack by natives. It was also a story of two peoples, native and European, each organized into a form of government, formally agreeing to establish a boundary between them—and of the Europeans repeatedly breaking those agreements to accommodate the desires of Europeans for farmland.

Things to remember while reading the Treaty of Fort Stanwix:

- The Treaty of Fort Stanwix was not the first attempt to avoid conflict between settlers and Indians by promising

Native Americans a halt to European settlement. Not long after the French and Indian War ended, the Proclamation of 1763 had forbidden English colonists from moving west of the Appalachian Mountains. The intent of the proclamation, an official public announcement sometimes in the form of a rule or law, was to reserve the land between the Appalachians and the Mississippi River for Native Americans. From the British viewpoint, the proclamation was a means of keeping peace. To the British colonialists, the proclamation was merely a slight stumbling block to achieving economic success in the New World.

- In 1768, the British had signed an earlier treaty with the Six Nations at Fort Stanwix. In that agreement, the Iroquois Indians agreed to give up lands east and south of the Ohio River, in exchange for being left alone in their territory. The 1768 treaty was unsuccessful for two reasons: English settlers largely ignored it, and some Native Americans living in the territory did not recognize the rights of the Iroquois to negotiate on their behalf. Among the tribes that did not agree to the 1768 treaty were the Delaware, the Mintos, and the Shawnees. By 1774, violence had broken out between the two sides. The natives, especially the Shawnee tribe, tried to drive the whites east of the Appalachian Mountains.

- Possession of farmland was not the only source of friction between the white settlers and native inhabitants. Most Native Americans in the region depended on hunting deer and other wild animals for their food. Some white men took up hunting as a means of earning a living, killing animals and selling them for meat to fellow Europeans. Some Native American leaders in the disputed territories viewed this as an intrusion on Indian hunting grounds, every bit as objectionable to them as it was for the white settlers when Native Americans killed one of their cows or hogs for meat. The arrival of Europeans in North America did not represent simply a clash of possession; it was also a clash between an ancient culture of hunters and gatherers with a more modern culture of farmers. For the Native Americans, possession of land was not important; their lives revolved around following herds of animals. For the European settlers, possession of land for farming was the essence of their civilization. It was, perhaps, inevitable that the two sides would clash, regardless of diplomatic efforts to avoid violence.

The Treaty of Fort Stanwix

*Articles concluded at **Fort Stanwix**, on the twenty-second day of October, one thousand seven hundred and eighty-four, between*

Fort Stanwix: A British, and later, American fortification located near Rome, New York.

Oliver Wolcott, Richard Butler, and Arthur Lee, Commissioners Plenipotentiary from the United States, in Congress assembled, on the one Part, and the **Sachems** and Warriors of the Six Nations, on the other.

The United States of America give peace to the **Senecas, Mohawks, Onondagas,** and **Cayugas,** and receive them into their protection upon the following conditions:

ARTICLE 1.

Six hostages shall be immediately delivered to the commissioners by the said nations, to remain in possession of the United States, till all the prisoners, white and black, which were taken by the said Senecas, Mohawks, Onondagas, and Cayugas, or by any of them, in the late war, from among the people of the United States, shall be delivered up.

ARTICLE 2.

The **Oneida** and **Tuscarora** nations shall be secured in the possession of the lands on which they are settled.

ARTICLE 3.

A line shall be drawn, beginning at the mouth of a creek about four miles east of Niagara, called Oyonwayea, or Johnston's Landing-Place, upon the lake named by the Indians Oswego, and by us Ontario; from thence southerly in a direction always four miles east of the carrying path, between Lake Erie and Ontario, to the mouth of Tehoseroron or Buffalo Creek on Lake Erie; thence south to the north boundary of the state of Pennsylvania; thence west to the end of the said north boundary; thence south along the west boundary of the said state, to the river Ohio; the said line from the mouth of the Oyonwayea to the Ohio, shall be the western boundary of the lands of the Six Nations, so that the Six Nations shall and do yield to the United States, all claims to the country west of the said boundary, and then they shall be secured in the peaceful possession of the lands they inhabit east and north of the same, reserving only six miles square round the fort of Oswego, to the United States, for the support of the same.

ARTICLE 4.

The Commissioners of the United States, in consideration of the present circumstances of the Six Nations, and in **execution** of the **humane** and **liberal** views of the United States upon the signing of the above articles, will order goods to be delivered to the said Six Nations for their use and comfort.

Oliver Wolcott: A member of the U.S. Constitutional Congress and a signer of the Declaration of Independence.

Richard Butler: Revolutionary War soldier who was appointed Indian commissioner by the U.S. Congress.

Arthur Lee: A member of the U.S. Constitutional Congress.

Commissioners Plenipotentiary: Diplomatic representatives given power to conduct business.

Sachems: Chiefs.

Senecas: A native tribe that originally lived in western New York.

Mohawks: A native tribe that lived in the Mohawk River valley of New York.

Onondagas: A native tribe that once lived in New York and Canada.

Cayugas: A native tribe that once lived in New York.

Oneida: A tribe of Native Americans originally of New York.

Tuscarora: A native American tribe that once lived in North Carolina and later moved to New York and thhe Canadian province of Ontario.

Execution: Carrying out.

Humane: Kind; compassionate.

Liberal: Open-minded; tolerant.

Modern-day Tuscarora Indians at a wedding feast.
Library of Congress.

Oliver Wolcott

Richard Butler

Arthur Lee

Otyadonenghti, his x mark (Oneida)

Dagaheari, his x mark (Oneida)

What happened next...

The Treaty of Fort Stanwix made little difference in the European rush westward. Five years after it was signed and almost entirely ignored, the United States negotiated another formal treaty with the Six Nations. The governor of what was then called the Northwest Territory (roughly present-day Ohio), Arthur St. Clair (1734–1818), signed another agreement with the Six Nations at Fort Harmar, "for removing all causes of controversy, regulating trade, and settling boundaries, between the Indian nations in the northern department and the said United States, of the one part, and the sachems and warriors of the Six Nations, of the other part." This treaty, like the one at Fort Stanwix, promised peace and friendship between the United States and the Six Nations. But like the Treaty of Fort Stanwix, the Treaty of Fort Harmar was soon to be ignored.

Some of the tribes that signed the treaty, notably the Shawnee, tried to strike back when it became obvious that the U.S. government either could not or would not stem the flood of Europeans. In so doing, the Native Americans effectively played into the hands of the Europeans, who sent troops to protect settlers, making it even easier and safer for the settlers to ignore their treaties with the natives and push the borders of the United States westward.

Did you know ...

- Fort Stanwix was designated a national historical monument in 1935 and has been developed into a tourist attraction. The fort played an important role both before and after the Revolutionary War (1775–83) in guarding an important route, called the "Carrying Path," that linked the headwaters of the Hudson River with Lake Erie. The fort is not far from the route of the Erie Canal. The canal was built in the 1820s to aid hauling goods by water from New York to the Great Lakes and from there as far west as Chicago.

For More Information

Books

Costo, Rupert. *Indian Treaties: Two Centuries of Dishonor.* San Francisco: Indian Historian Press, 1977.

Jones, Dorothy V. *License for Empire: Colonialism by Treaty in Early America.* Chicago: University of Chicago Press, 1982.

Kappler, Charles J., ed. *Indian Treaties, 1778–1883.* New York: Interland Pub., 1972. (Reprint of *Indian Affairs: Laws and Treaties,* vol. 2. Washington, DC: Government Printing Office, 1904.)

Prucha, Francis Paul. *American Indian Treaties: The History of a Political Anomaly.* Berkeley: University of California Press, 1994.

Periodicals

Mullin, Michael J. "Personal Politics: William Johnson and the Mohawks." *The American Indian Quarterly* (Summer 1993): p. 350.

Web Sites

Haudenosaunee: People Building a Long House. http://www.sixnations.org/ (accessed on January 21, 2004).

"1784—Treaty with the Six Nations (Treaty of Fort Stanwix)." *Oneida Indian Nation.* http://oneida-nation.net/treat-1784-stand.html (accessed on January 16, 2004).

Act of March 26, 1790

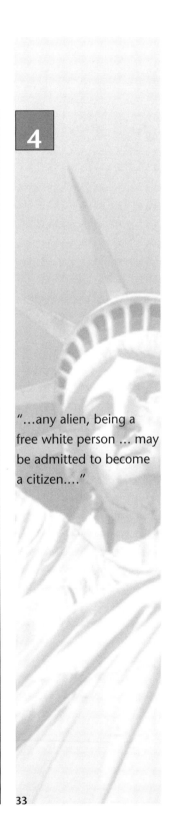

Enacted by U.S. Congress on March 26, 1790

Excerpt reprinted from *U.S. Immigration and Naturalization Laws and Issues: A Documentary History*

Congress passes a law that sets the tone for naturalization laws for over a century

4

S oon after the Constitution was adopted as the basic law of the newly organized United States, Congress passed a law governing the question of how immigrants could become voting citizens with the same rights as people born in the country, a process called naturalization. It was an important issue in one of the first countries ruled by democracy, the will of the citizens as expressed through voting.

The issue of naturalization had not been a problem when the states had been colonies of England. People living in the English colonies had no voice in selecting members of the British legislature, called the Parliament. Even in England, voting for members of Parliament was limited to a relatively few wealthy property owners. In the newly independent United States, political power lay in the hands of citizens (initially, limited to white men). North America seemed destined to be a magnet for people in many different countries who were looking for new economic opportunities. The question of political rights for immigrants had to be addressed.

The men who drafted the U.S. Constitution in the summer of 1788 realized that citizenship was bound to be-

"...any alien, being a free white person ... may be admitted to become a citizen...."

come an issue. They also realized that their newly independent country already had a rich mix of non-English people, including Native Americans, slaves from Africa, and immigrants from European countries other than England, especially France.

Consequently, Article I, Section 8 of the new Constitution listed the powers given to the new Congress. The third item on the list was the power to "establish a uniform rule of naturalization ... throughout the United States."

A year after the Constitution was adopted, Congress passed the first law that established a "uniform rule of naturalization": The Act of March 26, 1790. The act was just the first in a series of laws addressing the issue of naturalization, which is a companion to the question of immigration, or admitting people from abroad to live in the United States. The 1790 law set the tone for such laws for well over a century.

Things to remember while reading an excerpt from the Act of March 26, 1790:

- The 1790 law allowed any immigrant who was a "free white person" to become a citizen after living in the United States for two years. Most obviously, this clause excluded Africans brought to the United States as slaves. This law was just the first of many laws that openly discriminated against people of color. Beginning around 1860, similar restrictions were placed on people from Asia, although these limitations focused on the right to come to the United States in the first place, rather than on the right to become a citizen. As late as 1906, the U.S. Supreme Court ruled that the government had the power to prevent Asians from becoming citizens on the grounds that they were not "white," as specified in the 1790 law.

- The law of 1790 did not distinguish between men and women; it referred to "white persons." In reality, however, the law was largely irrelevant to women, since the only practical advantage of becoming a citizen was the right to vote, which was denied to all American women until 1920. During the nineteenth century, wives and children of naturalized male citizens became citizens automatically. The 1790 law specifically mentioned that

the children of American citizens who were born "beyond the sea," or overseas, were considered as natural citizens. This provision would apply to a child of a diplomat or merchant who was traveling abroad at the time a child was born, for example.

- The Act of March 26, 1790, left many questions unanswered. For example, the act said that new citizens must swear an oath, but it did not specify what the oath should say, exactly. It also stated that people becoming new citizens should appear before a "court of record," without specifying exactly what such a court was. Because these statements could be interpreted in different ways, one result was that the process of becoming a citizen was different across the country, contrary to the expectation of the men who had drafted the Constitution. Many different oaths were accepted—and in some cases, the oaths were not even recorded—in both federal and state courts. The first naturalization law provides a good

The Act of March 26, 1790, covered only white people, which excluded Africans brought to the United States as slaves, such as those shown above at a slave auction. *Getty Images.*

example of how a law that seems simple on the surface can become complicated when it is put into practice.

Excerpt from the Act of March 26, 1790

*Section 1: Be it **enacted** by the Senate and House of Representatives of the United States in Congress assembled, That any **alien**, being a free white person, who shall have resided within the **limits** and under the **jurisdiction** of the United States for the term of two years, may be admitted to become a citizen thereof, on application to any **common law court of record**, in any one of the States wherein he shall have resided for the term of one year at least, and making proof to the satisfaction of such court, that he is a person of good character, and taking the oath or **affirmation prescribed** by law, to support the Constitution of the United States, which oath or affirmation such court shall administer; and the clerk of such court shall record such application, and the proceedings thereon; and thereupon such person shall be considered as a citizen of the United States. And the children of such persons so **naturalized**, dwelling within the United States, being under the age of twenty-one years at the time of such naturalization, shall also be considered as citizens of the United States. And the children of citizens of the United States, that may be born **beyond sea**, or out of the limits of the United States, shall be considered as natural born citizens: Provided, that the right of citizenship shall not **descend** to persons whose fathers have never been resident in the United States; Provided also, That no person **heretofore proscribed** by any state, shall be admitted a citizen as **aforesaid**, except by an act of the legislature in the state in which such person was proscribed.*

Enacted: Voted into law.

Alien: One who is not a citizen.

Limits: Boundaries.

Jurisdiction: Area subject to the laws of a government.

Common law court of record: A normal court of law; here, both state and federal courts.

Affirmation: A solemn oath.

Prescribed: Established.

Naturalized: Given the rights of a citizen born in a country.

Beyond sea: Overseas; outside the United States.

Descend: Pass down.

Heretofore: Previously.

Proscribed: Prohibited.

Aforesaid: Previously mentioned.

What happened next ...

The 1790 act mentioned nothing about the attitudes of new citizens toward government policy in the new democracy. Soon after the 1790 act was passed, however, politics became an important consideration in giving immigrants the right to vote. During the two terms of the nation's first president, George Washington (1732–1799; served 1789–97), two distinct political parties had begun to emerge. (Political parties are groups of people who broadly agree on sets of political issues and act together in order to bring about their ideas through the election to office of favored politicians.) One party, led by Washington's successor, John Adams (1797–1801; served 1797–1801), was known as the Federalists. The Federalist Party included Washington, Adams, and the nation's first secretary of the treasury, Alexander Hamilton (c. 1755–1804). The Federalists supported a strong central (federal) government and were generally sympathetic to the interests of merchants in the cities. An opposing faction, the Anti-Federalists (also called the Democratic-Republicans), were led by the country's third president, Thomas Jefferson (1743–1826; served 1801–9). The Anti-Federalists opposed giving the federal government more power than was absolutely needed.

George Washington, taking the oath of office as the United States' first president.
© Bettmann/Corbis.

In January 1795, the act of 1790 was repealed and replaced by another law. The new law required immigrants to wait five years (instead of two) to become a citizen and to make a declaration of intention to become a citizen three years before becoming naturalized. An immigrant who failed to make the declaration might have to wait more than five years after arrival in the United States to become a voter. The 1795 law also required naturalized citizens to renounce any noble titles they might hold (such as "duke" or "countess") and to promise not to be loyal to any foreign king or queen. These measures were intended to ensure that new citizens would not secretly want to restore a king and an aristocracy, or individuals who inherit great wealth and special political privileges.

In 1798, the law on naturalization was changed again. The Federalists feared that many new immigrants favored their political foes, the Democratic-Republicans. The Federalists, therefore, wanted to reduce the political influence of immigrants. To do so, the Federalists, who controlled Congress, passed a law that required immigrants to wait fourteen years before becoming naturalized citizens and thereby gaining the right to vote. The 1798 act also barred naturalization for citizens of countries at war with the United States. At the time, the United States was engaged in an unofficial, undeclared naval war with France. The French government thought the United States had taken the side of Britain in the ongoing conflict between Britain and France. A related law passed in 1798, the Alien Enemy Act, gave the president the power during a time of war to arrest or deport any alien thought to be a danger to the government.

After Jefferson became president (in 1801), the 1798 naturalization law was repealed, or overturned (in 1802). The basic provisions of the original 1790 law were restored except for the period of residency before naturalization. The residency requirement, that is, the amount of time the immigrant had to reside, or live, in the United States, was put back to five years, as it had been in 1795.

The 1802 law remained the basic naturalization act until 1906, with two notable exceptions. In 1855, the wives of American citizens were automatically granted citizenship. In 1870, people of African descent could become naturalized citizens, in line with constitutional amendments passed after the American Civil War (1861–65) that banned slavery and gave African American men the right to vote. Other laws were passed to limit the number of people (if any) allowed to enter the United States from different countries, especially Asian countries, but these laws did not affect limits on naturalization.

Within a decade of adopting the Constitution, immigration, and naturalization in particular, had become hot political issues. They have remained political issues for more than two centuries.

Did you know ...

- Naturalization laws relate to the process of immigrants becoming a citizen. Other laws have provided for losing citizenship—by getting married! In 1907, Congress passed a law that said a woman born in the United States (and therefore a citizen) would lose her citizenship if she married an alien (who was therefore not a citizen). In 1922, two years after women won the right to vote, this provision was repealed and a woman's citizenship status was separated from her husband's.

For More Information

Books

Franklin, Frank G. *The Legislative History of Naturalization in the United States*. New York: Arno Press, 1969.

Jasper, Margaret C. *The Law of Immigration*. Dobbs Ferry, NY: Oceana Publications, 2000.

LeMay, Michael, and Elliot Robert Barkan, eds. *U.S. Immigration and Naturalization Laws and Issues: A Documentary History*. Westport, CT: Greenwood Press, 1999.

Periodicals

DeConcini, Christina, Jeanine S. Piller, and Margaret Fisher. "The Changing Face of Immigration Law." *Social Education* (November-December 1998): p. 462.

Web Sites

History, Genealogy and Education, U.S. Bureau of Citizenship and Immigration Services. http://uscis.gov/graphics/aboutus/history/ (accessed on January 22, 2004).

"A Know Nothing" (Anonymous)

Excerpt from the Know Nothing Platform
About 1855

An upstart political party reveals its platform

In the mid-1840s, the United States witnessed a sudden increase in the number of immigrants from Europe, particularly from Germany and Ireland. Political strife and widespread crop failures in Germany sent tens of thousands of immigrants to the United States. In Ireland, a devastating failure of the potato crop resulted in starvation for thousands; those who could afford a ticket out of Europe sailed to the United States, many virtually penniless.

The Irish immigrants in particular were overwhelmingly Roman Catholic, the Christian church headed by the pope in Rome, Italy. The arrival of the Irish immigrants in eastern cities like New York, Boston, and Philadelphia marked the first significant number of Catholics in a country that previously had been primarily Protestant. This sudden inflow of immigrants sparked a sharp reaction among some Americans, who feared that the character of the United States might change dramatically if large numbers of Catholics became citizens. The result was an anti-immigrant movement called the Know Nothings, so called because members of the variety of organizations that constituted the movement customarily replied "I know nothing" when asked about their association.

Until the mid-1830s, most immigrants to the United States were from England or Scotland or were African slaves kidnapped and transported against their will to the United States. The majority of European immigrants were Protestants, whose religious beliefs were based on a three-hundred-year-old opposition to teachings of the Roman Catholic Church. Some Protestants feared that the Catholic Church, which had played an important political role in European history, wanted to exert political influence in the United States. These Protestants worried that the Church would use Catholic immigrants as a tool to accomplish this goal by influencing immigrants' votes. Even without any evidence of Church interference in politics, some Protestants were persuaded that a plot existed and were anxious to put a stop to it. To do so, these Protestants formed several organizations with names like the Order of United Americans and the Order of the Star-Spangled Banner. (The term "order" was used in the sense of a group of people united for a particular cause, often implying use of secret rituals, which characterized the anti-immigrant, anti-Catholic Know-Nothing movement.)

Under U.S. immigration laws dating from the 1790s, newcomers had to wait five years before they could become citizens and obtain the right to vote. Children born in the United States of immigrant parents were full-fledged citizens at birth. There were several organizations devoted to limiting the rights of immigrants, principally by denying them the right to vote. The so-called Know-Nothing organizations also supported banning immigrants from holding public office (the U.S. Constitution required that the president be born in the United States, but other offices were open to any citizen, regardless of place of birth). Additionally, they provided strong support for public, nonreligious (and, therefore, non-Catholic) schools.

Just as the new wave of immigrants was arriving, one of the two dominant political parties in the United States, the Whigs, was rapidly losing influence. (A political party is a group of like-minded people who work together to elect people to office and to influence government policy.) The other major political party, the Democratic Party, actively sought support from new citizens, which was another cause of concern for Know Nothings: that in order to attract votes from people born outside of the United States who became American (a process known as naturalization), the Democratic Party might adopt policies that favored the Catholic Church. Despite a U.S. constitutional ban on laws that favored one religion over another, such bans were not in place for state governments. In Massachusetts, for example, taxes supported the Protestant church until 1833. As late as 1877, the constitution of New Hampshire contained a clause disqualifying Catholics from holding public office. The Whigs were losing influence, largely because the party was divided over the issue of whether slavery should be abolished. In the congressional elections of 1852, some Whigs, in an effort to retain power, also began appealing to Catholic immigrants—a move that shocked and dismayed members of the Know-Nothing groups.

To combat the suspected political influence of the Catholic Church among naturalized immigrant voters, the Know Nothings began organizing their own political parties. Starting in the early 1840s, a party called the National Republican Party (not the same as the Republican Party that was formed in 1852 and continues into the twenty-first century) elected some local officials in New York, as well as a congressman from Philadelphia, Louis Levin (1808–1860). In 1849, the American Party was formally organized in New York to represent the Know-Nothing agenda. Over the next six years, the party attracted significant support in state elections, especially in New England and New York, states where large numbers of Irish immigrants had settled. In the elections of 1854 and 1856, American Party candidates were elected governor in California, Connecticut, Kentucky, Maryland, Massachusetts, and New Hampshire. The party also controlled state legislatures in Connecticut, Kentucky, Maryland, New Hampshire, and Rhode Island, and was the leading opposition party in other states. In the U.S. Congress, an American Party congressman, Nathaniel Banks (1816–1894), was elected to the highly influential position of Speaker of the House of Representatives.

Things to remember while reading an excerpt from the *Know Nothing Platform*:

- The Know-Nothing movement reflected two different trends in American politics during the middle of the nineteenth century: opposition to the Catholic Church and concern about the sudden rise in immigrants. Anti-Catholic feelings were not new in the United States; some of the earliest settlers from Britain, the Puritans and pilgrims, came to North America to escape what they viewed as Roman Catholic influence over the official Church of England. As reflected in this excerpt from the *Know-Nothing Platform: Containing an Account of the Encroachments of the Roman Catholic Hierarchy on the Civil and Religious Liberties on the People in Europe, Asia, Africa and America, Showing the Necessity of the Order of Know Nothings, with a Valuable and Interesting Appendix,* prejudice against Catholics was extreme and unjustified. Whatever the history of religion in Europe, there was no evidence in nineteenth-century America that the Catholic Church was trying to seize power in the United States. The anti-Catholic sentiments expressed by the anonymous author of the *Know Nothing Platform* would hardly be tolerated in twenty-first-century America, but they were not so uncommon in the middle of the nineteenth century, which was a period marked by a revival of strong religious feelings throughout much of the country.

- In parallel with anti-Catholic feelings was suspicion of "foreigners." Although most Americans could trace their ancestry to immigrants, the immigration of the mid-1840s was different. Many of the newcomers did not speak English as a first language. Moreover, many of those coming to the United States, especially from Ireland, were extremely poor, barely able to afford the cost of a ticket on a ship across the Atlantic Ocean. Once they arrived, the immigrants were willing to take nearly any job that paid money, and were willing to work for relatively low wages, which was a source of annoyance to workers already living in the United States. Underlying some of the bitterness towards immigrants was the economic issue of low wages and competition for jobs.

- In California, the Gold Rush of 1848 attracted many newcomers, including large numbers of Chinese immigrants who came to the United States in search of instant riches. Like their Irish counterparts on the East Coast, Chinese immigrants were often willing to work for low wages. Combined with obvious cultural differences between Chinese and Americans, Asian immigration added support to the Know-Nothing movement in California.

- The author of the *Know Nothing Platform* points to no specific instances in which Catholic immigrants have acted against the interests of the United States while under the influence of church leaders. The "platform" substitutes labels and insults for facts, a technique common in political propaganda. (Propaganda is writing intended to sway people's opinions without presenting a balanced argument.) The author assumes that Catholics are influenced by their religious leaders to act against the interests of the United States, but also takes for granted that Protestants are not subject to similar influences by their religious leaders. The fact that the *Know Nothing Platform* appeared in print does not automatically give it legitimacy.

Excerpt from the Know Nothing Platform

The spirit of **denationalization** was fast proceeding, under the policy of the leaders of **the two great political parties** of the union. Each [party] had **degraded** the American nationality, by calling to its aid the votes of foreigners, as such, and in **invoking** the aid of a church [the Catholic church] which, while she **exacts** the most implicit obedience of her **laity**, refuses, in her priesthood, allegiance to any **temporal** authority, save that of the Pope of Rome, as is evidenced by the oath of her bishops, and the oaths taken by the **novitiates** of the order of Jesus.... The rank and file, the masses of both parties, true to their American instincts, and deeply **venerating** the institutions of their fathers, had, previously to the formation of the "Order of Know Nothings," shown their **abhorrence** of the principles of their leaders, by refusing **sanction** to the same by their **suffrages**. The democratic party of Pennsylvania refused to degrade the judiciary of Pennsylvania, by elevating to the dignity of the **ermine**, a man, whose only recommendation was his anti-American sentiments, and a blind devotion to the **despotic** principles of **popery**. The whig leaders did not blush while the newspapers of the party were singing **paeans** of praise in favor of the racy **brogue** of

Denationalization: The process of becoming part of another country.

The two great political parties: The Democratic and Whig parties.

Degraded: Cheapened.

Invoking: Drawing upon.

Exacts: Demands.

Laity: Non-clergy.

Temporal: Earthly.

Novitiates: Beginners.

Venerating: Honoring.

Abhorrence: Extreme dislike.

Sanction: Permission.

Suffrages: Votes.

Ermine: Weasel.

Despotic: Acting like a ruler with absolute power.

Popery: A negative reference to the pope.

Paeans: Joyous songs.

Brogue: Accent.

the Irish, and the **sonorous guttural** of the Germans. The time had arrived when the American of all parties must, of necessity, give birth to an American party, a party that would not only concentrate the principles of nationality, which were burning in their hearts, but that would devise measures and means that would effectually relieve the country from danger of the degrading **serfdom** to which it was about to be subjected.

The **tocsin of alarm**, that our institutions were in danger, had resounded from the pulpit, but the danger was despised; in fact, it would not be comprehended, how a people, inheriting a soil of freedom from their fathers, blest with institutions which, while conservative in their nature, gave the largest political liberty to the people, sanctioned by law, that the world, either in ancient or modern times, has ever beheld, could ever be betrayed by an **effete** and worn out despotism. The **wily** serpent approached our **Eden** with such caution, that even his slimy tracks were invisible, for a long time, to our sight. Scarce had he raised his head to hiss out his temptations, **ere** the whole country was aroused. Hearts strong in patriotism, **imbued** with wisdom from on high, banded themselves together, and with solemn vows of devotion to country, on the altar of their God, resolved to free their soil from the poisonous pollution of its slimy trail. To this original band of patriotic worthies, have been, and still are, associated, hundreds of thousands of Americans, knit together by holy ties of brotherhood, and a common devotion to country, for the support of national honor, of national rights, and the common freedom of man.

The great questions are:—1. Whether the principles of "Know Nothings," are thoroughly American, and such as will add force, vigor and vitality to our institutions. 2. Will this concentration of American sentiment, lead to such measures as will render **innoxious**, the efforts of a foreign church, with her innumerable forces, and **despotic** centralization, as well as the efforts of the secret traitors to our midst?

Both of these objects, the "Order of Know Nothings" will achieve. Armed with the consciousness of right, each day will increase their strength, and add fresh vigor to their blows.

The first principle of the "order" is self-reliance. Like the majestic oak of our own soil, the "order," self-reliant, raises its lofty head, and bids defiance to the blast. It takes to its **embrace** none but of American birth, those who have been reared in the lap of freedom, and whose principles of liberty are interwoven with their beings. As

Sonorous guttural: A negative connotation referring to the full, deep throaty sound of the German language.

Serfdom: A form of virtual slavery common in Europe between about 500 and 1700.

Tocsin of alarm: A warning bell.

Effete: Weak.

Wily: Calculating; scheming.

Eden: In the Bible, the place where Adam and Eve first lived.

Ere: Before.

Imbued: Filled.

Innoxious: Harmless.

Despotic: Characteristic of a dictatorial ruler.

Embrace: Grip.

Americans, but one common sentiment of liberty can find a **lodgment** in their breasts. They **snuff** the breeze, tainted with slavery, afar off, and **disinfect** it of its poisonous quality. They, by their united action, give body, force, and concentration to American sentiment, regardless of all former party ties, as the principles of a party essentially American in its origin, growth and future progress. They **disdain**, and will not receive foreign aid, not even the aid of those **degenerate** Americans who look to foreign aid, to give tone and support to American interests.

Among their resolves, they will the repeal of all those naturalization laws, which by their tolerant and too liberal principles, have invited the despotisms of the old world, to vomit upon our shores, not only the refuse of their own countries, comprising the **paupers, vagrants,** and criminals, the outcasts of society, but also those who swell the rank and file that are offered in the market to politicians, by **Archbishop Hughes,** through the columns of his paper, the "Freeman's Journal." This alteration contemplated in the naturalization laws, is not intended, as is falsely alleged, to deprive these emigrants of any right, civil or religious, but will take from them the right of interfering with the civil, literary, and religious institutions of the country, by taking from the future immigrant the **donation** of citizenship; it will deprive them of all motive and right of interfering with the laws and institutions of the country. The emigrant from foreign shores has no claim to the right of foreigners who are unwilling to become **denizens** upon the terms of our laws, many remain away, and if any do come, it will be with the full understanding, that they must be satisfied to enjoy the rights we are willing to give, without expecting them either to rule over us, or take any part in the regulation of our political arrangements. When they come here, they will be protected in the same enjoyments of the rights of property, the accumulation of their own industry, as ourselves. They may expect that their children, after becoming Americanized by American instruction, may have the rights of full citizenship conferred on them. They will be tolerated in their religious worship, whether of sticks and stones, the relics of **barbarous monks,** or any other **pagan superstition,** but will not be permitted to destroy the American system of common school education, based upon the word of God, without note or comment. Still less will we permit them to arrange the system of instruction for American youth, as to cause them to be false to the allegiance due to our own country, for either a spiritual or temporal foreign head. The American youth, as the future hope of our country, must and shall receive an American education alone.

Lodgment: Place of rest.

Snuff: Sniff at, in order to investigate.

Disinfect: Cleanse of germs.

Disdain: Despise.

Degenerate: Degraded, corrupt.

Paupers: Poor people.

Vagrants: Wanderers.

Archbishop Hughes: John Hughes (1797–1864), the leader of the Catholic church in New York.

Donation: Gift.

Denizens: Foreigners given rights of citizenship.

Barbarous monks: Uncivilized religious leaders.

Pagan superstition: Primitive religious belief not supported by science, such as a belief in magic.

It is also the firm resolve of the "order," that from this time **henceforth,** no foreigner shall hold office under the American government, neither shall any degenerate Americans be elected by our suffrages, who may so **desecrate** the American principle, as to **endeavor,** by their votes or influence, to place any foreigner in any office of honor, trust, or profit. The Americans may, without **vanity,** act upon the belief, that they who have been instructed from their youth, in the principles of free government, as founded by their fathers, are better able to conduct the business of the great political **firm,** than any foreigner whatever, be his abilities what they may. That a foreigner, admitted to the firm as a junior partner, without a knowledge of its general scope, and its practical details, would be as competent to conduct the affairs of the firm, as the senior partners, who had laid the foundation of the house and had erected the **superstructure,** would be contrary to all experience. Where is there an old and well established **mercantile** firm in the whole country that would admit a junior partner, totally unacquainted with the business, and whose habits, and training, and associations, during all his previous life, had been such as to make him, in principle, totally ignorant of its principles, that would be received not only as such partner, but placed at the end of the firm, and the management and direction of its complicated and **multifarious** transactions? Would not such arrangement stamp the senior partners with insanity and justify a **commission** of lunacy? And is it to be supposed that an ignorant, **bog-trotting** Irishman, who after years of instruction, can scarcely be taught to shoe a horse—the moment he is imported from Ireland, under the **auspices** of Archbishop Hughes, to be put up for sale, to the highest bid of **profligate** politicians—is competent to understand and control, for the good of the community, our complicated system of government and policy? Is it not a fact notoriously known to every school-boy of this country, that the comments upon our laws and institutions, by the most celebrated **savans** of Europe, are not only miserable failures, but that their ignorance is apparent on every pages? How then, I ask, can the bigoted ignorant **Papist** from the south of Ireland, who knows no God but his priest, who has surrendered the right of private judgment to an ignorant and vicious priesthood, in things spiritual, be competent to wield the affairs of this great nation, in things temporal? Is he acquainted with the principles of international law? Does he understand, and is he capable of directing the complicated machinery of federal and state governments? Can he do this intuitively, without long previous instruction, when the teachings of a life would scarcely be sufficient, with any re-

Henceforth: Hereafter.

Desecrate: Treat disrespectfully.

Endeavor: Attempt.

Vanity: Pride.

Firm: Organization.

Superstructure: The basic framework of a structure.

Mercantile: Commercial; referring to merchants.

Multifarious: Diverse.

Commission: Certification.

Bog-trotting: Walking on wet spongy ground; a word that derives from Gaelic, the language of Ireland and Scotland.

Auspices: Support; protection.

Profligate: Wild and extravagant.

Savans: Savants; people of learning and wisdom.

Papist: Someone who accepts the pope as the leader of the church.

*gard to the safety of life, to entrust him with the working of an ordinary steam engine, propelling a boat on our navigable streams? Of what right then is he deprived, if the law of the land should compel him, before he sets up the trade of ruler, to qualify himself for the vocation by years of proper training? Does not the law of his own country require a seven years' service as an **apprentice** before he can exercise any **mechanic art**, as master? Could he exercise, in his own country, any of the **learned professions**, before he had been qualified by an adequate training? Is it not the daily and universal practice for every parent to endeavor, by all the means in his power, to train his offspring, by education and unwearied instruction, to fit them for the great battle of life, that they may be well able to perform their parts upon the great **theatre** of future action? Can fault be found with the "Order of Know Nothings" for insisting upon carrying out the principles of common sense, in excluding from the control of the junior partner of the firm, until, by a series of years of instruction, and by years of obedience to the laws of the firm, they become qualified for a higher trust?*

*It is also the firm and unyielding resolve of the "Order of Know Nothings," to have a system of common school education, on strictly American principles, **commensurate** with the wants of the country. By this they mean, not merely schools, where the **rudiments** of knowledge may be obtained, but schools of regular graduations, where will be taught knowledge in all its branches, and common to all the youth of the country and of both sexes. It is the determination that these democratic schools shall be the very best in the land. That the instruction, there received, shall be of the very highest order, as schools, suited for the education of princes. That hereafter, none shall be esteemed an American imbued with the learning and knowledge which an American ought to possess, unless he or she has been educated at those nurseries of national greatness. Here shall be taught no **dogmas** of superstition, but the rules of moral conduct and religious belief shall be fully drawn from the fountain of inspiration, the pure word of God, without note or comment. The language of its instruction is democratic equality, in the sight of God, as this government of the United States recognizes the equality of its own citizens. To preserve this equality, each of the youth of the country must have equality of rights, in education, as the most important, being the foundation of all other rights. Upon the good education of the youth of the country, depend not only their political rights, but the rights of property can only be respected and maintained, either by the general **diffusion** of knowledge, or [by] **bayonets**. In Europe, their peace establishment for the smallest king-*

Apprentice: A trainee in a job or profession.

Mechanic art: A task or job that requires training, such as dealing with machines.

Learned professions: Careers that require specialized learning, such as medicine or law.

Theatre: Scene.

Commensurate: On a compatible scale, such as an appropriate size.

Rudiments: Basics.

Dogmas: Beliefs taught as rules without question.

Diffusion: Circulation.

Bayonets: Knifelike blades attached to the end of rifles.

doms, equals the largest military force ever embodied by this country. Is it not the conservative arm of government, the only protection to the rights of property? For what purpose are such armies kept up in times of peace? Is it not the conservative arm of government, the only protection to the rights of property? In a **pecuniary** point of view, is it not more costly to keep up one army of soldiery, than ten armies of school masters? We are therefore determined, at whatever cost, that the system of common school education shall be kept up, and enlarged to such an extent, that every child of the Union shall be educated as princes, that they may be able to give a reason for their political and every other faith; that the avenues of wealth, consideration and respect, based upon worth, shall be open to every child of the Union; that the incalculable wealth of **dormant** talent shall be cultivated and brought out in bold relief, and made **subservient,** not only to the production of all that dignifies and adorns humanity, but will, in its eventual progress, raise the American people to the highest pinnacle of human happiness and greatness. The child of poverty shall no longer have occasion to mourn, that he is excluded from the temple of science, but to him will be afforded the means for the full development of all the talent and excellencies of his nature, as well as the repression of the rank growth of weeds, which will **encumber,** and choke the fruitfulness of every uncultivated field.…

In order to carry out the reforms contemplated by the "Order of Know Nothings," and **effect** the purification of American sentiment, they contemplate, and will carry through, a complete re-organization of the naturalization laws.… The introduction of foreigners, as citizens, with all the privileges of citizenship, could be of no detriment, if they honestly, in taking the oaths of allegiance to our constitution, could feel and act as if they were Americans, and had cast their lot with us for good or for evil; and would join heart and hand in support of these leading measures which have elevated the American name, and made it, throughout the civilized world, a more powerful shield of protection than the assertion of ancient times—"I am a Roman citizen!" These foreigners, as their conduct has shown, still, while claiming the rights of American citizens, are unwilling, even on our own soil, to discard the principles and name of a **precedent** nationality.

They form associations, exclusively confined to those emigrants claiming the same common origin with themselves. The feuds and **animosities** of their own country, their **antipathies** and **enmities** are by them endeavored to be acclimated here. Hence our peace is disturbed by the barbarous feud of **Corkonians and Far Downs,** the

Pecuniary: Financial.

Dormant: Undiscovered.

Subservient: Inferior.

Encumber: Obstruct.

Effect: Bring about.

Precedent: Previous.

Animosities: Dislikes or hatreds.

Antipathies: Dislikes.

Enmities: Hostilities.

Corkonians and Far Downs: Immigrant Roman Catholics from different parts of Ireland who were involved in gang violence during work on canal projects.

formation of societies of foreign growth, and for the promotion of foreign principles and views, in our midst. Societies, with the names of their patron saint—such as St. Patrick and St. David, as well as St. George—are instituted for the express purpose of keeping alive in their bosoms the love of the father land. To a patriotic recollection of the land of their fathers we do not object; on the contrary, the want of such patriotic feeling would be disgraceful to their character; and perhaps it is impossible for humanity to **eradiate** such feeling.

Does not this show, that such a divided allegiance, due by them to this country and their father land, is incompatible, on principle? How or on what principle of political ethics can we suppose, in case of collision of interests of the two countries, they will give an undivided allegiance to this? It is contrary to the law of nature to expect the same. Is not such divided allegiance, or rather open hostility, to be expected from them, to our institutions, when, in addition to the temporal allegiance due to their former sovereign, is added the **sanction** and requirements of religion itself? Does not the fact warrant the conclusion of their hostility? If not, why the undivided front presented by the Catholics, led on by their priests and bishops, against the educational interests of the country? Why the banding themselves together, as volunteer military corps, with distinctive national names, foreign to our own, made up on rank and file, of distinct nationalities? Were they worthy of the national name of American—were they sincere in their professed allegiance to this country—at all times, and under all possible circumstances, they would rally under the **stars and stripes**, with the recognized nationality of Americans alone, and would rejoice, as Americans, when the national eagle was borne in triumph o'er every sea, and was gallantly borne aloft, as the **"avant courier"** of victory on every battle field of American principles.

Had the European emigration, now swarming to our shores, been as limited as heretofore, they would have been absorbed and lost among our countrymen, but they have not only recently flooded us with their numbers, but they already boast, that such will soon be their increase, that preserving their distinct nationality and faithful allegiance to the Bishop of Rome, they will be able, by the peaceful action of the ballot box, to revolutionize the country—to enact such laws as will enable them to uproot and overturn our educational institutions and make us **panders** to the superstition and despotism of Rome.

Forewarned, we are doubly armed. The "Order of Know Nothings," leaving to them every avenue of honorable industry open, and securing to them the rights of person, property, and the free ex-

Eradiate: Eradicate; remove all traces.

Sanction: Approval.

Stars and stripes: American flag.

Avant courier: Advanced messenger.

Panders: People who encourage and profit from others' weaknesses.

Forewarned: Be advised.

ercise of their religion, are determined so to modify the terms of American political partnership that they shall be excluded from full admission to the control of the firm, until they show by the training that they have full knowledge and capacity, as well as political integrity, to conduct the business of the firm.

The soil of the United States was either fairly acquired by purchase from the **aborigines,** or won by the **valor** and blood of our fathers and our own. We have acquired both the legal and equitable title to the soil, by purchase and by conquest, while the right of independent political government is the legitimate fruit of the hardships, efforts and victories of the wars [against Britain] of 1776 and 1812. Those efforts gave us the undoubted right to model our political constitutions as we thought best. We formed the state and federal constitutions embodying the most enlarged principles of personal freedom compatible with due subordination to social order. Having formed our federal constitution, it is true that we enacted laws to **ascertain** and define the terms upon which foreigners should be admitted into the family compact. Many have availed themselves of those terms, and have become part of ourselves, and would do honor to any community; while others, and **their name is legion**, although with us, are not of us. They … will not be parted from their idols. They preserve a distinct nationality, as a nucleus for the disaffected; and openly **deriding** the institutions of the country, threaten, by their increasing numbers, to place us in the same degrading **vassalage** to the church of Rome as themselves.

If we had the right—and how can it be questioned?—to enact naturalization laws, have we not the same right to **abrogate** them? Cannot the power that creates, also destroy? Are not all legislative enactments temporary in their nature, dependent alone upon the will of the legislature? Will not this legislative will be exercised in a free government for the good of the constituency, and according to their declared views? Has a foreigner any right of citizenship, **inchoate** or complete, except by virtue of the naturalization laws? May not that **boon** be legitimately withdrawn, except so far as rights are already acquired and **vested** under those laws? If the boon of citizenship of hereafter to be given to foreigners, may not the terms be remodeled and better suited to prevent abuse? Of this there can be no doubt.

The "Order of Know Nothings," therefore, are resolved to have the laws of naturalization so modified, that hereafter, none of foreign birth shall be entitled to the full rights of citizens, and that the boon shall be refused even to the children of foreigners born on our

Aborigines: Original inhabitants, such as Native Americans, as distinguished from an invading people.

Valor: Bravery.

Ascertain: Determine.

Their name is legion: There are many of them.

Deriding: Scoffing at.

Vassalage: Captivity.

Abrogate: Abolish.

Inchoate: Partially form.

Boon: Benefit or advantage.

Vested: Given or endowed with a particular right.

*soil, unless educated and prepared for the legitimate exercises of those rights, by a suitable training in the common schools of the country. The children of foreigners trained in our common schools, taught with the youth of the country, imbued by their associations with American sentiments, will look to this as their only country, to it they will cheerfully give their allegiance, and trained in American freedom of thought, they will be Americans in birth, thought and action, and as such can never be made the **servile** tools of foreign despots, either under the **garb** of politics or religion.*

*The emigrant of the first generation, if he really casts his lot with us, and with an honest intent to benefit his offspring, will readily yield his assent to a policy which will qualify his child to become the recipient of the highest honors of the country, while he himself is protected in every legitimate rights, not **subversive** of the honor or interest of the nation.*

*It is to accomplish these leading measures of reform, that the "Order of Know Nothings" has been formed. They are Americans by birth, the descendants of those who laid the foundation of our national greatness, and therefore feel that it is a pious duty **devolved** upon them to transmit the liberties of our country unimpaired, to the remotest posterity. To maintain our institutions in pristine **vigor**, to transmit them unimpaired, to protect them from foreign aggression, to **eschew** all foreign assistance, they know that their own right arm is sufficient, aided and directed by the God of their fathers. They appeal not to force, to effect the reforms intended; they are satisfied that the fraternal associations, banded by the brotherhood of the order, will be sufficient for them by constitutional means, and the sacredness of the ballot box, to effect every reformation for the regeneration of the country. To the laws and constitution they will appeal, and with effect.*

A "Know Nothing."

Servile: Servant-like.

Garb: Appearance.

Subversive: Disloyal.

Devolved: Passed.

Vigor: Strength.

Eschew: Avoid.

What happened next ...

In 1856, the American Party nominated former president Millard Fillmore (1800–1874) as its candidate for president. Fillmore had been vice president when President Zachary Taylor (1785–1850) died suddenly. But in the next presidential election, of 1852, Fillmore was not nominated to

MILLARD FILLMORE,

AMERICAN CANDIDATE FOR PRESIDENT OF THE UNITED STATES.

run by his own Whig Party, which instead nominated former Army general Winfield Scott (1786–1866). Four years later, in 1856, Fillmore was the candidate of the American Party, representing the Know-Nothing cause. He won a majority of votes in just one state, Maryland, and after the election he retired to his home near Buffalo, New York.

The election of 1856 was the last time the Know-Nothing movement played a decisive role in national politics. Instead, national attention shifted to the issue of slavery. In the next election, in 1860, the Republican Party candidate, Abraham Lincoln (1809–1865), was elected president. A few months later, the United States plunged into civil war.

Campaign poster for Millard Fillmore, the former U.S. president who ran in 1856 as the presidential nominee of the American Party, also known as the Know-Nothing Party.
© Corbis.

Did you know ...

- One politician of the 1850s who opposed the Know Nothing movement was Abraham Lincoln, a member of the U.S. House of Representatives and future president. In a

letter written in August 1855 to his life-long friend Joshua Speed (1814–1882), Lincoln wrote: "I am not a Know-Nothing. That is certain. How could I be? How can any one who abhors the oppression of negroes, be in favor of degrading classes of white people? Our progress in degeneracy [decline] appears to me to be pretty rapid. As a nation, we begin by declaring that 'all men are created equal.' We now practically read it 'all men are created equal, except negroes.' When the Know-Nothings get control, it will read 'all men are created equal, except negroes, and foreigners, and catholics.' When it comes to this I should prefer emigrating to some country where they make no pretence of loving liberty—to Russia, for instance, where despotism can be taken pure, and without the base alloy of hypocracy (sic)."

U.S. representative Abraham Lincoln of Illinois, a future president, was very much against the Know Nothing movement.

- Lincoln was a leader of the newly emerging Republican Party, which in 1855 was competing with the American Party for influence. By 1856, the Republicans had largely replaced the American Party as the second major political party, alongside the Democratic Party. Many Know Nothings joined the Republicans, where they influenced the Republican position on issues of immigration for the rest of the nineteenth century and beyond.

For More Information

Books

Anbinder, Tyler. *Nativism and Slavery: The Northern Know Nothings and the Politics of the 1850s.* New York: Oxford University Press, 1992.

Beals, Carleton. *Brass-Knuckle Crusade; the Great Know-Nothing Conspiracy, 1820–1860.* New York: Hastings House, 1960.

Billington, Ray Allen. *The Protestant Crusade, 1800–1860: A Study of the Origins of American Nativism.* Chicago: Quadrangle Books, 1964.

Periodicals

Watson, Harry L. "The American Party Battle: Election Campaign Pamphlets, 1828–1876 (book review)." *Journal of Southern History* (May 2001): p. 448.

Wernick, Robert. "The Rise, and Fall, of a Fervid Third Party." *Smithsonian* (November 1996): p. 150.

Web Sites

Anonymous. *Know Nothing Platform.* Philadelphia: Published for the Author, c. 1855. Also available at *Schoenberg Center for Electronic Text and Image, University of Pennsylvania.* http://dewey.library.upenn.edu/sceti/printedbooksNew/index.cfm?textID=51242_O_12 (accessed on February 25, 2004).

Griffin, Roger A. "American Party." *The Handbook of Texas Online.* http://www.tsha.utexas.edu/handbook/online/articles/print/AA/waa1.html (accessed on February 25, 2004).

Lincoln, Abraham. "On the Know Nothing Party." *Lincoln Home, National Park Service.* http://www.nps.gov/liho/writer/immigran.htm (accessed on February 25, 2004).

Homestead Act of 1862

Enacted by U.S. Congress, May 20, 1862
Reprinted from *Our Documents* **(Web site)**

An act to secure homesteads to settlers in the West

> "Upon filing the said affidavit with the register or receiver, and on payment of ten dollars, he or she shall thereupon be permitted to enter the quantity of land specified...."

In 1862, the U.S. Congress offered to sell public lands to citizens and to immigrants at the cost of $1.25 per acre, or less. The law was designed to attract people to settle vast stretches of territory in the Midwest and West, and it was highly effective. The promise of land at a low price attracted hundreds of thousands of people from the East and from Europe. The offer greatly increased the numbers of people migrating westward.

In the middle of the nineteenth century, owning land was a dream of hundreds of thousands of people, both in the United States and in Europe. Owning land, rather than working on someone else's property, was an ancient sign of wealth and held the promise of future prosperity.

In Europe, farmland was not readily available. Men of high rank still controlled vast tracts, or areas, of land, as they had for hundreds of years. Details of land ownership varied from one country to another, but the idea of owning 160 acres was an impossible dream for many. In the eastern United States, most suitable farmland had long since been settled. Immigrants or young Americans could seldom afford to buy a good-sized farm on their own in the nineteenth century.

On the other hand, enormous tracts of land in the West were largely empty of European settlers. Most of the land was owned by the federal government; much of it was still occupied by Native Americans. For much of the nineteenth century, many Americans urged the government to make publicly owned land available to settlers for free, or at very low cost.

Finally, Congress passed the Homestead Act. This act enabled people to claim 160 acres for 10 dollars. After farming and living on the land for five years, homesteaders would be given title to, or legal ownership of, the land. Traditionally, it has been thought that Daniel Freeman (1826–1908) was the first person to file a claim under the Homestead Act near Brownville, Nebraska, at 12:10 A.M. on January 1, 1863, the first day the Act took effect. Freeman had traveled from Illinois to Nebraska to take advantage of the law. He was the first of tens of thousands to travel west in search of free land. The site of Freeman's claim later became the site of the Homestead National Monument.

Homestead Act settlers stand outside their farmhouse in Custer County, Nebraska, in the late 1800s.
© Bettmann/Corbis.

A steam train sits at a railway station. Many settlers desired land near railroads in the West to make shipping crops back east easier. © *Corbis.*

Things to remember while reading the Homestead Act of 1862:

- The Homestead Act covered a very large area. About 10 percent of the land area of the United States, or 270 million acres, would eventually be claimed and settled under terms of the Homestead Act. It was the largest transfer of property in U.S. history.

- Although a homesteader, a person who settled on land in order to gain title to it, could get the land for no cost, it was not exactly free. The homesteader had to build a home and to farm the land for five years. Farming unbroken prairie land in the mid-1800s was far from easy. Harsh weather, unfriendly natives, and the threat of drought were added to the back-breaking labor required.

- Before the Homestead Act, most land in the West was empty of settlers. The government gave away thousands of acres as a kind of bonus to companies, to make it more attractive for them to build railroads. Much of this land was later sold to settlers who wanted to have farms near the rails that could ship crops back east. Nevertheless, this did not stop thousands of people from claiming free land from the government.

- Not everyone favored the idea behind homesteading. For years, politicians in the Southern states opposed the distribution of public land in the West. Southerners were afraid that such bills would lead to rapid population of the West with settlers who would then demand statehood and would also oppose slavery. Southerners also feared that a large number of free whites on farms would make an unfortunate contrast to their large plantations worked by slaves. Only after the Southern states had begun leaving the Union in 1861 during the American Civil War (1861–65) era was Congress able to pass the Homestead Act the next year.

The Homestead Act of 1862

*An Act to Secure **Homesteads** to Actual Settlers on the Public Domain.*

*Be it enacted by the Senate and House of Representatives of the United States of America in Congress assembled, That any person who is the head of a family, or who has arrived at the age of twenty-one years, and is a citizen of the United States, or who shall have filed his declaration of intention to become such, as required by the **naturalization** laws of the United States, and who has never **borne** arms against the United States Government or given aid and comfort to its enemies, shall, from and after the first January, eighteen hundred and sixty-three, be entitled to enter one quarter section or a less quantity of **unappropriated** public lands, upon which said person may have filed a **preemption** claim, or which may, at the time the application is made, be subject to preemption at one dollar and twenty-five cents, or less, per acre; or eighty acres or less of such unappropriated lands, at two dollars and fifty cents per acre, to be located in a body, in conformity to the legal subdivisions of the public lands, and after the same shall have*

Homesteads: Houses and surrounding land, especially a farm established by a settler for five years in exchange for title to the land from the government.

Naturalization: A process that gives a person from another country the rights of a citizen born in the United States.

Borne: Carried.

Unappropriated: Not having been taken possession of by someone else.

Preemption: Right of purchasing before someone else.

been surveyed: *Provided, That any person owning and residing on land may, under the provisions of this act, enter other land lying **contiguous** to his or her said land, which shall not, with the land so already owned and occupied, exceed in the **aggregate** one hundred and sixty acres.*

*SEC. 2. And be it further enacted, That the person applying for the benefit of this act shall, upon application to the register of the land office in which he or she is about to make such entry, make **affidavit** before the said register or receiver that he or she is the head of a family, or is twenty-one years or more of age, or shall have performed service in the army or navy of the United States, and that he has never borne arms against the Government of the United States or given aid and comfort to its enemies, and that such application is made for his or her exclusive use and benefit, and that said entry is made for the purpose of actual settlement and **cultivation**, and not either directly or indirectly for the use or benefit of any other person or persons whomsoever; and upon filing the said affidavit with the register or receiver, and on payment of ten dollars, he or she shall thereupon be permitted to enter the quantity of land specified: Provided, however, That no certificate shall be given or **patent** issued therefor until the expiration of five years from the date of such entry; and if, at the expiration of such time, or at any time within two years thereafter, the person making such entry; or, if he be dead, his widow; or in case of her death, his heirs or **devisee**; or in case of a widow making such entry, her heirs or devisee, in case of her death; shall prove by two **credible** witnesses that he, she, or they have resided upon or cultivated the same for the term of five years immediately succeeding the time of filing the affidavit **aforesaid**, and shall make affidavit that no part of said land has been **alienated**, and that he has borne due allegiance to the Government of the United States; then, in such case, he, she, or they, if at that time a citizen of the United States, shall be entitled to a patent, as in other cases provided for by law: And provided, further, That in case of the death of both father and mother, leaving an Infant child, or children, under twenty-one years of age, the **right and fee** shall ensure to the benefit of said infant child or children; and the executor, administrator, or guardian may, at any time within two years after the death of the surviving parent, and in accordance with the laws of the State in which such children for the time being have their **domicil[e]**, sell said land for the benefit of said infants, but for no other purpose; and the purchaser shall acquire the absolute title by the purchase, and be entitled to a patent from the United States, on payment of the office fees and sum of money herein specified.*

Contiguous: Touching.

Aggregate: Total.

Affidavit: A sworn statement in writing.

Cultivation: Farming.

Patent: A legal document supporting a right or a privilege.

Devisee: A person who receives property as a result of a will.

Credible: Believable.

Aforesaid: Previously mentioned.

Alienated: Separated.

Right and fee: Right to the land and the value of the land upon selling it.

Domicile: In legal matters, where a person lives.

U.S. Immigration and Migration: Primary Sources

SEC. 3. *And be it further enacted,* That the register of the land office shall note all such applications on the **tract books** and **plats** of his office, and keep a register of all such entries, and make return thereof to the General Land Office, together with the proof upon which they have been founded.

SEC. 4. *And be it further enacted,* That no lands acquired under the provisions of this act shall in any event become liable to the satisfaction of any debt or debts contracted prior to the issuing of the patent therefor.

SEC. 5. *And be it further enacted,* That if, at any time after the filing of the affidavit, as required in the second section of this act, and before the expiration of the five years aforesaid, it shall be proven, after due notice to the settler, to the satisfaction of the register of the land office, that the person having filed such affidavit shall have actually changed his or her residence, or abandoned the said land for more than six months at any time, then and in that event the land so entered shall **revert** to the government.

SEC. 6. *And be it further enacted,* That no individual shall be permitted to acquire title to more than one quarter section under the provisions of this act; and that the Commissioner of the General Land Office is hereby required to prepare and issue such rules and regulations, consistent with this act, as shall be necessary and proper to carry its provisions into effect; and that the registers and receivers of the several land offices shall be entitled to receive the same compensation for any lands entered under the provisions of this act that they are now entitled to receive when the same quantity of land is entered with money, one half to be paid by the person making the application at the time of so doing, and the other half on the issue of the certificate by the person to whom it may be issued; but this shall not be **construed** to enlarge the maximum of compensation now prescribed by law for any register or receiver: Provided, That nothing contained in this act shall be so construed as to impair or interfere in any manner whatever with existing preemption rights: And provided, further, That all persons who may have filed their applications for a preemption right prior to the passage of this act, shall be entitled to all privileges of this act: Provided, further, That no person who has served, or may hereafter serve, for a period of not less than fourteen days in the army or navy of the United States, either regular or volunteer, under the laws thereof, during the existence of an actual war, domestic or foreign, shall

Tract books: Books recording the details about areas of land.

Plats: Maps and charts representing a particular piece of land.

Revert: Go back.

Construed: Understood.

be deprived of the benefits of this act on account of not having attained the age of twenty-one years.

SEC. 7. And be it further enacted, That the fifth section of the act entitled "An act in addition to an act more effectually to provide for the punishment of certain crimes against the United States, and for other purposes," approved the third of March, in the year eighteen hundred and fifty-seven, shall extend to all oaths, affirmations, and affidavits, required or authorized by this act.

SEC. 8. And be it further enacted, That nothing in this act shall be so construed as to prevent any person who has availed him or herself of the benefits of the first section of this act, from paying the minimum price, or the price to which the same may have graduated, for the quantity of land so entered at any time before the expiration of the five years, and obtaining a patent therefor from the government, as in other cases provided by law, on making proof of settlement and cultivation as provided by existing laws granting preemption rights.

APPROVED, May 20, 1862.

What happened next ...

About two million people filed claims for free land during the 124 years the Homestead Act was in effect. Fewer than half of them, or about 783,000 people, succeeded in gaining title to their land by staying five years and fulfilling the other requirements. The fact that so many others gave up was a measure of how difficult it was to build a house and a farm from scratch.

Among well-known Americans with close links to homesteaders were author Willa Cather (1873–1947); frontier lawman Virgil Earp (1843–1905); politician Jeannette Rankin (1880–1973), the first woman elected to Congress; and *Little House on the Prairie* author Laura Ingalls Wilder (1867–1957).

Did you know ...

• Although homesteading is widely viewed as an activity of the nineteenth century, it was possible to claim public land under the 1862 law as recently as 1986, in Alaska. Elsewhere, the Homestead Act was repealed in 1976. The Act remains responsible for one of the largest shifts in land ownership in history. Its impact is visible throughout the Midwest and West today.

For More Information

Books
DuBois, James T., and Gertrude S. Mathews. *Galusha A. Grow, Father of the Homestead Law.* Boston: Houghton Mifflin, 1917.

Hauswald, Carol. *Westward Movement; Expanding America's Boundaries: 1800–1900.* Tucson, AZ: Zephyr Press, 1998.

Stein, R. Conrad. *The Story of the Homestead Act.* Chicago: Children's Press, 1978.

Periodicals
Trimm, Warren P. "Two Years in Kansas." *American Heritage* (February-March 1983): p. 65.

Web Sites
"Homestead Act (1862)." *Our Documents.* http://www.ourdocuments. gov/doc.php?doc=31 (accessed on February 26, 2004).

PBS. *New Perspectives on the West.* http://www.pbs.org/weta/thewest/ (accessed on February 21, 2004).

U.S. National Park Service. *Homestead National Monument of America.* http://www.nps.gov/home/home.html (accessed on February 21, 2004).

John A. Johnson

Excerpt from **Concerning Emigration**

Originally published in *Billed-Magazin,* **January through March, 1869; also available on** *Norwegian-American Historical Association* **(Web site)**

A U.S. businessman from Norway gives immigration suggestions to the natives back home

"In answer to the question as to what prospects an immigrant laborer has in America, we can state briefly and directly: daily wages in Wisconsin are high; employment will not be lacking for those who have the will and ability to work; food and lodging are good; and the labor is not unendurable."

Nearly a million people emigrated from Norway to the United States from 1825 to 1925. For each family that came, the decision was important and often difficult: To leave a familiar country and relatives for a strange country thousands of miles away was one of the most important decisions of their lives. In 1869, John Anders Johnson (1832–1901), a Norwegian emigrant who became a successful businessman in the United States, offered his advice to Norwegians in *Billed-Magazin,* the first illustrated monthly magazine in the Norwegian language published in America. Johnson's message: If you are prepared to work hard, you can succeed in the United States.

Most of the Norwegians who came to the United States after the American Civil War (1861–65) were from southern Norway. There, the land was relatively crowded, and it was difficult for many people to acquire enough land to support a family. Asked why they were leaving their native land, most Norwegian emigrants said they were looking for a better economic opportunity.

Relative to the size of its population, Norway was a major contributor to the flow of immigrants to the United

States, second only to Ireland. Although Norway did not experience the starvation that drove many Irish emigrants to come to the United States, times were often hard in Norway, especially in the southern part of the country.

A wagon train of emigrants pulled by oxen makes a stop in 1887. *© Corbis.*

Johnson's articles offered very practical advice, ranging from what sort of ship to take to what sort of trunks to pack possessions in. He advised Norwegians not to settle on the East Coast, but rather to keep going west until they reached Wisconsin. Many people in Wisconsin, Minnesota, and North and South Dakota can trace their ancestry to relatives who emigrated from Norway and nearby Scandinavian countries, such as Sweden and Denmark.

Things to remember while reading an excerpt from *Concerning Emigration:*

- Johnson offered Norwegians some practical advice, such as packing possessions in sturdy trunks or saving money by taking a sailing ship instead of a steamship. He also had another motivation: to convince his audience that the way to success is through hard work. It is clear from his advice that Johnson firmly believed that hard work was the solution to life's problems, rather than, for example, relying on a policy of government assistance or believing in rearranging ownership of property to achieve a more equal distribution of wealth. Johnson himself became a successful businessman in the United States. Despite Johnson's advice, one of the major attractions for Europeans, including Norwegians, of moving to the United States after 1862 was the Homestead Act of 1862, which gave 160 acres of free land to settlers who built a house on the land and farmed it for five years. The Homestead Act of 1862 amounted to an enormous giveaway of government land to anyone willing to remain on the land for five years. This was not easy: "homesteaders" had to face harsh weather, drought, and even hostile Native Americans who were being driven off of their traditional hunting territory.

- Going to America was not the only choice of poor Norwegians in the 1860s. The northern part of the country was much less crowded than the south, and many Norwegians decided to move north, in their own country, instead of sailing to the United States. For most of the nineteenth century, Norway was ruled by Sweden. Norway became an independent country in 1905.

- This article first appeared in *Billed-Magazin,* published in the United States for the benefit of Norwegian immigrants. It was Johnson's intention that copies of the magazine would be sent to Norway to inform potential immigrants of the opportunities, and potential pitfalls, of making the journey. Johnson originally signed the articles with his original name in Norway, J. A. Johnsen Skibsnæs.

Excerpt from Concerning Emigration

Why I Write

Emigration is a question which at present especially occupies men's minds both in the old world and the new. When I learned that many of Billed-Magazin's subscribers send it home to relatives and friends in Norway I concluded that a brief discussion concerning conditions in this country would be well received by the readers—particularly by those who send the magazine to acquaintances in the homeland where all information about far-off America is read with great interest....

Some Important Questions

What shall I do? Shall I go to America? Is it true that over there people are not **plagued** by the agonizing question of how to make a living? Can I believe those who tell me that in America hard work and **frugality** will unfailingly lead to wealth and economic independence? Thus the Norwegian day laborer often ponders when, with a sorrow-laden mind, he realizes that the only reward for all his sweat and toil is a miserable **subsistence**, void of any prospects for better days. Thus **queries** the **destitute**, still **robust** laborer when he considers his desperate situation. He dreads approaching old age and often sees no other solution than the humiliation of **poor-relief**, unless a merciful death puts an end to his existence while he still enjoys the gift of good health and the undiminished strength of an able body. The same questions haunt the family breadwinner who considers the future of his children. Memories of a past life full of woe and want fill his thoughts with concern for the future of those dependent on him. He knows that they, like him, must take up the struggle for existence and, matured in the school of experience, he lets his thoughts roam abroad to see if he might possibly discover some place in this wide world which offers better prospects for happiness and well being than does the same spot where he first saw the light of day and his children were cradled as well. Servants are now beginning to ask whether there might not be a country where toil is better rewarded than in Norway—whether in America, even in a servant's humble position, they may have hopes of better days and a happier future than in the homeland. A humble form of existence and wages which barely **suffice** to provide the most modest demands for clothing—this is the whole reward which a Norwegian servant **garners** from all his labors; and the future seldom offers him any other prospect than entry into the **cotter**'s or the day laborer's unenviable form of life.

Who Tells the Truth?

The Norwegian newspapers look upon all those who emigrate as merely **duped** fools, while in no uncertain terms they imply that Norwegian laborers have themselves to blame for their **depressed condition**. America is pictured as the land of seduction, an immoral **Sodom**;

Plagued: Burdened or annoyed constantly.

Frugality: The practice of being careful in using resources.

Subsistence: The minimum amount of food to live on.

Queries: Questions.

Destitute: Poor or penniless.

Robust: Healthy and thriving.

Poor-relief: Welfare in the form of money or necessities given to the poor.

Suffice: Meet a need.

Garners: Earns.

Cotter: A peasant or farm laborer who occupies a cottage and perhaps a small piece of land, usually in return for services to a landlord.

Duped: Fooled.

Depressed condition: Economic hardship.

Sodom: A city in the Bible destroyed for its wickedness.

and those who dare raise their voices against **manifest** lies are **well-nigh** put in a class with traitors. Because of confused patriotism, many otherwise decent men rave against emigration, which, in their blindness, they believe to be a misfortune for the country; and without any show of mercy they pass the most damning judgment over anyone whom they suspect of furthering emigration by giving information about the true state of affairs on the other side of the Atlantic.

The Ne'er-Do-Well in Alliance with Politicians

In order to check the flow of emigration, the Norwegian government has evidently not resorted to such **sordid** means as several of the small German states adopted in earlier days: that is, with the aid of hired **shysters** to spread warped accounts about conditions and circumstances in America. But there are other **obliging spirits** who believe themselves ordained to curb emigration, and like fanatics in general they are immune to all rationality; their **zeal** grows in proportion to the proofs of the indefensibility of the arguments on which they base their contentions. Now and then they are joined by some **ne'er-do-well** whose hopes of living at other people's expense were wrecked in America. Our fanatics are, of course, past masters at exploiting such gold mines to **buttress** their own biased judgments about life and conditions in the New World.

Do Not Misunderstand Me

It is by no means my intention, with the present articles, to promote emigration. My purpose is purely and simply to give a true picture of America as a possible place of residence for Norwegians; and if someone should ask: "Shall I leave my native land in order to seek a new home beyond the Atlantic?" then I will merely answer: "Do as you may deem best." I can only promise to give such guidance as emigrants and newcomers need; and the accounts I render shall be **transfused** with the spirit of truth. If they can be of some service to my fellow countrymen, then my aim has been achieved.

Reasons for the Differing Impressions

In the first place, different people can interpret or understand one and the same thing in highly divergent ways. In the second place, we must bear in mind that America covers a vast expanse, so that an account which may fit one particular place cannot, without making an exception to the rule, be applied to districts with quite different natural conditions and opportunities for achieving success and well-being.... While the former, during their first year abroad, often sadly yearn for Old Norway and cannot adjust to life in the New

Manifest: Obvious.

Well-nigh: Close to being.

Sordid: Dirty or filthy.

Shysters: People who are dishonest in practicing law.

Obliging spirits: Those who do good for others.

Zeal: Enthusiasm for an idea or a goal.

Ne'er-do-well: A lazy, irresponsible person.

Buttress: Prop up.

Transfused: Injected.

World, you will scarcely find one out of a hundred of the old settlers who does not bless the day when he resolved to leave for America....

Who Ought Not to Emigrate?

*Work is the foundation of society. From this fountain flow the wealth and general prosperity of the country. Work is honored and the person with initiative is respected and can count on being supported in his endeavors. In "Help wanted" advertisements in Norwegian newspapers we often read: "Those without good recommendations need not apply." Similarly, the proposition should be driven home that no one should enlist for emigration unless he is a good worker. The only quality demanded is two able hands and a willingness to use them. **Idlers and loafers** had better remain at home. Such persons are not tolerated here. They must either starve or get themselves a job. There is no poor-relief here which serves as a pillow for idlers to rest on. The Americans know that anyone who can and will work does not need help from others. Those who are sick or those who—because of no fault of their own—are suffering **want** can count on generous support. Americans gladly extend a helping hand to their fellowmen when they are certain that the gift reaches someone worthy of aid. But the drunkard and the **shirker** find no mercy in their eyes.*

A Promising Future for Craftsmen

*There are well-paid jobs for **craftsmen**. It may happen that at some certain place there are no openings for newcomers, whether because of a great inrush of emigrants or other chance circumstances. But a person can generally find employment here in the western states by changing his place of residence for a while or by temporarily accepting whatever job may present itself. In the eastern states conditions are somewhat different. There it frequently happens that a newcomer cannot find work during the winter months. The emigrant should, therefore, go as far west as Wisconsin. Great numbers come here every year and no complaints are heard about want of employment. At first the language causes some inconvenience; but no other immigrants master English as readily as the Norwegians: after a few months the difficulties will be overcome. To be sure, working methods differ a bit from what the **artisans** are used to in the home country. They will discover that work is less **arduous** here and that much of it is done by machines, thus reducing the amount of manual labor. But our countrymen are gifted to a high degree with the ability to learn and "catch on." Many of them have gained so much expertise after a few years that*

Idlers and loafers: Those who are lazy, unoccupied, or unemployed.

Want: Deprivation and hardship.

Shirker: Someone who avoids work.

Craftsmen: Workers with specific skills, such as carpentry.

Artisans: Craftsmen.

Arduous: Exhausting.

*as independent masters, operating their own establishments, they can compete on equal terms with the most skilled of our native craftsmen. **Wheelwrights**, carpenters, smiths, and masons can expect good wages: the job seeks the man. Ability is the only thing that counts. Good workers who behave decently do not need to worry about making a living, even if they are fathers who must support and bring up a group of children....*

What Does America Offer the Day Laborer?

In answer to the question as to what prospects an immigrant laborer has in America, we can state briefly and directly: daily wages in Wisconsin are high; employment will not be lacking for those who have the will and ability to work; food and lodging are good; and the labor is not unendurable. It should also be noted that many railways are being built and that other improvements in the means of communication are being planned, such as making rivers more navigable and building canals and roads. Such undertakings will, presumably, call for a great number of laborers next summer.

Prospects for Norwegian Servant Girls in America

There will always be positions open for able Norwegian servant girls. They are held to be industrious and dependable, and the Yankees prefer them to servant girls of other nationalities. Wages are high: up to $100 per year and at times even higher. We know of instances where servant girls in Chicago earn six dollars per week. This is, of course, exceptional. Norwegian women are highly respected in this country, and I have as yet never heard of any one being idled by lack of opportunity for employment....

The East Compared with the West

What I have said refers especially to the western states. As already indicated, conditions in the East are somewhat different. The emigrant ought, therefore, to go at least as far west as Wisconsin. There he can meet fellow countrymen who will welcome him with open arms and gladly help him with advice and assistance.... Decades of experience have convinced the Scandinavians that out here, more easily than anywhere else, they can win economic independence and a bright future....

Comparison Between Norway and America

The day laborer in Norway can rarely get beyond the hand to mouth stage; over here he can put aside cash and be respected as highly as his employer because everyone knows that within a short time he himself may be hiring men. In Norway a laborer toils year

Wheelwrights: Those who make wheels or repair wheeled vehicles, especially wagons or carriages pulled by animals.

*after year and earns nothing for his sweat beyond the bare necessities for existence while here he can, within two or three years, become the owner of a farm large enough to support a family. Even the most able cotter or landless tenant in Norway may, throughout his entire life, continue the labors of **Sisyphus** without making any headway. Barely has the rock been wrestled to the top of the mountain before it hurtles back into the valley, and the labor must begin all over again.*

*Year follows year but the **spectre** of **famine** will not leave the cotter's cabin. And when his strength fades, the poor-law officials begin casting **furtive** glances at him as if they fear that death will not soon enough relieve the cotter of his misery and he will remain a burden on the community. If all the work which a cotter performs during some twenty or thirty years were expended on a good farm here in the West it would generally yield him $500 for every year of labor. Among the settlers here in Wisconsin we can point to numerous individuals as verification of this statement. Many of them came here without a penny in their pockets. Now they live free of debt on their good farms, and not a few have money on deposit, drawing interest....*

Preparations for the Journey

*Chests or boxes made of strong boards—well joined and reinforced with iron fittings—should be secured for storage of the goods an immigrant expects to bring along to America. The owner's name and destination should be painted on the boxes in large and clear letters. And the boxes should be of such dimensions that when fully packed they can be carried by two men. Too heavy boxes cause much inconvenience when they are to be reloaded at the railroad stations. Handles at each end will **expedite** transportation. We hear frequent complaints about the recklessness with which immigrant property is treated by employees of steamships and railroads. And it is true that these fellows do not wear silk gloves or treat things as if they were glass. The thousands upon thousands of articles they have to handle call for speed, and it may well happen that proper care is not always exercised. But it should also be remembered that the boxes are often so fragile that they scarcely bear touching without falling apart. Much trouble, many inconveniences and misunderstandings could be avoided if everyone would have his belongings packed in strong cases well marked with the owner's name and place of destination. How much and which kinds of provisions the passengers should take along can best be explained by the shipping agents, so I will merely add that the chests or boxes in which the*

Sisyphus: A figure in Greek mythology, condemned to push a rock up a hill only to have it roll down again when it nears the top.

Spectre: Horrible vision or possibility.

Famine: Hunger.

Furtive: Secret.

Expedite: Help move along efficiently.

provisions are to be kept should be provided with locks because there could well be someone in the group of travelers whose conception of property rights might be somewhat dim.

Some Matters to Consider Before Departure

Those emigrants who can raise enough money to pay for their passage without selling all their belongings ought to bring along wearing apparel of all sorts, as well as bedclothes, and table service such as tablecloths, knives, forks, and silverware. In Norway there are many who want to sell but comparatively few buyers. The emigrant would therefore be well advised to keep those articles rather than sell them at too low a price. Fur items such as caps, collars, and **muffs** *will be useful here because the winters are cold and furs are expensive in this country. Craftsmen might also bring along their tools, provided they are not too heavy or bulky. No doubt the implements used here in America are as a rule better than the ones the immigrant brings along from Norway. But it is possible that he may be unable to buy new tools immediately on arrival and in the meantime the ones he brought along from home may come in handy....*

How Shall I Travel?

Shall I secure quarters aboard a steamship or shall I go with a sailing vessel? This question is usually raised by the emigrant as soon as he has decided to leave the homeland. Here advice is difficult to give: there are as many opinions as there are heads. It might well happen that an emigrant would get quite contradictory answers if he directed this question to several persons familiar with the field—all of whom, naturally, would be able to substantiate their reasoning with apparently sound arguments.

Nevertheless, this can not deter me from expressing my own opinion. If the emigrant has a large family or is not flush with money, then I would unhesitatingly advise him to go by sail. The money he thus saves by making use of this cheaper means of transportation will stand him in good stead after his arrival in this country.

Muffs: Hand warmers shaped like a cylinder open at both ends.

What happened next ...

Several hundred thousand Norwegians took Johnson's advice and emigrated to the United States. Once here,

however, Scandinavians participated in creating societies that were among the most liberal in America. States where many Scandinavians settled, such as Minnesota and Wisconsin, eventually had governments that favored social welfare programs to assist the poor and needy—a somewhat different picture than the one painted by the author.

Eventually, the flow of emigrants from Norway slowed in the twentieth century. There were many reasons, including improved conditions of living in Norway and increased difficulty in finding good jobs in the United States.

Norwegians from two counties in South Dakota gather at a farm.
© *Minnesota Historical Society/Corbis.*

Did you know …
- Farming was not the only occupation of Norwegian immigrants; many also worked in factories or as sailors. A sailor on an American ship in the 1860s was paid about three or four times as much as a Norwegian sailor on a

Norwegian ship. A laborer—a low-skilled person who might dig ditches, for example—only earned around $40 a year in Norway. In America, a laborer could earn around $4 to $5 a day, or $800 to $1,000 a year. It was little wonder that the United States beckoned to Europeans as the land of opportunity.

For More Information

Books

Andersen, Arlow W. *The Norwegian-Americans*. Boston: Twayne Publishers, 1975.

Bergmann, Leola Nelson. *Americans from Norway*. New York: J. B. Lippincott, 1950.

Larsen, Agnes M. *John A. Johnson: An Uncommon American*. Northfield, MN: Norwegian-American Historical Association, 1969.

Lovoll, Odd Sverre. *The Promise of America: A History of the Norwegian-American People*. Rev. ed. Minneapolis: University of Minnesota Press in cooperation with the Norwegian-American Historical Association, 1999.

Semmingsen, Ingrid. *Norway to America: A History of the Migration*. Minneapolis: University of Minnesota Press, 1978.

Web Sites

Johnson, John A. "Concerning Emigration." *The Norwegian-American Historical Association.* http://www.naha.stolaf.edu/publications/volume33/vol33_07.htm (accessed on February 21, 2004). Originally published in *Billed-Magazin,* January 23, 30; February 6, 13; March 13, 20, 1869.

Chinese Exclusion Act of 1882

Enacted by U.S. Congress, May 6, 1882

Reprinted from *U.S. Immigration and Naturalization Laws and Issues: A Documentary History*

The United States begins a ban on Chinese immigrants

The Chinese Exclusion Act of 1882 barred any more Chinese workers from coming to the United States for ten years, the beginning of a ban on Chinese immigrants that lasted for sixty years. It was the first time the United States had enacted a law aimed at a specific national or ethnic group.

For much of the 1870s, the United States experienced difficult economic times. Jobs were hard to find. Many businesses failed as a result of a financial crisis that started in New York on September 18, 1873. On that day, a major bank in New York City, Jay Cooke and Company, closed its doors. The bank declared bankruptcy, meaning it could not afford to give depositors their money back. Railroads that had borrowed money from the bank to expand their network of tracks were unable to repay their loans. Consequently, the bank did not have money to give depositors making withdrawals. People with money deposited in other banks, fearing they might also lose their money, rushed to withdraw their deposits. Without money on hand to turn over to depositors, other banks also closed their doors. (In the 1870s, there was no government guarantee of deposits, as there is

"In the opinion of the Government of the United States the coming of Chinese laborers to this country endangers the good order of certain localities...."

today.) The result was widespread panic by depositors, which led to several years of slow economic growth, as banks were unable to lend money to businesses to expand.

The effects of the economic slowdown were especially severe on the West Coast, where three railroad routes from the east to the west (a northern route ending in Washington; the middle route through Sacramento, California; and a southern route to Los Angeles) had been recently completed. Railroad construction workers, both Chinese and European American, were no longer needed and consequently became unemployed. Some unemployed workers blamed Chinese immigrants for their economic plight, on grounds that Chinese workers had taken jobs that might otherwise have been available to European American workers. In reality, the Chinese were blamed for an economic crisis caused by overly enthusiastic expansion by the railroads, over which Chinese immigrants had no control or responsibility.

The economic slowdown also changed the perceptions of many politicians toward Chinese immigration. In the 1850s and 1860s, Chinese workers had established a reputation as reliable, hard workers. They were credited with much of the dangerous, backbreaking work involved in building the Central Pacific railroad through the steep California Sierra Nevada mountains. The important role of Chinese laborers was recognized by the government in 1868, a year before the first railroad link between California and the East Coast was completed, when the United States signed the Burlingame Treaty with China. The treaty specifically protected the right of the Chinese to immigrate into the United States.

Attitudes toward Chinese workers were not universally positive, however, even before the economic crisis of 1873. Chinese immigrants tended to associate exclusively with each other. They had little interaction with European American workers. Some Europeans, such as miners and explosives experts from Wales, felt that Chinese workers competed with them for the same jobs and that the Chinese held down wages by their willingness to work for lower wages. At the celebrations in Utah marking completion of the transcontinental railroad (the railroad across the continent) in 1869, Chinese workers were excluded. This exclusion can be seen as

Chinese immigrants stand outside a butcher shop in Chinatown in San Francisco, California. © *Bettmann/Corbis.*

a symbol of an already well-established discrimination against Chinese people.

As economic hard times dragged on in the 1870s, some workers in California increasingly focused their anger and despair on immigrants from China. In the summer of 1877, a mob of European Americans in San Francisco attacked and killed Chinese workers and wrecked Chinese-owned laundries. That summer, an Irish immigrant named Denis Kearney (1847–1907), who owned a small hauling company, became the leader of a local association of workers called the Workingmen's Party. The organization was initially formed to protest a lack of jobs and to support a strike (a work stoppage aimed at gaining better pay and benefits) by railroad workers. But, as noted in *The American Commonwealth,* in fiery speeches to disenchanted workers, Kearney cast blame on Chinese workers (whom he sometimes called "Asiatic pests") for keeping wages low and making jobs scarce. He gave speeches that several times ended with the crowd turning into a mob and rampaging through San Francisco's Chinatown. Kearney was arrested several times, accused of urging a crowd to violence, but juries repeatedly found him not guilty.

Kearney's political influence grew, and in 1879, voters in San Francisco elected one of Kearney's followers, the Reverend Isaac Kalloch (1832–1887), as mayor. The Workingman's Party spread to other parts of California. The party replaced the Democratic Party as the chief challenger to the Republican Party, which controlled the state government. (Political parties are organizations of like-minded people who organize to get sympathetic politicians elected to office.)

Faced with growing unrest, California politicians in Washington urged the U.S. Congress to pass legislation banning more Chinese from entering the United States. The Congress passed such a law in 1879, which in effect blamed the victims of riots for causing disorder. President Rutherford B. Hayes (1822–1893; served 1877–81) vetoed the act, or refused to sign it into law, on grounds that it violated an 1868 treaty with China guaranteeing the right of Chinese to enter the United States as immigrants.

In 1880, faced with continuing anti-Chinese violence in California that the U.S. government seemed helpless or unwilling to prevent, the government of China agreed to modify the earlier treaty and allow the United States to suspend immigration of Chinese workers. In May 1882, Congress passed the Chinese Exclusion Act of 1882.

The act had five main provisions: (1) Chinese workers were barred from coming to the United States for ten years; (2) Chinese workers already in the United States were allowed to stay, and those who had been in the United States before the act was passed were allowed to return after a short absence; (3) Chinese workers who were in the United States illegally could be deported; (4) Chinese were barred from becoming naturalized citizens, or those who gain the rights of people who were born in the United States, such as the right to vote; and (5) some Chinese, such as students and merchants, could visit the United States temporarily. The act also made captains of ships pay fines if they helped Chinese immigrate illegally to the United States.

Passage of the 1882 Chinese Exclusion Act marked the first time that a specific national group was singled out for special treatment by being barred from entering the United States. There seems little doubt that racial prejudice also played a

Pedestrians walk along the streets of Chinatown in San Francisco, California, in the early twentieth century.
© *Corbis*.

large role in passage of the law. The Chinese were viewed as being fundamentally different than Europeans and as somehow inferior. They were not Christians, for example, which most European Americans had in common. Instead of letters, the Chinese language used characters (drawings that stood for whole words), which were unreadable to non-Chinese. Chinese immigrants tended to wear traditional Chinese costumes and to wear their hair in long braids; their appearance emphasized the difference between Chinese and Europeans in general. Most Chinese immigrants lived together in Chinatowns, where they regulated their own business and social affairs through associations apart from government institutions.

Things to remember while reading the Chinese Exclusion Act of 1882:

- In its preamble, or introduction, the act declared that it was the opinion of the government that "the coming of

Chinese laborer ... endangers the good order of certain localities...." This phrase refers to the riots in California directed against Chinese immigrants. Instead of focusing on controlling the riots, Congress decided it would be easier to ban any more Chinese from coming to the United States.

• The number of Chinese who had immigrated to the United States by 1882 was relatively small, compared with other national groups. The 1880 census counted only about one hundred thousand Chinese in the United States. Most lived in their own communities, usually called Chinatowns. Many Chinese immigrants maintained the clothing and customs of their native land. They seemed strange and separate from European Americans—and therefore were an easy target for politicians looking for someone to blame for economic hard times.

• One of the qualities that made many employers eager to hire Chinese workers for work in mines, construction projects, and in some factory jobs—their willingness to work hard for low wages—aroused the anger of European workers, who thought the Chinese were responsible for keeping wages low and jobs scarce.

Chinese Exclusion Act of 1882

Forty-Seventh Congress. Session I. 1882. Chapter 126.-An act to execute certain treaty stipulations relating to Chinese

Preamble.

*Whereas, in the opinion of the Government of the United States the coming of Chinese laborers to this country endangers the **good order** of certain localities within the territory thereof: Therefore,*

Be it enacted by the Senate and House of Representatives of the United States of America in Congress assembled, *That from and after the expiration of ninety days next after the passage of this act, and until the expiration of ten years next after the passage of this act, the coming of Chinese laborers to the United States be, and the*

Preamble: Introduction.

Good order: Peaceful environment, not marked by rioting or violence.

same is hereby, suspended; and during such suspension it shall not be lawful for any Chinese laborer to come, or, having so come after the expiration of said ninety days, to remain within the United States.

Sec. 2. That the **master of any vessel** who shall knowingly bring within the United States on such vessel, and land or permit to be landed, any Chinese laborer, from any foreign port of place, shall be **deemed** guilty of a **misdemeanor**, and on conviction thereof shall be punished by a fine of not more than five hundred dollars for each and every such Chinese laborer so brought, and may be also imprisoned for a term not exceeding one year.

Sec. 3. That the two foregoing sections shall not apply to Chinese laborers who were in the United States on the seventeenth day of November, eighteen hundred and eighty, or who shall have come into the same before the expiration of ninety days next after the passage of this act, and who shall produce to such master before going on board such vessel, and shall produce to the **collector of the port** in the United States at which such vessel shall arrive, the evidence hereinafter in this act required of his being one of the laborers in this section mentioned; nor shall the two foregoing sections apply to the case of any master whose vessel, being bound to a port not within the United States by reason of being in distress or in stress of weather, or touching at any port of the United States on its voyage to any foreign port of place: Provided, That all Chinese laborers brought on such vessel shall depart with the vessel on leaving port.

Sec. 4. That for the purpose of properly [identifying] Chinese laborers who were in the United States on the seventeenth day of November, eighteen hundred and eighty, or who shall have come into the same before the expiration of ninety days next after the passage of this act, and in order to furnish them with the proper evidence of their right to go from and come to the United States **of their free will and accord,** as provided by the treaty between the United States and China dated November seventeenth, eighteen hundred and eighty, the collector of customs of the district from which any such Chinese laborer shall depart from the United States shall, in person or by deputy, go on board each vessel having on board any such Chinese laborer and cleared or about to sail from his district for a foreign port, and on such vessel make a list of all such Chinese laborers, which shall be entered in registry-books to be kept for that purpose, in which shall be stated the name, age, occupation, last place of residence, physical marks or peculiarities, and all facts necessary for the [identification] of each of such Chinese laborers,

Master of any vessel: Ship captain.

Deemed: Judged.

Misdemeanor: A relatively minor crime.

Collector of the port: Government official who collects taxes on imports and regulates international shipping in a seaport.

Of their free will and accord: Voluntarily and in agreement.

*which books shall be safely kept in the custom-house; and every such Chinese laborer so departing from the United States shall be entitled to, and shall receive, free of any charge or cost upon application therefor, from the collector or his deputy, at the time such list is taken, a certificate, signed by the collector or his deputy and **attested** by his seal of office, in such form as the Secretary of the Treasury shall prescribe, which certificate shall contain a statement of the name, age, occupation, last place of residence, personal description, and fact of identification of the Chinese laborer to whom the certificate is issued, corresponding with the said list and registry in all particulars. In case any Chinese laborer after having received such certificate shall leave such vessel before her departure he shall deliver his certificate to the master of the vessel, and if such Chinese laborer shall fail to return to such vessel before her departure from port the certificate shall be delivered by the master to the collector of customs for cancellation. The certificate herein provided for shall entitle the Chinese laborer to whom the same is issued to return to and re-enter the United States upon producing and delivering the same to the collector of customs of the district at which such Chinese laborer shall seek to re-enter; and upon delivery of such certificate by such Chinese laborer to the collector of customs at the time of re-entry in the United States, said collector shall cause the same to be filed in the custom house and duly canceled.*

Sec. 5. That any Chinese laborer mentioned in section four of this act being in the United States, and desiring to depart from the United States by land, shall have the right to demand and receive, free of charge or cost, a certificate of [identification] similar to that provided for in section four of this act to be issued to such Chinese laborers as may desire to leave the United States by water; and it is hereby made the duty of the collector of customs of the district next adjoining the foreign country to which said Chinese laborer desires to go to issue such certificate, free of charge or cost, upon application by such Chinese laborer, and to enter the same upon registry-books to be kept by him for the purpose, as provided for in section four of this act.

*Sec. 6. That in order to the **faithful execution** of articles one and two of the treaty in this act before mentioned, every Chinese person other than a laborer who may be entitled by said treaty and this act to come within the United States, and who shall be about to come to the United States, shall be identified as so entitled by the Chinese Government in each case, such identity to be evidenced by a certificate issued under the authority of said govern-*

Attested: Affirmed to be true, usually by the signature or stamp of an official.

Faithful execution: Carrying out of an act in line with a law or a request.

ment, which certificate shall be in the English language or (if not in the English language) accompanied by a translation into English, stating such right to come, and which certificate shall state the name, title, or official rank, if any, the age, height, and all **physical peculiarities**, former and present occupation or profession, and place of residence in China of the person to whom the certificate is issued and that such person is entitled **conformably to** the treaty in this act mentioned to come within the United States. Such certificate shall be **prima-facie evidence** of the fact set forth therein, and shall be produced to the collector of customs, or his deputy, of the port in the district in the United States at which the person named therein shall arrive.

Sec. 7. That any person who shall knowingly and falsely alter or substitute any name for the name written in such certificate or forge any such certificate, or knowingly utter any forged or fraudulent certificate, or falsely personate any person named in any such certificate, shall be deemed guilty of a misdemeanor; and upon conviction thereof shall be fined in a sum not exceeding one thousand dollars, and imprisoned in a **penitentiary** for a term of not more than five years.

Sec. 8. That the master of any vessel arriving in the United States from any foreign port or place shall, at the same time he delivers a **manifest of the cargo,** and if there be no cargo, then at the time of making a report of the entry of vessel **pursuant to** the law, in addition to the other matter required to be reported, and before landing, or permitting to land, any Chinese passengers, deliver and report to the collector of customs of the district in which such vessels shall have arrived a separate list of all Chinese passengers taken on board his vessel at any foreign port or place, and all such passengers on board the vessel at that time. Such list shall show the names of such passengers (and if accredited officers of the Chinese Government traveling on the business of that government, or their servants, with a note of such facts), and the name and other particulars, as shown by their respective certificates; and such list shall be sworn to by the master in the manner required by law in relation to the manifest of the cargo. Any willful refusal or neglect of any such master to comply with the provisions of this section shall incur the same penalties and forfeiture as are provided for a refusal or neglect to report and deliver a manifest of cargo.

Sec. 9. That before any Chinese passengers are landed from any such vessel, the collector, or his deputy, shall proceed to examine such passengers, comparing the certificates with the list and

Physical peculiarities: Unique physical features.

Conformably to: In accordance with.

Prima-facie evidence: In law, a demonstration that is legally sufficient on its appearance to establish a fact.

Penitentiary: Prison.

Manifest of the cargo: List of the goods on board a ship.

Pursuant to: According to.

with the passengers; and no passenger shall be allowed to land in the United States from such vessel in violation of law.

*Sec. 10. That every vessel whose master shall knowingly violate any of the provisions of this act shall be **deemed forfeited** to the United States, and shall be liable to seizure and condemnation on any district of the United States into which such vessel may enter or in which she may be found.*

*Sec. 11. That any person who shall knowingly bring into or cause to be brought into the United States by land, or who shall knowingly **aid or abet** the same, or aid or abet the landing in the United States from any vessel of any Chinese person not lawfully entitled to enter the United States, shall be deemed guilty of a misdemeanor, and shall, on conviction thereof, be fined in a sum not exceeding one thousand dollars, and imprisoned for a term not exceeding one year.*

Sec. 12. That no Chinese person shall be permitted to enter the United States by land without producing to the proper officer of customs the certificate in this act required of Chinese persons seeking to land from a vessel. And any Chinese person found unlawfully within the United States shall be caused to be removed therefrom to the country from whence he came, by direction of the United States, after being brought before some justice, judge, or commissioner of a court of the United States and found to be one not lawfully entitled to be or remain in the United States.

*Sec. 13. That this act shall not apply to diplomatic and other officers of the Chinese Government traveling upon the business of that government, whose **credentials** shall be taken as equivalent to the certificate in this act mentioned, and shall exempt them and their body and household servants from the provisions of this act as to other Chinese persons.*

Sec. 14. That hereafter no State court or court of the United States shall admit Chinese to citizenship; and all laws in conflict with this act are hereby repealed.

Sec. 15. That the words "Chinese laborers," whenever used in this act, shall be construed to mean both skilled and unskilled laborers and Chinese employed in mining.

Approved, May 6, 1882.

Deemed forfeited: Considered to have been given over to the government.

Aid or abet: Help or actively support.

Credentials: Official papers describing a person's position.

What happened next …

The Chinese Exclusion Act immediately reduced the number of Chinese immigrants from around forty thousand in 1881 to less than a thousand in the year after the act was passed. One impact was to create an oddly imbalanced society in Chinese neighborhoods, where men outnumbered women by a ratio of about twenty to one. Because Chinese men who had come to work were no longer able to bring wives into the United States, many Chinatown communities continued for many years with men living as permanent bachelors. Forty years later, in 1920, the ratio of men to women in Chinese communities was still about seven to one.

In 1892, Congress passed the Geary Act, which excluded Chinese immigrants for ten more years. In 1902, the exclusion of Chinese immigrants was made permanent. Chinese residents were required to obtain special certificates; without one, any Chinese found in the United States could be deported to China.

In 1942, the exclusion of Chinese immigrants had become an embarrassment. The United States had entered World War II (1941–45) against Japan after the Japanese navy bombed the U.S. Pacific fleet at Pearl Harbor, Hawaii, on December 7, 1941. China had been invaded by Japan a few years earlier, and consequently the United States and China became allies. The United States had to correct the uncomfortable situation of having an ally whose citizens were the subject of discrimination in immigration. On December 17, 1943, Congress repealed the Chinese exclusion laws. In their place, Congress set a numerical quota on Chinese immigrants, just as other countries had

An editorial cartoon in 1882 shows a Chinese man hanging from a branch, symbolizing the moratorium on Chinese immigration. © *Hulton Getty/Liaison Agency.*

been assigned numerical quotas on the number of people allowed to enter the United States. The spirit of the old laws, remained, however: The quota for Chinese was set at just 105 people per year.

Finally, in 1965, explicit discrimination against Chinese immigrants was lifted. A new immigration law got rid of numerical quotas and concentrated on other standards for acceptance, such as family ties or a person having skills judged to be in short supply in the United States.

Did you know ...

• The treatment of Chinese immigrants was the subject of intense diplomacy between the United States and China for many years, with the Chinese government taking an active interest in the fate of citizens who had emigrated to the United States.

Anson Burlingame, a U.S. diplomat who specialized in Chinese relations. *Library of Congress.*

• In 1868, the United States and China signed a treaty governing Chinese immigration. The treaty was called the Burlingame Treaty. It was named after Anson Burlingame (1820–1870), one of the diplomats who negotiated the agreement. A native of Berlin, New York, Burlingame was a congressman from 1855 to 1861, when he was appointed to represent the United States in China. His tact and understanding of Chinese issues was appreciated by the Chinese government. In 1867, he was named to represent China in a mission that included visits to several European countries and the United States.

• In 1868, Burlingame represented China in negotiations for a treaty with the United States. One clause of the treaty protected the right of Chinese to immigrate to the United States and assured that China would not be treated differently than other countries with respect to immigration. The treaty was effective for a decade, but in the late 1870s, anti-Chinese feelings ran so strong in California that the Congress tried to exclude Chinese immigrants altogether. China finally consented, in 1880, to modify the Burlingame Treaty, paving the way for the Chinese Exclusion Act of 1882.

For More Information

Books

Bryce, James. *The American Commonwealth.* London and New York: Macmillan, 1889. Multiple reprints.

Chin, Ko-lin. *Smuggled Chinese: Clandestine Immigration to the United States.* Philadelphia: Temple University Press, 1999.

Lee, Erika. *At America's Gates: Chinese Immigration During the Exclusion Era, 1882–1943.* Charlotte: University of North Carolina Press, 2003.

LeMay, Michael, and Elliot Robert Barkan, eds. *U.S. Immigration and Naturalization Laws and Issues: A Documentary History.* Westport, CT: Greenwood Press, 1999.

Web Sites

"Asian American History Timeline." *Ancestors in the Americas: A PBS Series Exploring the History and Legacy of Asians in the Americas.* http://www.cetel.org/timeline.html#1 (accessed on February 21, 2004).

Mark Twain

Excerpt from "Concerning the Jews"
Published in *Harper's Magazine*, March 1898

*A well-known writer tries to explain
why prejudice against Jews exists*

"I am quite sure that … I have no race prejudices, and I think I have no color prejudices nor caste prejudices nor creed prejudices. Indeed, I know it. I can stand any society. All that I care to know is that a man is a human being—that is enough for me."

In 1898, Samuel Clemens (1835–1910), writing under the name Mark Twain, wrote an article in which he tried to explain the widespread prejudice against Jews, both in the United States and in Europe. Though he claimed to have no personal prejudices against any group, the attitudes expressed in his article were similar to those of many Americans. But as he demonstrated in his essay, Twain's perceptions of Jews were the very essence of prejudice, even if he kept it hidden from himself. A strong case can be made that Twain's attitudes were a reflection of the attitudes of many Americans, in his time and since: strong prejudice hidden behind a screen of self-deceiving acceptance.

Twain, who gained celebrity as the author of such American classics as *The Celebrated Jumping Frog of Calaveras County, and Other Sketches; The Adventures of Tom Sawyer;* and *Adventures of Huckleberry Finn,* wrote his essay about Jews while living in Vienna, Austria. Like many European cities at the end of the nineteenth century, Vienna had a large Jewish population marked by official prejudice. In addressing the question, Twain seemed to like to think that America was different than

Europe; he looked at the United States as a country in which ancient religious hatreds and prejudices had been replaced by freedom of religion and an attitude that judged every individual on his or her own merits.

The subject was highly meaningful in 1898, when the essay was written, because significant numbers of Jewish immigrants were arriving in the United States from Russia, where Jews experienced official restrictions and physical attacks against them, making life unbearable. Most of the Jewish immigrants between 1880 and 1910 were from Russia and Poland. Most were poor, unlike an earlier wave of Jewish immigration from Germany during the 1840s, which consisted of mostly middle-class and professional Jews. Many young Jewish women went to work in clothing factories where they worked under difficult conditions and for low pay. To Twain, these recent Jewish immigrants seemed almost invisible. His essay was based on his perceptions of the earlier wave of middle-class professionals from Germany.

Writer Mark Twain, author of "Concerning the Jews."
AP/Wide World Photos.

Twain professed, in his essay, to admire Jews. They made good citizens. They seldom committed crimes. They were generous in giving to charities. He attributed the prejudice against them to jealousy on the part of other Americans who thought they could not effectively compete with Jews in business. He also assessed the failure of Jews to establish political power for themselves by acting as a group in their own self-interest.

What Twain ignored was the strong desire of many Jews in America to identify themselves as Americans, rather than as Jews in America. For Jewish immigrants, establishing political influence by acting as a group of Jews would mean continuing in their role as outsiders in European society. The idea of America as a "melting pot"—where people from different nations could come together and create a new type of individual, the American—was one that Jewish immigrants appreciated. One such Jew was Emma Lazarus (1849–1887), whose poem "The New Colossus" was later attached to the Statue of Liberty: "Give me your tired, your poor, Your huddled masses yearning to breathe free, The wretched refuse of your teeming shore. Send these, the homeless, tempest-tost to me, I lift my lamp beside the golden door!"

Things to remember while reading an excerpt from "Concerning the Jews":

- Twain painted a picture of Jews as successful businessmen, disliked by their neighbors because of their success. In fact, at the time Twain wrote his essay, many recent Jewish immigrants in the United States were extremely poor. Many clothing factories in New York City were staffed with young Jewish immigrant women who were hardly successful in business.

- Twain refers to an incident that occurred in the Austrian Reichstrath, or Imperial Parliament, in 1897. Twain was in the gallery watching, as Hungarian and German members of Parliament engaged in fierce disagreements, resulting in one member speaking for twelve straight hours so that opposing sides could not get their points across.

Excerpt from "Concerning the Jews"

Some months ago I published a magazine article ["Stirring Times in Austria," Harper's New Monthly Magazine (March 1898)] descriptive of a remarkable scene in the Imperial Parliament in Vienna. Since then I have received from Jews in America several letters of inquiry. They were difficult letters to answer, for they were not very definite. But at last I have received a definite one. It is from a lawyer, and he really asks the questions which the other writers probably believed they were asking. By help of this text I will do the best I can to publicly answer this correspondent, and also the oth-

ers—at the same time apologizing for having failed to reply private-ly. The lawyer's letter reads as follows:

"I have read 'Stirring Times in Austria.' One point in particular is of vital import to not a few thousand people, including myself, being a point about which I have often wanted to address a question to some disinterested person. The show of military force in the Austrian Parliament, which **precipitated** the riots, was not introduced by any Jew. No Jew was a member of that body. No Jewish question was involved in the **Ausgleich** or in the language proposition. No Jew was insulting anybody. In short, no Jew was doing any mischief toward anybody whatsoever. In fact, the Jews were the only ones of the nineteen different races in Austria which did not have a party—they are absolutely non-participants. Yet in your article you say that in the rioting which followed, all classes of people were unanimous only on one thing, **viz.,** in being against the Jews. Now will you kindly tell me why, in your judgment, the Jews have thus ever been, and are even now, in these days of supposed intelligence, the butt of baseless, vicious **animosities**? I dare say that for centuries there has been no more quiet, undisturbing, and well-behaving citizen, as a class, than that same Jew. It seems to me that ignorance and **fanaticism** cannot alone account for these horrible and unjust persecutions.

"Tell me, therefore, from your vantage-point of cold view, what in your mind is the cause. Can American Jews do anything to correct it either in America or abroad? Will it ever come to an end? Will a Jew be permitted to live honestly, decently, and peaceably like the rest of mankind? What has become of the **Golden Rule?**"

I will begin by saying that if I thought myself prejudiced against the Jew, I should hold it fairest to leave this subject to a person not crippled in that way. But I think I have no such prejudice. A few years ago a Jew observed to me that there was no uncourteous reference to his people in my books, and asked how it happened. It happened because the **disposition** was lacking. I am quite sure that (bar one) I have no race prejudices, and I think I have no color prejudices nor **caste** prejudices nor **creed** prejudices. Indeed, I know it. I can stand any society. All that I care to know is that a man is a human being—that is enough for me....

In the present paper I shall allow myself to use the word Jew as if it stood for both religion and race. It is handy; and, besides, that is what the term means to the general world.

Precipitated: Caused.

Ausgleich (1867): A German word meaning "compromise"; the Ausgleich of 1867 transformed the Habsburg Empire into a "dual monarchy" known as Austria-Hungary, two separate states with equal rights under a common ruler.

Viz.: Namely; an abbreviation for Latin *videlicet.*

Animosities: Active hate or hostility.

Fanaticism: Excessive attachment to a view or an ideal.

Golden Rule: In the New Testament of the Bible, the teaching that states, "Do unto others as you would have them do unto you."

Disposition: Inclination.

Caste: Class.

Creed: Religion.

In the above letter one notes these points:

1. The Jew is a well-behaved citizen.

2. Can ignorance and fanaticism alone account for his unjust treatment?

3. Can Jews do anything to improve the situation?

4. The Jews have no party; they are non-participants.

5. Will the persecution ever come to an end?

6. What has become of the Golden Rule?

Point No. 1.

*We must grant proposition No. 1 for several sufficient reasons. The Jew is not a disturber of the peace of any country. Even his enemies will concede that. He is not a **loafer,** he is not a **sot,** he is not noisy, he is not a brawler nor a rioter, he is not quarrelsome. In the statistics of crime his presence is **conspicuously** rare—in all countries. With murder and other crimes of violence he has but little to do: he is a stranger to the hangman. In the police court's daily long roll of "assaults" and "**drunk and disorderlies**" his name seldom appears. That the Jewish home is a home in the truest sense is a fact which no one will dispute. The family is knitted together by the strongest affections; its members show each other every due respect; and reverence for the elders is an **inviolate** law of the house. The Jew is not a burden on the charities of the state nor of the city; these could cease from their functions without affecting him. When he is well enough, he works; when he is **incapacitated,** his own people take care of him. And not in a poor and stingy way, but with a fine and large **benevolence.** His race is entitled to be called the most benevolent of all the races of men. A Jewish beggar is not impossible, perhaps; such a thing may exist, but there are few men that can say they have seen that spectacle....*

*These facts are all on the credit side of the proposition that the Jew is a good and orderly citizen. Summed up, they **certify** that he is quiet, peaceable, industrious, unaddicted to high crimes and brutal dispositions; that his family life is commendable; that he is not a burden upon public charities; that he is not a beggar; that in benevolence he is above the reach of competition. These are the very quint-essentials of good citizenship. If you can add that he is as honest as the average of his neighbors—But I think that question is affirmatively answered by the fact that he is a successful business man. The basis of successful business is honesty; a business cannot thrive where the parties to it cannot trust each other. In the matter of numbers the Jew counts for little in the overwhelming population*

Loafer: Lazy person.

Sot: Drunkard.

Conspicuously: Obviously.

"Drunk and disorderlies": People arrested by police for being drunk and acting disorderly; their names were often listed in police logs published in the newspaper.

Inviolate: Pure and intact; unbroken.

Incapacitated: Sick or disabled.

Benevolence: Charity; kindness.

Certify: Confirm.

Quint-essentials: The essence of a thing in its purest and most concentrated form.

of New York; but that his honesty counts for much is guaranteed by the fact that the immense wholesale business houses of Broadway, from the Battery to Union Square, is substantially in his hands....

The Jew has his other side. He has some **discreditable** ways, though he has not a **monopoly** of them, because he cannot get entirely rid of **vexatious** Christian competition. We have seen that he seldom **transgresses** the laws against crimes of violence. Indeed, his dealings with courts are almost restricted to matters connected with commerce. He has a reputation for various small forms of cheating, and for practising oppressive **usury,** and for burning himself out to get the insurance, and for arranging **cunning** contracts which leave him an exit but lock the other man in, and for smart evasions which find him safe and comfortable just within the strict letter of the law, when court and jury know very well that he has violated the spirit of it. He is a frequent and faithful and capable officer in the civil service, but he is charged with an unpatriotic **disinclination** to stand by the flag as a soldier—like the **Christian Quaker.**

Now if you offset these discreditable features by the creditable ones summarized in a preceding paragraph beginning with the words, "These facts are all on the credit side," and strike a balance, what must the verdict be? This, I think: that, the merits and demerits being fairly weighed and measured on both sides, the Christian can claim no superiority over the Jew in the matter of good citizenship.

Yet in all countries, from the dawn of history, the Jew has been persistently and **implacably** hated, and with frequency persecuted.

Point No. 2.

"Can fanaticism alone account for this?" Years ago I used to think that it was responsible for nearly all of it, but **latterly** I have come to think that this was an error. Indeed, it is now my conviction that it is responsible for hardly any of it....

When I was a boy, in the back settlements of the Mississippi Valley, where a gracious and beautiful Sunday-school simplicity and unpracticality prevailed, the **"Yankee"** was hated with a splendid energy. But religion had nothing to do with it. In a trade, the Yankee was held to be about five times the match of the Westerner. His shrewdness, his insight, his judgment, his knowledge, his **enterprise,** and his formidable cleverness in applying these forces were frankly confessed, and most competently cursed....

The Jew is being **legislated out** of Russia. The reason is not concealed. The movement was instituted because the Christian peasant

Discreditable: Disgraceful.

Monopoly: Full and exclusive control.

Vexatious: Irritating or troubling.

Transgresses: Disobeys.

Usury: Charging high interest on loans.

Cunning: Crafty; shrewd.

Disinclination: Reluctance.

Christian Quaker: A member of the Society of Friends, a religious group that does not believe in war.

Implacably: Unable to be changed.

Latterly: Lately; recently.

"Yankee": Citizen of the New England states.

Enterprise: Drive; initiative.

Legislated out: Forced out by the law.

Jewish exiles from Russia arrive in New York.
© Bettmann/Corbis.

Banish: Remove; deport.

Curtail: Cut short; lessen.

Exploited: Capitalized on.

Statute: Law.

and villager stood no chance against his commercial abilities. He was always ready to lend money on a crop, and sell vodka and other necessaries of life on credit while the crop was growing. When settlement day came he owned the crop; and next year or year after he owned the farm....

For the like reasons Spain had to **banish** him four hundred years ago, and Austria about a couple of centuries later.

In all the ages Christian Europe has been obliged to **curtail** his activities. If he entered upon a mechanical trade, the Christian had to retire from it. If he set up as a doctor, he was the best one, and he took the business. If he **exploited** agriculture, the other farmers had to get at something else. Since there was no way to successfully compete with him in any vocation, the law had to step in and save the Christian from the poor-house. Trade after trade was taken away from the Jew by **statute** till practically none was left. He was forbidden to engage in agriculture; he was forbidden to practise law; he was forbidden to practise medicine, except among Jews; he was forbidden the handicrafts. Even the seats of learning and the schools of science had to be closed against this tremendous **antagonist.** Still, almost **bereft** of employments, he found ways to make money, even ways to get rich. Also ways to invest his takings well, for usury was not denied him. In the hard conditions suggested, the Jew without brains could not survive, and the Jew with brains had to keep them in good training and well sharpened up, or starve. Ages of restriction to the one tool which the law was not able to take from him—his brain—have made that tool singularly competent; ages of **compulsory** disuse of his hands have **atrophied** them, and he never uses them now. This history has a very, very commercial look, a most **sordid** and practical commercial look, the business aspect of a Chinese cheap-labor crusade. Religious prejudices may account for one part of it, but not for the other nine.

Protestants have persecuted Catholics, but they did not take their livelihoods away from them. The Catholics have persecuted the Protestants with bloody and awful bitterness, but they never closed agriculture and the handicrafts against them. Why was that? That has the candid look of genuine religious persecution, not a trade-union boycott in a religious disguise....

I am persuaded that in Russia, Austria, and Germany nine-tenths of the hostility to the Jew comes from the average Christian's inability to compete successfully with the average Jew in business—in either straight business or the questionable sort....

With most people, of a necessity, bread and meat take first rank, religion second. I am convinced that the persecution of the Jew is not due in any large degree to religious prejudice.

No, the Jew is a money-getter; and in getting his money he is a very serious obstruction to less capable neighbors who are on the same quest. I think that that is the trouble. In estimating worldly values the Jew is not shallow, but deep. With **precocious** wisdom he found out in the morning of time that some men worship rank, some worship heroes, some worship power, some worship God, and that over these ideals they dispute and cannot unite—but that they all worship money; so he made it the end and aim of his life to get it....

Point No. 4.

"The Jews have no party; they are non-participants."

Perhaps you have let the secret out and given yourself away. It seems hardly a credit to the race that it is able to say that; or to you,

Antagonist: One who competes with another; opponent.

Bereft: Lonely; left wanting.

Compulsory: Mandatory.

Atrophied: Withered.

Sordid: Unpleasant; corrupt.

Precocious: Showing unusually early development, especially in mental abilities.

sir, that you can say it without remorse; more than you should offer it as a plea against maltreatment, injustice, and oppression. Who gives the Jew the right, who gives any race the right, to sit still, in a free country, and let somebody else look after its safety? The oppressed Jew was entitled to all pity in the former times under brutal **autocracies**, for he was weak and friendless, and had no way to help his case. But he has ways now, and he has had them for a century, but I do not see that he has tried to make serious use of them…. In the United States he was created free in the beginning—he did not need to help, of course. In Austria and Germany and France he has a vote, but of what considerable use is it to him? He doesn't seem to know how to apply it to the best effect. With all his splendid capacities and all his fat wealth he is to-day not politically important in any country….

Point No. 3.

"Can Jews do anything to improve the situation?"

I think so. If I may make a suggestion without seeming to be trying to teach my grandmother **how to suck eggs,** I will offer it. In our days we have learned the value of combination. We apply it everywhere—in railway systems, in trusts, in trade unions, in Salvation Armies, in minor politics, in major politics, in European Concerts. Whatever our strength may be, big or little, we organize it. We have found out that that is the only way to get the most out of it that is in it. We know the weakness of individual sticks, and the strength of the concentrated **fagot.** Suppose you try a scheme like this, for instance. In England and America put every Jew on the census-book as a Jew (in case you have not been doing that). Get up volunteer regiments composed of Jews solely, and, when the drum beats, fall in and go to the front, so as to remove the **reproach** that you have few **Massenas** among you, and that you feed on a country but don't like to fight for it. Next, in politics, organize your strength, band together, and deliver the casting vote where you can, and, where you can't, compel as good terms as possible. You huddle to yourselves already in all countries, but you huddle to no sufficient purpose, politically speaking. You do not seem to be organized, except for your charities….

Point No. 5.

"Will the persecution of the Jews ever come to an end?"

On the score of religion, I think it has already come to an end. On the score of race prejudice and trade, I have the idea that it will continue. That is, here and there in spots about the world, where a

Autocracies: Governments in which a single ruler has unlimited power.

How to suck eggs: An expression meaning to attempt to teach someone how to do something he or she already knows how to do.

Fagot: A bundle of sticks or twigs tied together.

Reproach: Criticism.

Massenas: A reference to André Massena (1758–1817), a French general and military hero.

barbarous ignorance and a sort of mere animal civilization prevail; but I do not think that elsewhere the Jew need now stand in any fear of being robbed and raided. Among the high civilizations he seems to be very comfortably situated indeed, and to have more than his proportionate share of the prosperities going. It has that look in Vienna. I suppose the race prejudice cannot be removed; but he can stand that; it is no particular matter....

Point No. 6.

"What has become of the Golden Rule?"

It exists, it continues to sparkle, and is well taken care of. It is Exhibit A in the Church's assets, and we pull it out every Sunday and give it an airing. But you are not permitted to try to smuggle it into this discussion, where it is irrelevant and would not feel at home. It is strictly religious furniture, like an **acolyte**, or a contribution-plate, or any of those things. It has never been intruded into business; and Jewish persecution is not a religious passion, it is a business passion.

To conclude. If the statistics are right, the Jews constitute but one per cent of the human race. It suggests a **nebulous** dim puff of star-dust lost in the blaze of the Milky Way. Properly the Jew ought hardly to be heard of; but he is heard of, has always been heard of. He is as prominent on the planet as any other people, and his commercial importance is extravagantly out of proportion to the smallness of his bulk. His contributions to the world's list of great names in literature, science, art, music, finance, medicine, and **abstruse** learning are also away out of proportion to the weakness of his numbers. He has made a marvellous fight in this world, in all the ages; and has done it with his hands tied behind him. He could be vain of himself, and be excused for it. The Egyptian, the Babylonian, and the Persian rose, filled the planet with sound and splendor, then faded to dream-stuff and passed away; the Greek and the Roman followed, and made a vast noise, and they are gone; other peoples have sprung up and held their torch high for a time, but it burned out, and they sit in twilight now, or have vanished. The Jew saw them all, beat them all, and is now what he always was, exhibiting no **decadence**, no **infirmities** of age, no weakening of his parts, no slowing of his energies, no dulling of his alert and aggressive mind. All things are mortal but the Jew; all other forces pass, but he remains. What is the secret of his immortality?

Acolyte: Trainee, especially in a church.

Nebulous: Vague; without form or limits; like a nebula, a mass of interstellar dust or gas.

Abstruse: Difficult to understand.

Decadence: A period of decline, especially in morals.

Infirmities: Bodily weaknesses or the diseases that cause them.

What happened next ...

Twain's article was widely criticized, especially on actual grounds. He had asserted that Jews were reluctant to defend their country. Readers of *Harper's* were eager to correct the record. When Twain's essay was later collected into a book, he printed a correction to his oversight:

"When I published the above article in *Harper's Monthly,* I was ignorant—like the rest of the Christian world—of the fact that the Jew had a record as a soldier. I have since seen the official statistics, and I find that he furnished soldiers and high officers to the Revolution, the War of 1812, and the Mexican War. In the Civil War he was represented in the armies and navies of both the North and the South by 10 per cent of his numerical strength—the same percentage that was furnished by the Christian populations of the two sections. This large fact means more than it seems to mean; for it means that the Jew's patriotism was not merely level with the Christian's, but overpassed it."

Two decades after Twain's essay appeared, the U.S. Congress began passing a series of laws to restrict immigration from southern and eastern Europe, laws that were aimed especially at Catholic and Jewish immigrants. The laws never proclaimed prejudice against religious groups. They were based on restricting immigration from specific countries in proportion to the number of Americans whose ancestors came from these countries. This meant, in practice, that the number of immigrants from predominantly Catholic countries like Italy was sharply limited. Immigrants from Russia—which in practice meant Jews—also were sharply restricted.

Did you know ...

- In his essay, Twain assumed that Jews were unwilling to fight in the armed forces, either of the United States or of other countries. In fact, just the opposite was true. In the nineteenth century, Jews regarded fighting in the army as a sign of acceptance. On the other hand, they were not always welcomed as soldiers. In the Dutch colony of New Amsterdam, later New York, Jews volunteered to stand armed guard. They were told instead they should depart, "whenever and whither it pleases them."

For More Information

Books

Twain, Mark. *The Complete Essays of Mark Twain Now Collected for the First Time*. Edited by Charles Neider. Garden City, NY: Doubleday, 1963.

Periodicals

Gilman, Sander L. "Mark Twain and the Diseases of the Jews." *American Literature* (March 1993): p. 95.

Web sites

Levy, M. S. "A Rabbi's Reply to Mark Twain." *Overland Monthly* (October 1899). http://www.boondocksnet.com/twaintexts/levy99.html (accessed on February 21, 2004).

Twain, Mark. "Stirring Times in Austria." *Harper's New Monthly Magazine* (March 1898). http://www2.h-net.msu.edu/~habsweb/sourcetexts/twain1.htm (accessed on February 21, 2004).

Zwick, Jim. "Mark Twain's Vienna and 'Concerning the Jews.'" *Boondocksnet.com*. http://www.boondocksnet.com/twainwww/essays/twain_vienna9705.html (accessed on February 21, 2004).

Jane Addams

Excerpt from **Twenty Years at Hull-House**
Originally published by the Macmillan Company, 1912

A Chicago woman writes of her experiences as owner of a house primarily designed to help immigrants

> "Her mother's whole life had been spent in a secluded spot under the rule of traditional and narrowly localized observances ... and then suddenly she was torn from it all and literally put out to sea ... and she now walked timidly but with poignant sensibility upon a new and strange shore."

Chicago by 1890 had become the great "melting pot" of the Midwest. People from many different nationalities found themselves mixed together, living in grimy industrial neighborhoods during a period of rapid expansion of factories and meat-processing plants. Immigrants came from Russia, Germany, Italy, Bohemia (later called the Czech Republic), and Greece. They crowded in an urban, or city, environment far removed from the rural, or country, villages from which they had emigrated to live in the United States. For many immigrant families, moving to the United States meant not only moving to a new country but also moving from the countryside to a city, and from an agricultural society to an industrial one.

Jane Addams (1860–1935), an upper-middle-class woman from Cedarville, Illinois, bought a house in Chicago, named Hull-House after a previous owner, and opened its doors to working people, both native-born Americans and immigrants, to help them adjust to their radically new surroundings. Addams had visited a settlement house called Toynbee Hall in the East End of London, where many poor people struggled to adjust to the new industrial age. In settlement houses such as Toynbee, university students and other upper-class, educated people "settled," or came to live in the houses, to help improve the lives of the underprivileged people in the neighborhood. Addams's memoir of the first two decades running Hull-House as a settlement house in Chicago provides a glimpse of the impact felt by immigrants trying to adjust to a completely different way of life.

In Chapter 11 of her book *Twenty Years at Hull-House,* Addams observed that a cultural gap had opened between immigrant parents and their own children. Watching immigrant women using ancient handcrafted techniques for making "thread," or yarn, Addams realized that the women's children did not appreciate the skills their mothers brought with them to their new country—skills that were an essential part of life in the villages of European countries that had not experienced the Industrial Revolution, the decades-long process by which large factories replaced smaller home-based workshops in manufacturing. In what Addams called a "desire to reveal the humbler immigrant parents to their own children," Addams established a small "Labor Museum" in Hull-House. The "museum" was not a large building devoted to the subject. Instead, the museum consisted of a small display of traditional tools and methods familiar to immigrants but utterly foreign to their children living in Chicago around the turn of the twentieth century.

The display demonstrated how large-scale immigration to the United States in the period from 1880 to 1920 occurred at the same time as the technological progression of simple tools and the rapid growth of American industry. On a personal level, immigrant mothers enjoyed coming to Hull-House to see the exhibits that displayed the skills and methods they had practiced in their home countries. Unknowingly, immigrant women had brought these skills with them to America as part of a way of life that had been rendered virtually useless, not just by the voyage across the Atlantic to Chicago but also by the voyage across an era from an agricultural society to an industrial one. The museum allowed immigrant parents to show their children that these tools and skills provided the basis for the new industrial machines.

Addams also noticed how life had changed for immigrant teenagers. Young people, traditionally closely controlled by their parents, were torn between the temptations of their new American society and their desire to obey their parents, who were often clinging to long-established practices of raising children. The tension between the new world and the old world sometimes led young men and women not only into trouble with parents but into trouble with the law. Addams viewed their misdeeds not as a sign of "bad" behavior but as the result of unreasonable expectations in the midst of confusing and highly difficult living circumstances.

Hull-House founder Jane Addams. © *Bettmann/Corbis.*

Things to remember while reading an excerpt from *Twenty Years at Hull-House:*

• In many societies, women play the central role in binding together families. This was certainly the case among immigrants from southern and eastern Europe living in Chicago at the time *Twenty Years at Hull-House* was written. The woman's role in the family was made vastly more difficult in the new setting. Many immigrant women did not know how to function in an urban environment, much less one in which they did not speak the language well. Their clothing and headscarves set them apart, too.

• For many women, even the smallest details of life, such as baking bread, were different. For example, Addams told the story of an Italian woman who had baked her bread in a community oven. Because her daughter had had cooking lessons in school, the bewildered mother would learn how to use the oven at home from her child. There were many cases of such a role reversal: in America, it was the English-speaking, more streetwise children who had to show immigrant parents how things worked in their new world.

• Jane Addams realized that setting up a little "Labor Museum" in Hull-House was part of an educational experience for immigrant children, enabling them to relate to their cultural roots. In this excerpt from Addams's book, she refers to "Dr. Dewey." At the time Addams was running Hull-House, John Dewey (1859–1952) was appointed to be the head of a new department of philosophy, psychology, and education at the University of Chicago. Dewey believed that people should learn by experience, not just by repetitive, mechanical memorization of facts. His ideas have long been controversial since they challenged the predominant method of instruction in use at the time, and still prevalent in the twenty-first century. Dewey became friends with Addams and other social reformers at Hull-House and was one of the educators recruited by Addams to give lectures there. He frequently visited Hull-House, praised it as a model for what schools should be like, and became a trustee, or administrator, of the house for seven years.

University of Chicago educator John Dewey, a friend of Hull-House founder Jane Addams. *Special Collections Research Center, Morris Library, Southern Illinois University.*

• At the beginning of this excerpt, Addams refers to seeing "an old Italian woman, her distaff against her homesick face, patiently spinning a thread by the simple stick spindle so reminiscent of all southern Europe." In just a sentence, Addams evoked the essence of leaving home and coming to a new country for many women in the late nineteenth century. A distaff is a stick, or rod, used as part of the process of turning sheep's wool into yarn that can later be woven into material. A "simple stick spindle" is a hand-held tool used by women to spin the fibers of wool, a technique that existed for hundreds of years before modern industrial machinery in factories took over the task. Seeing an immigrant woman patiently spinning yarn using an ancient technique called to mind for Addams a sense of the woman's homesickness. The woman's longing was not just for the sunny climate of southern Italy, as opposed to the often cloudy, windy, and cold climate of Chicago, but also for a bygone time when life followed a familiar pattern. The word "distaff" refers not only to a tool for spinning, but it had also come to mean the more general concept of a "woman's work." The familiar, essential role of women in rural life had been abandoned by immigrants in the bustle of industrial Chicago. In carrying out her lifelong habit, the elderly woman encountered by Addams conveyed the sense of loss—of a familiar place, of familiar habits, and even of a familiar role in her family—that many immigrant women must have felt living in their adopted country.

- The sense of loss felt by immigrants was not limited to women. Addams tells the story of a man who used to be a skilled goldsmith, capable of making beautiful jewelry, who could only find work in a factory in Chicago. The loss of being able to do the work he loved drove him to heavy drinking and eventually to kill himself. The struggle to live—to earn money for food and shelter—robbed some immigrants of their joy in work and the joy of life itself.

Excerpt from Twenty Years at Hull-House

Chapter XI: Immigrants and Their Children

*An overmastering desire to reveal the humbler immigrant parents to their own children lay at the base of what has come to be called the Hull-House Labor Museum. This was first suggested to my mind one early spring day when I saw an old Italian woman, her **distaff** against her homesick face, patiently spinning a thread by the simple stick **spindle** so reminiscent of all southern Europe. I was walking down Polk Street, **perturbed** in spirit, because it seemed so difficult to come into genuine relations with the Italian women and because they themselves so often lost their hold upon their Americanized children. It seemed to me that Hull-House ought to be able*

Distaff: A staff, or rod, for holding the wool in spinning; also implies the larger topic of a woman's work, since spinning was traditionally done by women.

Spindle: A round stick with tapered ends used to form and twist the yarn in hand spinning.

Perturbed: Irritated.

to devise some educational *enterprise* which should build a bridge between European and American experiences in such wise as to give them both more meaning and a sense of relation. I meditated that perhaps the power to see life as a whole is more needed in the immigrant quarter of a large city than anywhere else, and that the lack of this power is the most fruitful source of misunderstanding between European immigrants and their children, as it is between them and their American neighbors; and why should that *chasm* between fathers and sons, yawning at the feet of each generation, be made so unnecessarily cruel and impassable to these bewildered immigrants? Suddenly I looked up and saw the old woman with her distaff, sitting in the sun on the steps of a *tenement house*. She might have served as a model for one of *Michael Angelo's Fates*, but her face brightened as I passed and, holding up her spindle for me to see, she called out that when she had spun a little more yarn, she would knit a pair of stockings for her goddaughter. The occupation of the old woman gave me the clue that was needed. Could we not interest the young people working in the neighborhood factories in these older forms of industry, so that, through their own parents and grandparents, they would find a dramatic representation of the inherited resources of their daily occupation. If these young people could actually see that the complicated machinery of the factory had been evolved from simple tools, they might at least make a beginning toward that education which *Dr. Dewey* defines as a "continuing reconstruction of experience." They might also lay a foundation for reverence of the past which *Goethe* declares to be the basis of all sound progress....

We found in the immediate neighborhood at least four varieties of these most primitive methods of spinning and three distinct variations of the same spindle in connection with *wheels*. It was possible to put these seven into historic sequence and order and to connect the whole with the present method of factory spinning. The same thing was done for weaving, and on every Saturday evening a little exhibit was made of these various forms of labor in the textile industry. Within one room a Syrian woman, a Greek, an Italian, a Russian, and an Irishwoman enabled even the most casual observer to see that there is no break in *orderly evolution* if we look at history from the industrial standpoint; that industry develops similarly and peacefully year by year among the workers of each nation, heedless of differences in language, religion, and political experiences....

I recall a number of Russian women working in a sewing room near Hull-House, who heard one Christmas week that the House

Enterprise: Program.

Chasm: Gap; also used as a metaphor for a distance separating two people or two generations.

Tenement house: An apartment house, usually poorly constructed and offering crowded, but inexpensive, quarters for poor immigrants.

Michel Angelo's Fates: A depiction of women by Italian sculptor and painter Michelangelo (1475–1564).

Dr. Dewey: John Dewey (1859–1952), a leading philosopher, psychologist, and educator from the University of Chicago and a friend of Addams.

Goethe: Johann Wolfgang von Goethe (1749–1832), a leading German novelist and playwright.

Wheels: Spinning wheels; another method of spinning thread.

Orderly evolution: Development.

*was going to give a party to which they might come. They arrived one afternoon, when, unfortunately, there was no party on hand and, although the residents did their best to entertain them with impromptu music and refreshments, it was quite evident that they were greatly disappointed. Finally it was suggested that they be shown the Labor Museum—where gradually the thirty **sodden**, sluggish tired women were transformed. They knew how to use the spindles and were delighted to find the Russian spinning frame. Many of them had never seen the spinning wheel, which has not penetrated to certain parts of Russia, and they regarded it as a new and wonderful invention. They turned up their dresses to show their homespun petticoats; they tried the looms; they explained the difficulty of the old patterns; in short, from having been stupidly entertained, they themselves did the entertaining. Because of a direct appeal to former experiences, the immigrant visitors were able for the moment to instruct their American hostesses in an old and honored craft, as was indeed becoming to their age and experience....*

*There has been some testimony that the Labor Museum has revealed the charm of woman's **primitive** activities. I recall a certain Italian girl who came every Saturday evening to a cooking class in the same building in which her mother spun in the Labor Museum exhibit; and yet Angelina always left her mother at the front door while she herself went around to a side door because she did not wish to be too closely identified in the eyes of the rest of the cooking class with an Italian woman who wore a kerchief over her head, **uncouth** boots, and short petticoats. One evening, however, Angelina saw her mother surrounded by a group of visitors from the School of Education who much admired the spinning, and she concluded from their conversation that her mother was "the best stick-spindle spinner in America." When she inquired from me as to the truth of this **deduction**, I took occasion to describe the Italian village in which her mother had lived, something of her free life, and how, because of the opportunity she and the other women of the village had to drop their spindles over the edge of a **precipice**, they had developed a skill in spinning beyond that of the neighboring towns. I **dilated** somewhat on the freedom and beauty of that life—how hard it must be to exchange it all for a two-room tenement, and to give up a beautiful homespun kerchief for an ugly department store hat. I intimated it was most unfair to judge her by these things alone, and that while she must depend on her daughter to learn the new ways, she also had a right to expect her daughter to know something of the old ways.*

Sodden: Wet.

Primitive: Original or primary.

Uncouth: Crude or uncultivated.

Deduction: Conclusion.

Precipice: Cliff.

Dilated: Added details.

That which I could not convey to the child, but upon which my own mind persistently dwelt, was that her mother's whole life had been spent in a secluded spot under the rule of traditional and narrowly localized observances, until her very religion clung to local **sanctities**—to the shrine before which she had always prayed, to the pavement and walls of the low vaulted church-and then suddenly she was torn from it all and literally put out to sea, straight away from the solid habits of her religious and domestic life, and she now walked timidly but with **poignant** sensibility upon a new and strange shore.

It was easy to see that the thought of her mother with any other background than that of the tenement was new to Angelina, and at least two things resulted; she allowed her mother to pull out of the big box under the bed the beautiful homespun garments which had been previously hidden away as uncouth; and she openly came into the Labor Museum by the same door as did her mother, proud at least of the mastery of the craft which had been so much admired....

These women and a few men, who come to the museum to utilize their European skill in pottery, metal, and wood, demonstrate that immigrant colonies might yield to our American life something very valuable, if their resources were intelligently studied and developed. I recall an Italian, who had decorated the doorposts of his tenement with a beautiful pattern he had previously used in carving the **reredos** of a Neapolitan church [in Naples], who was "fired" by his landlord on the ground of destroying property. His feelings were hurt, not so much that he had been put out of his house, as that his work had been so disregarded; and he said that when people traveled in Italy they liked to look at wood carvings but that in America "they only made money out of you."

Sometimes the suppression of the instinct of workmanship is followed by more disastrous results. A **Bohemian** whose little girl attended classes at Hull-House, in one of his periodic drunken spells had literally almost choked her to death, and later had committed suicide when in **delirium tremens.** His poor wife, who stayed a week at Hull-House after the disaster until a new tenement could be arranged for her, one day showed me a gold ring which her husband had made for their **betrothal.** It exhibited the most exquisite workmanship, and she said that although in the old country he had been a goldsmith, in America he had for twenty years shoveled coal in a furnace room of a large manufacturing plant; that whenever

Sanctities: The quality of being holy.

Poignant: Painfully affecting the feelings.

Reredos (RARE-a-dose): An ornamental wood or stone screen or partition behind the altar in a church.

Bohemian: A person from a region of Europe called Bohemia, situated in what is now called the Czech Republic.

Delirium tremens: A violent and life-threatening reaction to excessive use of alcohol, characterized by mental confusion and shaking of the body.

Betrothal: Engagement.

A group of small children stand in front of Hull-House in Chicago, Illinois. *AP/Wide World Photos.*

*she saw one of his "restless fits," which preceded his drunken periods, "coming on," if she could provide him with a bit of metal and persuade him to stay at home and work at it, he was all right and the time passed without disaster, but that "nothing else would do it." This story threw a flood of light upon the dead man's struggle and on the stupid maladjustment which had broken him down. Why had we never been told? Why had our interest in the remarkable musical ability of his child blinded us to the hidden artistic ability of the father? We had forgotten that a long-established occupation may form the very foundations of the moral life, that the art with which a man has **solaced** his toil may be the salvation of his uncertain temperament.*

*There are many examples of touching **fidelity** to immigrant parents on the part of their grown children; a young man who day after day attends ceremonies which no longer express his religious convictions and who makes his vain effort to interest his Russian Jewish father in social problems; a daughter who might earn much more money as a **stenographer** could she work from Monday morning till*

Solaced: Comforted.

Fidelity: Faithfulness; loyalty.

Stenographer: Bookkeeper; typist.

Saturday night, but who quietly and **docilely** makes neckties for low wages because she can thus **abstain from** work Saturdays to please her father; these young people, like poor **Maggie Tulliver**, through many painful experiences have reached the conclusion that pity, memory, and faithfulness are natural ties with paramount claims.

This faithfulness, however, is sometimes ruthlessly imposed upon by immigrant parents who, eager for money and accustomed to the **patriarchal** authority of peasant households, hold their children in a stern bondage which requires a surrender of all their wages and concedes no time or money for pleasures.

There are many convincing illustrations that this parental harshness often results in **juvenile delinquency.** A Polish boy of seventeen came to Hull-House one day to ask a contribution of fifty cents "towards a flower piece for the funeral of an old Hull-House club boy." A few questions made it clear that the object was fictitious, whereupon the boy broke down and half-defiantly stated that he wanted to buy two twenty-five cent tickets, one for his girl and one for himself, to a dance of the Benevolent Social Twos [a social club]; that he hadn't a penny of his own although he had worked in a brass foundry for three years and had been advanced twice, because he always had to give his pay envelope unopened to his father; "just look at the clothes he buys me" was his concluding remark.

Perhaps the girls are held even more rigidly. In a recent investigation of two hundred working girls it was found that only five per cent had the use of their own money and that sixty-two per cent turned in all they earned, literally every penny, to their mothers. It was through this little investigation that we first knew Marcella, a pretty young German girl who helped her widowed mother year after year to care for a large family of younger children. She was content for the most part although her mother's old-country notions of dress gave her but an **infinitesimal** amount of her own wages to spend on her clothes, and she was quite sophisticated as to proper dressing because she sold silk in a neighborhood department store. Her mother approved of the young man who was showing her various attentions and agreed that Marcella should accept his invitation to a ball, but would allow her not a penny toward a new gown to replace one impossibly plain and shabby. Marcella spent a sleepless night and wept bitterly, although she well knew that the doctor's bill for the children's **scarlet fever** was not yet paid. The next day as she was cutting off three yards of shining pink silk, the thought came to her that it would make her a fine new waist to wear to the ball. She

Docilely: Willingly; gently.

Abstain from: Avoid.

Maggie Tulliver: A character in the 1860 novel *Mill on the Floss,* by George Eliot, who serves as an example of how women were often expected to make personal sacrifices to sustain appearances for their families.

Patriarchal: Fatherly.

Juvenile delinquency: Minor crimes committed by children.

Infinitesimal: Extremely small.

Scarlet fever: A childhood disease common in the nineteenth century.

wistfully saw it wrapped in paper and carelessly stuffed into the muff of the purchaser, when suddenly the parcel fell upon the floor. No one was looking and quick as a flash the girl picked it up and pushed it into her blouse. The theft was discovered by the relentless department store detective who, for "the sake of example," insisted upon taking the case into court. The poor mother wept bitter tears over this downfall of her "frommes Mädchen" [pious daughter] and no one had the heart to tell her of her own blindness.

I know a Polish boy whose earnings were all given to his father who gruffly refused all requests for pocket money. One Christmas his little sisters, having been told by their mother that they were too poor to have any Christmas presents, appealed to the big brother as to one who was earning money of his own. Flattered by the implication, but at the same time quite impecunious, the night before Christmas he nonchalantly walked through a neighboring department store and stole a manicure set for one little sister and a string of beads for the other. He was caught at the door by the house detective as one of those children whom each local department store arrests in the weeks before Christmas at the daily rate of eight to twenty. The youngest of these offenders are seldom taken into court but are either sent home with a warning or turned over to the officers of the Juvenile Protective Association. Most of these premature law breakers are in search of Americanized clothing and others are only looking for playthings. They are all distracted by the profusion and variety of the display, and their moral sense is confused by the general air of openhandedness.

These disastrous efforts are not unlike those of many younger children who are constantly arrested for petty thieving because they are too eager to take home food or fuel which will relieve the distress and need they so constantly hear discussed. The coal on the wagons, the vegetables displayed in front of the grocery shops, the very wooden blocks in the loosened street paving are a challenge to their powers to help out at home. A Bohemian boy who was out on parole from the old detention home of the Juvenile Court itself, brought back five stolen chickens to the matron for Sunday dinner, saying that he knew the Committee were "having a hard time to fill up so many kids and perhaps these fowl [chickens] would help out." The honest immigrant parents, totally ignorant of American laws and municipal regulations, often send a child to pick up coal on the railroad tracks or to stand at three o'clock in the morning before the side door of a restaurant which gives away broken [unused] food, or to collect grain for the chickens at the base of elevators and

Muff: A cylinder of material or fur open at both ends for hands to be inserted for warmth; used in place of gloves.

Impecunious: Penniless.

Nonchalantly: Casually.

Manicure set: Scissors and files used to care for fingernails.

Profusion: Abundance.

Matron: Supervisor of the detention center.

standing cars. The latter custom accounts for the large number of boys arrested for breaking the seals on grain freight cars. It is easy for a child thus trained to accept the proposition of a junk dealer to bring him bars of iron stored in freight yards. Four boys quite recently had thus carried away and sold to one man two tons of iron.

Four-fifths of the children brought into the Juvenile Court in Chicago are the children of foreigners. The Germans are the greatest offenders, Polish next. Do their children suffer from the excess of virtue in those parents so eager to own a house and lot? One often sees a grasping parent in the court, utterly broken down when the Americanized youth who has been brought to grief clings as piteously to his peasant father as if he were still a frightened little boy in the **steerage.**

Many of these children have come to grief through their premature fling into city life, having thrown off parental control as they have impatiently discarded foreign ways. Boys of ten and twelve will refuse to sleep at home, preferring the freedom of an old **brewery vault** or an empty warehouse to the obedience required by their parents, and for days these boys will live on the milk and bread which they steal from the back porches after the early morning delivery. Such children complain that there is "no fun" at home. One little chap who was given a vacant lot to cultivate by the City Garden Association insisted upon raising only popcorn and tried to present the entire crop to Hull-House "to be used for the parties," with the stipulation that he would have "to be invited every single time." Then there are little groups of **dissipated** young men who pride themselves upon their ability to live without working and who despise all the honest and sober ways of their immigrant parents. They are at once a menace and a center of demoralization. Certainly the bewildered parents, unable to speak English and ignorant of the city, whose children have disappeared for days or weeks, have often come to Hull-House ... as if they had discovered a new type of suffering, devoid of the healing in familiar sorrows. It is as if they did not know how to search for the children without the assistance of the children themselves. Perhaps the most pathetic aspect of such cases is their **revelation** of the premature dependence of the older and wiser upon the young and foolish, which is in itself often responsible for the situation because it has given the children an undue sense of their own importance and a false security that they can take care of themselves.

On the other hand, an Italian girl who has had lessons in cooking at the public school will help her mother to connect the entire

Steerage: A section of inferior accommodations in a passenger ship for passengers paying the lowest fares.

Brewery vault: A storage facility in a beer factory.

Dissipated: Extravagant in the pursuit of pleasure, especially in pursuit of drinking.

Revelation: Sudden awareness.

family with American food and household habits. That the mother has never baked bread in Italy—only mixed it in her own house and then taken it out to the village oven—makes all the more valuable her daughter's understanding of the complicated cooking stove....

What happened next ...

Jane Addams was a pioneer in a profession that came to be called social work. Her efforts to help people struggling to cope with life in Chicago were not limited to immigrants; programs of Hull-House were open to all nationalities. Over the next century, social work became a highly respected profession, often sponsored by state governments to address the social problems of modern industrial society.

The dramatic flow of immigrants from southern and eastern Europe largely stopped after 1921, when new federal laws imposed restrictions on what had previously been a largely unregulated flow of poor rural people into the United States. The children and grandchildren of immigrants gradually became used to American customs, a process called "becoming Americanized."

People from other countries were not the only "immigrants" coming to northern industrial cities like Chicago. During World War II (1939–45), when many U.S. factory workers left to serve in the Army, rural residents of the South, many of them African Americans, migrated to northern cities to fill factory jobs. Their experiences were very similar to the experiences of immigrants from European rural societies fifty years earlier.

Did you know ...

- In 1931, Jane Addams became the first woman to win the Nobel Peace Prize. Her efforts to improve social conditions were not limited to the industrial slums of Chicago. She also campaigned for women's right to vote, for government regulation of the conditions under which people worked, and for unemployment insurance (payments to people who lose their jobs).

- Addams was a "hands-on" reformer. Hull-House was not only the site of programs to benefit poor immigrants and other workers; it was also Addams's house, where she both lived and worked.

- Her work was widely admired during her lifetime. President Theodore Roosevelt (1858–1919; served 1901–9) once described Addams as "the most useful citizen in America."

For More Information

Books

Addams, Jane. *Twenty Years at Hull-House*. Boston: Bedford/St. Martin's, 1999.

Eliot, George. *The Mill on the Floss."* New York: Knopf, 1992.

Elshtain, Jean Bethke. *Jane Addams and the Dream of American Democracy: A Life*. New York: Basic Books, 2002.

Hovde, Jane. *Jane Addams*. New York: Facts on File, 1989.

Periodicals

Kornblatt, Mark, and Pamela Renner. "'Saint' Jane." *Scholastic Update* (February 23, 1990): p. 10.

Levinsohn, Florence Hamlish. "A Tribute to a Life of Caring; Halsted Street's Living Memorial to Jane Addams." *Chicago* (November 1986): p. 304.

Web Sites

Holli, Melvin G. "Hull House and the Immigrants." *Illinois Periodicals Online*. http://www.lib.niu.edu/ipo/iht1010323.html (accessed on February 25, 2004).

Jane Addams Hull House. http://www.hullhouse.org (accessed on February 25, 2004).

Willa Cather

Excerpt from My Antonia
Published in 1918

*A novel accurately relates the difficulties experienced
by European immigrants in the United States
in the late nineteenth century*

"They ain't got but one overcoat among 'em over there, and they take turns wearing it. They seem awful scared of cold, and stick in that hole in the bank like badgers."

My *Antonia* is a novel about life in Nebraska in the 1880s and 1890s, where author Willa Cather (1872–1947) lived from age nine. The Antonia in the title is fourteen-year-old Antonia Shimerda, whose family moved to Nebraska from Bohemia, in Europe, the land now known as the Czech Republic. Although *My Antonia* is fiction, it accurately represents how hard life was for European immigrants attracted to the United States in the last quarter of the nineteenth century.

Arriving with little money and unable to speak English, European immigrants were often attracted by the promise of free or inexpensive farmland made available through the Homestead Act of 1862 (see entry). But the Great Plains of North and South Dakota, Nebraska, and Kansas offered a difficult, hostile environment. Pioneers dug holes into the earth and heaped bricks made of sod (dirt held together by grass roots) to make low houses that were a combination of a hole in the ground and a mud hut. Trees were scarce on the prairie, and wooden houses were a sign of economic success.

The Shimerda family in *My Antonia* suffered greatly. They arrived in Nebraska without enough money to buy food until their first crops could be harvested. One child was mentally challenged. The father was not coping well in his new circumstances, and sometimes slid into depression, a mental disorder characterized by feelings of sadness and disinterest in everyday activities. The family did not speak English and had few friends.

Antonia, who is introduced in the part of the book excerpted here, was about twelve when the story opens with the arrival of the Shimerdas in Black Hawk, Nebraska. They had taken the same train from Chicago that carried the book's narrator, Jim Burden, who was moving from Virginia to join his grandparents, just as Willa Cather did as a young girl.

My Antonia is not only a story about immigrants; some people living in Nebraska were American-born, like the narrator. But many European immigrants who headed west after arriving in the United States did have experiences like the Shimerdas. More than half the pioneers who filed for free land under the Homestead Act of 1862 gave up and left their land before the five-year minimum stay required to obtain title to the property.

My Antonia author Willa Cather. *UPI/Corbis-Bettmann.*

Things to remember while reading an excerpt from *My Antonia:*

- Not all of history is about government institutions. Most immigrants to the United States were ordinary people in search of a better life. Most never wrote down their stories in detail. Sometimes it requires a writer of skill and talent, like Cather, to fill in the human touches of a great movement like the European migration to North America in the nineteenth century.

- Cather went to live with her grandparents in Nebraska at age nine, after a childhood spent in Virginia. She

The cover of *My Antonia*, by
Willa Cather. *Cover
illustration © John Collier.
Houghton Mifflin Company.*

spent about a year living on the prairie before her family moved into the town of Red Cloud, near Nebraska's southern border with Kansas. Her father opened a business lending money to buy land and houses. As a child, Cather was full of imagination, sometimes identifying herself as a doctor, "William Cather, M.D." She was interested in the many different immigrants she met, people from Denmark, Sweden, Bohemia, France, and Germany. They had followed the railroads west.

- The model for Antonia was a girl named Annie, who worked as a servant in the home of Cather's best friends, the Miner children.

- In the book, the narrator explains that Antonia's name is pronounced with an emphasis on the first syllable, like the name Anthony: AN-to-nia.

Excerpt from My Antonia

*On Sunday morning Otto Fuchs was to drive us over to make the acquaintance of our new Bohemian neighbors. We were taking them some provisions, as they had come to live on a wild place where there was no garden or chicken-house, and very little broken land. Fuchs brought up a sack of potatoes and a piece of cured pork from the cellar, and grandmother packed some loaves of Saturday's bread, a jar of butter, and several pumpkin pies in the straw of the wagon-box. We **clambered** up to the front seat and jolted off past the little pond and along the road that climbed to the big cornfield.*

I could hardly wait to see what lay beyond that cornfield; but there was only red grass like ours, and nothing else, though from the high wagon-seat one could look off a long way. The road ran

Clambered: Scrambled.

about like a wild thing, avoiding the deep draws, crossing them where they were wide and shallow. And all along it, wherever it looped or ran, the sunflowers grew; some of them were as big as little trees, with great rough leaves and many branches which bore dozens of blossoms. They made a gold ribbon across the prairie. Occasionally one of the horses would tear off with his teeth a plant full of blossoms, and walk along munching it, the flowers nodding in time to his bites as he ate down toward them.

The Bohemian family, grandmother told me as we drove along, had bought the homestead of a fellow countryman, Peter Krajiek, and had paid him more than it was worth. Their agreement with him was made before they left the old country, through a cousin of his, who was also a relative of Mrs. Shimerda. The Shimerdas were the first Bohemian family to come to this part of the county. Krajiek was their only interpreter, and could tell them anything he chose. They could not speak enough English to ask for advice, or even to make their most pressing wants known. One son, Fuchs said, was well-grown, and strong enough to work the land; but the father was old and frail and knew nothing about farming. He was a weaver by trade; had been a skilled workman on **tapestries** and **upholstery** materials. He had brought his fiddle with him, which wouldn't be of much use here, though he used to pick up money by it at home.

"If they're nice people, I hate to think of them spending the winter in that cave of Krajiek's," said grandmother. "It's no better than a **badger** hole; no proper dugout at all. And I hear he's made them pay twenty dollars for his old cookstove that ain't worth ten."

"Yes'm," said Otto; "and he's sold 'em his oxen and his two bony old horses for the price of good workteams. I'd have interfered about the horses—the old man can understand some German—if I'd 'a' thought it would do any good. But Bohemians has a natural distrust of Austrians."

Grandmother looked interested. "Now, why is that, Otto?"

Fuchs wrinkled his brow and nose. "Well, ma'm, it's politics. It would take me a long while to explain."

The land was growing rougher; I was told that we were approaching Squaw Creek, which cut up the west half of the Shimerdas' place and made the land of little value for farming. Soon we could see the broken, grassy clay cliffs which indicated the windings of the stream, and the glittering tops of the cottonwoods and ash trees that grew down in the ravine. Some of the cottonwoods

Tapestries: Woven materials, often showing a pattern and hung on a wall.

Upholstery: Woven material used to cover furniture.

Badger: A burrowing mammal, related to the weasel.

had already turned, and the yellow leaves and shining white bark made them look like the gold and silver trees in fairy tales.

As we approached the Shimerdas' dwelling, I could still see nothing but rough red **hillocks**, and draws with shelving banks and long roots hanging out where the earth had crumbled away. Presently, against one of those banks, I saw a sort of shed, thatched with the same wine-colored grass that grew everywhere. Near it tilted a shattered windmill frame, that had no wheel. We drove up to this skeleton to tie our horses, and then I saw a door and window sunk deep in the **draw-bank.** The door stood open, and a woman and a girl of fourteen ran out and looked up at us hopefully. A little girl trailed along behind them. The woman had on her head the same embroidered shawl with silk fringes that she wore when she had alighted from the train at Black Hawk. She was not old, but she was certainly not young. Her face was alert and lively, with a sharp chin and shrewd little eyes. She shook grandmother's hand energetically.

"Very glad, very glad!" she **ejaculated.** Immediately she pointed to the bank out of which she had emerged and said, "House no good, house no good!"

Grandmother nodded **consolingly.** "You'll get fixed up comfortable after while, Mrs. Shimerda; make good house."

My grandmother always spoke in a very loud tone to foreigners, as if they were deaf. She made Mrs. Shimerda understand the friendly intention of our visit, and the Bohemian woman handled the loaves of bread and even smelled them, and examined the pies with lively curiosity, exclaiming, "Much good, much thank!"—and again she wrung grandmother's hand.

The oldest son, Ambroz—they called it Ambrosch—came out of the cave and stood beside his mother. He was nineteen years old, short and broad-backed, with a close-cropped, flat head, and a wide, flat face. His hazel eyes were little and shrewd, like his mother's, but more sly and suspicious; they fairly snapped at the food. The family had been living on corncakes and **sorghum molasses** for three days.

The little girl was pretty, but Antonia—they accented the name thus, strongly, when they spoke to her—was still prettier. I remembered what the conductor had said about her eyes. They were big and warm and full of light, like the sun shining on brown pools in the wood. Her skin was brown, too, and in her cheeks she had a glow of rich, dark color. Her brown hair was curly and wild-looking. The little

Hillocks: Small hills.

Draw-bank: A ridge of earth surrounding a shallow gully.

Ejaculated: Spoke suddenly and vehemently.

Consolingly: Sympathetically.

Sorghum molasses: A thick syrup made from a form of grass called sorghum.

sister, whom they called Yulka (Julka), was fair, and seemed mild and obedient. While I stood awkwardly confronting the two girls, Krajiek came up from the barn to see what was going on. With him was another Shimerda son. Even from a distance one could see that there was something strange about this boy. As he approached us, he began to make **uncouth** noises, and held up his hands to show us his fingers, which were webbed to the first knuckle, like a duck's foot. When he saw me draw back, he began to crow delightedly, "Hoo, hoo-hoo, hoo-hoo!" like a rooster. His mother scowled and said sternly, "Marek!" then spoke rapidly to Krajiek in Bohemian.

"She wants me to tell you he won't hurt nobody, Mrs. Burden. He was born like that. The others are smart. Ambrosch, he make good farmer." He struck Ambrosch on the back, and the boy smiled knowingly.

At that moment the father came out of the hole in the bank. He wore no hat, and his thick, iron-gray hair was brushed straight back from his forehead. It was so long that it bushed out behind his ears, and made him look like the old portraits I remembered in Virginia. He was tall and slender, and his thin shoulders stooped. He looked at us understandingly, then took grandmother's hand and bent over it. I noticed how white and well-shaped his own hands were. They looked calm, somehow, and skilled. His eyes were **melancholy,** and were set back deep under his brow. His face was ruggedly formed, but it looked like ashes—like something from which all the warmth and light had died out. Everything about this old man was in keeping with his **dignified** manner. He was neatly dressed. Under his coat he wore a knitted gray vest, and, instead of a collar, a silk scarf of a dark bronze-green, carefully crossed and held together by a red coral pin. While Krajiek was translating for Mr. Shimerda, Antonia came up to me and held out her hand **coaxingly.** In a moment we were running up the steep **drawside** together, Yulka trotting after us.

When we reached the level and could see the gold tree-tops, I pointed toward them, and Antonia laughed and squeezed my hand as if to tell me how glad she was I had come. We raced off toward Squaw Creek and did not stop until the ground itself stopped—fell away before us so abruptly that the next step would have been out into the tree-tops. We stood panting on the edge of the ravine, looking down at the trees and bushes that grew below us. The wind was so strong that I had to hold my hat on, and the girls' skirts were blown out before them. Antonia seemed to like it; she held her little sister by the hand and chattered away in that language which

Uncouth: Rude, impolite.

Melancholy: Sad.

Dignified: Sedate, proper.

Coaxingly: Persuasively.

Drawside: The side or bank of a draw, which is a shallow ravine in the earth.

seemed to me spoken so much more rapidly than mine. She looked at me, her eyes fairly blazing with things she could not say.

"Name? What name?" she asked, touching me on the shoulder. I told her my name, and she repeated it after me and made Yulka say it. She pointed into the gold cottonwood tree behind whose top we stood and said again, "What name?"

We sat down and made a nest in the long red grass. Yulka curled up like a baby rabbit and played with a grasshopper. Antonia pointed up to the sky and questioned me with her glance. I gave her the word, but she was not satisfied and pointed to my eyes. I told her, and she repeated the word, making it sound like "ice." She pointed up to the sky, then to my eyes, then back to the sky, with movements so quick and impulsive that she distracted me, and I had no idea what she wanted. She got up on her knees and wrung her hands. She pointed to her own eyes and shook her head, then to mine and to the sky, nodding violently.

"Oh," I exclaimed, "blue; blue sky."

*She clapped her hands and murmured, "Blue sky, blue eyes," as if it amused her. While we snuggled down there out of the wind, she learned a score of words. She was alive, and very eager. We were so deep in the grass that we could see nothing but the blue sky over us and the gold tree in front of us. It was wonderfully pleasant. After Antonia had said the new words over and over, she wanted to give me a little chased silver ring she wore on her middle finger. When she coaxed and insisted, I **repulsed** her quite sternly. I didn't want her ring, and I felt there was something reckless and **extravagant** about her wishing to give it away to a boy she had never seen before. No wonder Krajiek got the better of these people, if this was how they behaved.*

*While we were disputing about the ring, I heard a mournful voice calling, "Antonia, Antonia!" She sprang up like a hare. "**Tatinek!** Tatinek!" she shouted, and we ran to meet the old man who was coming toward us. Antonia reached him first, took his hand and kissed it. When I came up, he touched my shoulder and looked searchingly down into my face for several seconds. I became somewhat embarrassed, for I was used to being taken for granted by my elders.*

We went with Mr. Shimerda back to the dugout, where grandmother was waiting for me. Before I got into the wagon, he took a book out of his pocket, opened it, and showed me a page with two

Repulsed: Fended off.

Extravagant: Excessive.

Tatinek: Bohemian for "father."

alphabets, one English and the other Bohemian. He placed this book in my grandmother's hands, looked at her **entreatingly,** and said, with an earnestness which I shall never forget, "Te-e-ach, te-e-ach my Antonia!"...

[Book One Part X]

For several weeks after my sleigh-ride, we heard nothing from the Shimerdas. My sore throat kept me indoors, and grandmother had a cold which made the housework heavy for her. When Sunday came she was glad to have a day of rest. One night at supper Fuchs told us he had seen Mr. Shimerda out hunting.

"He's made himself a rabbit-skin cap, Jim, and a rabbit-skin collar that he buttons on outside his coat. They ain't got but one overcoat among 'em over there, and they take turns wearing it. They seem awful scared of cold, and stick in that hole in the bank like badgers...."

After breakfast grandmother and Jake and I bundled ourselves up and climbed into the cold front wagon-seat. As we approached the Shimerdas', we heard the frosty whine of the pump and saw Antonia, her head tied up and her cotton dress blown about her, throwing all her weight on the pump-handle as it went up and down. She heard our wagon, looked back over her shoulder, and, catching up her pail of water, started at a run for the hole in the bank.

Jake helped grandmother to the ground, saying he would bring the provisions after he had blanketed his horses. We went slowly up the icy path toward the door sunk in the drawside. Blue puffs of smoke came from the stovepipe that stuck out through the grass and snow, but the wind whisked them roughly away.

Mrs. Shimerda opened the door before we knocked and seized grandmother's hand. She did not say "How do!" as usual, but at once began to cry, talking very fast in her own language, pointing to her feet which were tied up in rags, and looking about accusingly at everyone.

The old man was sitting on a stump behind the stove, crouching over as if he were trying to hide from us. Yulka was on the floor at his feet, her kitten in her lap. She peeped out at me and smiled, but, glancing up at her mother, hid again. Antonia was washing pans and dishes in a dark corner. The crazy boy lay under the only window, stretched on a gunny-sack stuffed with straw. As soon as we entered, he threw a grain-sack over the crack at the bottom of the door. The

Entreatingly: In the manner of begging.

air in the cave was stifling, and it was very dark, too. A lighted lantern, hung over the stove, threw out a feeble yellow glimmer.

Mrs. Shimerda snatched off the covers of two barrels behind the door, and made us look into them. In one there were some potatoes that had been frozen and were rotting, in the other was a little pile of flour. Grandmother murmured something in embarrassment, but the Bohemian woman laughed **scornfully**, a kind of whinny-laugh, and, catching up an empty coffee-pot from the shelf, shook it at us with a look positively **vindictive**.

Grandmother went on talking in her polite Virginia way, not admitting their stark need or her own **remissness**, until Jake arrived with the hamper, as if in direct answer to Mrs. Shimerda's **reproaches**. Then the poor woman broke down. She dropped on the floor beside her crazy son, hid her face on her knees, and sat crying bitterly. Grandmother paid no heed to her, but called Antonia to come and help empty the basket. Tony left her corner reluctantly. I had never seen her crushed like this before.

"You not mind my poor **mamenka**, Mrs. Burden. She is so sad," she whispered, as she wiped her wet hands on her skirt and took the things grandmother handed her.

The crazy boy, seeing the food, began to make soft, gurgling noises and stroked his stomach. Jake came in again, this time with a sack of potatoes. Grandmother looked about in perplexity.

"Haven't you got any sort of cave or cellar outside, Antonia? This is no place to keep vegetables. How did your potatoes get frozen?"

"We get from Mr. Bushy, at the post-office what he throw out. We got no potatoes, Mrs. Burden," Tony admitted mournfully.

When Jake went out, Marek crawled along the floor and stuffed up the door-crack again. Then, quietly as a shadow, Mr. Shimerda came out from behind the stove. He stood brushing his hand over his smooth gray hair, as if he were trying to clear away a fog about his head. He was clean and neat as usual, with his green neckcloth and his coral pin. He took grandmother's arm and led her behind the stove, to the back of the room. In the rear wall was another little cave; a round hole, not much bigger than an oil barrel, scooped out in the black earth. When I got up on one of the stools and peered into it, I saw some quilts and a pile of straw. The old man held the lantern. "Yulka," he said in a low, despairing voice, "Yulka; my Antonia!"

Scornfully: Full of open contempt or disrespect.

Vindictive: Full of revenge.

Remissness: Carelessness or negligence.

Reproaches: Expressions of disapproval.

Mamenka: Bohemian for "mother."

Grandmother drew back. "You mean they sleep in there—your girls?" He bowed his head.

Tony slipped under his arm. "It is very cold on the floor, and this is warm like the badger hole. I like for sleep there," she insisted eagerly. "My mamenka have nice bed, with pillows from our own geese in Bohemie. See, Jim?" She pointed to the narrow bunk which Krajiek had built against the wall for himself before the Shimerdas came.

Grandmother sighed. "Sure enough, where would you sleep, dear! I don't doubt you're warm there. You'll have a better house after while, Antonia, and then you will forget these hard times...."

What happened next ...

In the story, the Shimerda family does not recover and suffers even more. Eventually, Antonia moves into town to work as a servant, has a child, and eventually marries another Bohemian. Antonia's story is one of a hard life. The narrator, Jim Burden, goes to college at the University of Nebraska and eventually to Harvard University.

For the pioneers of Nebraska, like the Shimerdas, life was a mixed bag. Some families survived and even thrived. Many others were forced to abandon their farms, unable to make a living, especially in the 1890s when the American economy underwent a severe slowdown.

One result of the economic slowdown was the emergence of politician William Jennings Bryan (1860–1925) of Nebraska, who was elected governor and ran for president of the United States three times, in 1896, 1900, and 1908. Bryan represented the interest of struggling farmers on the Great Plains. Bryan insisted that the U.S. government should issue paper currency (money) that was backed by either gold or silver. At the time, paper money represented deposits of gold owned by the U.S. government; this meant that only a limited amount of currency could be issued, which Bryan thought made life hard for poor people. Bryan argued that using silver to back up paper currency would allow more money to

William Jennings Bryan, the former governor of Nebraska and three-time unsuccessful nominee for U.S. president. He was a friend of the struggling farmer. *Library of Congress.*

come into circulation, and thereby benefit ordinary people like the pioneer families of Nebraska. Bryan lost his elections, and the United States remained committed to currency backed by gold until World War I (1914–18).

Did you know ...

• The population of Nebraska surged between 1870 and 1890, the prime time for settlements under the Homestead Act of 1862 and the time in which *My Antonia* took place. In 1870, the census showed 122,993 people living in Nebraska. By 1880, the population had jumped to 454,402, and in 1890 it reached 1,062,656. Thereafter, the population grew at a much slower pace; there were only about 4,000 more people in the state in 1900 than had been counted ten years earlier. In the 2000 census, the population of Nebraska was about 1.7 million.

For More Information

Books

Cather, Willa. *My Antonia.* Boston, New York: Houghton Mifflin, 1918. Multiple reprints.

Cather, Willa. *O Pioneers!* Boston, New York: Houghton Mifflin, 1913. Multiple reprints.

Dary, David. *True Tales of the Old Time Plains.* Boston: Little, Brown, 1935. Reprint, New York: Crown Publishers, 1979.

Sandoz, Mari. *Old Jules.* Boston: Little, Brown, 1935. Multiple reprints.

Stout, Janis P. *Willia Cather: The Writer and Her World.* Charlottesville: University Press of Virginia, 2000.

Periodicals

Holmes, Catherine D. "Jim Burden's Lost Worlds: Exile in My Antonia." *Twentieth Century Literature* (Fall 1999): p. 336.

Web Sites

Cather, Willa. *My Antonia*. Project Gutenberg online edition. http://digital.library.upenn.edu/webbin/gutbook/lookup?num=242 (accessed on February 25, 2004).

University of Nebraska Lincoln. *The Willa Cather Electronic Archive*. http://www.unl.edu/Cather/ (accessed on February 25, 2004).

12

Ozawa v. United States

Excerpt from U.S. Supreme Court trial of 1922

Opinion written by U.S. Supreme Court justice George Sutherland on November 13, 1922

An upstanding twenty-year Japanese immigrant resident of the United States fails in his application to become a U.S. citizen

> "The intention was to confer the privilege of citizenship upon that class of persons whom the fathers knew as white, and to deny it to all who could not be so classified."

Takao Ozawa was born in Japan, moved to the territory of Hawaii, and later lived in California. Altogether he had lived in the United States continuously for twenty years when he applied in 1914 for naturalization, the process of becoming a U.S. citizen. At the time, he had graduated from high school in Berkeley, California, and had been a student at the University of California for three years. He had children, all born in the United States. The family spoke English at home and attended American churches. Nevertheless, the U.S. government opposed his application to become a citizen, on grounds that he was not "white." Eight years after his application was filed, the U.S. Supreme Court agreed with the government: Ozawa was not eligible to become a citizen.

Immigration of Asians to the United States had been an issue long before the U.S. Supreme Court took up the case of *Ozawa v. United States.* In California, where most Asian immigrants settled, opposition to Asian immigrants was especially strong. California's representatives persuaded the U.S. Congress in 1882 to pass the Chinese Exclusion Act, barring Chinese from entering the United States as immigrants. In

1894, as Japan was emerging as a strong military and industrial power in Asia, a treaty with the United States had guaranteed free immigration to the United States for Japanese. But six years later, in the midst of strong opposition to Japanese immigrants among European Americans in California, Japan agreed not to issue passports for laborers seeking to enter the United States. (A passport is the formal travel document issued by a country's government that allows a citizen of that country exit and reentry.) For the Japanese government, it was a way to cut off emigration and solve the problem without agreeing to treatment that would be regarded as discriminatory against Japanese. The cutoff of passports did not, however, include passports for laborers seeking to enter Hawaii, Canada, or Mexico, from any one of which it was easy for Japanese to enter the United States.

In 1907, the San Francisco Board of Education decided to segregate its Asian students. All Asian students, including Japanese students, were to be placed in a single "Asian school" that kept the students apart from "white" European American students. Seeing Japanese the objects of discrimination upset the government of Japan just at the moment when the administration of President Theodore Roosevelt (1858–1919; served 1901–9) wanted to maintain smooth diplomatic relations with Japan. Roosevelt, who was eager to increase U.S. influence in east Asia, was counting on Japan to counter the influence of Russia in the region.

To cool the diplomatic tensions with Japan created by the school board in San Francisco, Roosevelt persuaded the school board to drop its segregation plan in exchange for promises that the federal government would try to solve the issue of Japanese immigration. The result was the "Gentleman's Agreement" (an agreement that falls short of a formal treaty) of 1907 under which Japan agreed to cooperate in stemming the flow of Japanese workers to the United States. The Japanese government said it would continue to refuse to issue passports for all Japanese workers planning to go to the United States. In addition, it would not object to the removal of Japanese from the United States who held passports issued for travel elsewhere, such as Canada or Mexico. In return, San Francisco authorities discontinued segregating Japanese students in a special school for Asians. Officially, Japanese still had the right to immigrate, on an equal basis with citizens of other countries.

The San Francisco school board incident demonstrated how U.S. immigration laws and attitudes affected American diplomatic policies unrelated to immigration. The incident also served as a reminder of the long-standing controversy in California over the admission of people from Asia, whether Japanese or Chinese, and the importance of race in determining U.S. policy. As early as 1790, the Congress had passed a law limiting citizenship to immigrants who were "free white persons." At the time it was adopted, the law was intended to deny citizenship to slaves from Africa. Seventy-five years later, after slavery was abolished, the immigration law was amended to include Africans and people of African descent—but nothing was said about Asians.

With many Americans displeased with immigration from Asia (and also from southern and eastern Europe), the U.S. district attorney (prosecutor) had objected when Ozawa applied for citizenship. The government, in its arguments to the Supreme Court, admitted that Ozawa would make a good citizen: He was well educated; his family spoke English at home and attended church; and he had lived in the United States for most of his life. There was nothing in his conduct that might suggest he would make a poor citizen. Nevertheless, the government argued in court that U.S. law had been clear, since 1790: "Any alien being a free white person ... may be admitted to become a citizen." The only exception was made in the Naturalization Act of 1870, which also made Africans or people of African descent eligible to become naturalized citizens. Ozawa did not fit any of these categories, in the government's opinion.

Ozawa's lawyers cited inconsistencies in the way that U.S. immigration laws had been written. They argued that when Congress passed a new naturalization law in 1906, it intended to overhaul the immigration law completely. Since the 1906 law had not specifically barred citizenship for Japanese people (as other laws specifically barred Chinese people), Ozawa's lawyers argued that he deserved to become a naturalized citizen. But the Supreme Court said no, ruling that if Congress had intended to remove the racial limitations on naturalized citizenship, it would have done so explicitly and decisively, rather than simply ignoring the issue. The Supreme Court noted that limiting citizenship to free white persons had been the law since 1790 and that the law had only been amended to include people born in Africa or of African descent. No such exception was ever made for Japanese, which both sides on the argument described as being a separate "race."

The Supreme Court also ruled on two other questions raised in the case: first, whether someone from Japan could be considered "white" under the law; and second, whether Ozawa could be barred from becoming a citizen because of race.

On the first question, Ozawa's lawyers had argued that the original immigration laws referred to "free white persons" in order to distinguish them from enslaved Africans, or "black," people. The lawyers tried to persuade the court that "white" meant "not black," and that the phrase was not intended to exclude Asians. The court's opinion rejected the argument, holding that people from Japan were not considered to be "Caucasian," which was what the law meant by "white," and were therefore not eligible to become citizens.

On the second question, the court ruled that Congress did have the power under the Constitution to determine the basis on which immigrants could become citizens, even if the basis was a concept as vague as race.

The *Ozawa* decision was significant in the history of immigration to the United States because it reconfirmed the importance of race when deciding whether immigrants should be allowed to become citizens—a standard for eligibility that had existed since the very beginnings of the United States as an independent country. The ruling came at a period of history when prejudice against racial and religious minorities was very strong among European American citizens, a fact that was not lost on the justices of the Supreme Court.

Things to remember while reading an excerpt from *Ozawa v. United States:*

- The *Ozawa* case came before the court at a time when the United States had already begun to restrict immigrants, especially those from southern and eastern Europe. For the forty years preceding the case, a higher number of Europeans than ever before had come to the United States, including many from poor areas of southern and eastern Europe. The case was decided in an era when the idea of "race" seemed highly important to many Americans, who were disturbed by the large number of darker-skinned individuals from countries around the Mediterranean. Although the Supreme Court is intended to interpret what Congress might have meant in passing laws, and making sure those laws do not conflict with the U.S. Constitution (the basic law of the land), in reality justices of the court usually have a political background and are often sensitive to the public sentiments of the time.

- The concept of race has always been vague, as the court's opinion admits. What race is the child of a black mother and a white father, for example? The court's opinion brushes aside this fundamental issue by saying that such questions fall into a "zone of more or less debatable ground." But since Ozawa had been born in Japan, the issue of his race was not subject to question: He was not white, and therefore not eligible to become a citizen.

- The court's opinion carefully examined minute details of previous immigration laws in an effort to understand what Congress intended to do. On the subject of what constitutes a "white" person, the opinion in essence says the court did not have time to study the issue from a scientific basis. The court ruled that anyone who was not a "free white person" (or who was not born in Africa or of African descent) did not fall into the category of people eligible to become citizens, and that included people from Asia. On the question of whether the authors of the 1790 law intended to exclude Asians, the court simply said that it has no power to read the minds of the authors of the original law. Since no subsequent Congress changed the wording, the court had no power to rule otherwise.

Excerpt from Ozawa v. United States

The act of June 29, 1906, entitled "An act to establish a Bureau of Immigration and Naturalization, and to provide for a uniform rule for the naturalization of aliens throughout the United States," consists of 31 sections and deals primarily with the subject of procedure. There is nothing in the circumstances leading up to or accompanying the passage of the act which suggests that any modification of section 2169, or of its application, was contemplated.

The report of the House Committee on Naturalization and Immigration, recommending its passage, contains this statement:

"It is the opinion of your committee that the frauds and crimes which have been committed in regard to naturalization have resulted more from a lack of any uniform system of procedure in such matters than from any radical defect in the fundamental principles of existing law governing in such matters. The two changes which the committee has recommended in the principles controlling in naturalization matters and which are embodied in the bill submit-

ted herewith are as follows: First, the requirement that before an alien can be naturalized he must be able to read, either in his own language or in the English language and to speak or understand the English language; and, second, that the alien must intend to reside permanently in the United States before he shall be entitled to naturalization."

This seems to make it quite clear that no change of the fundamental character here involved was in mind....

In 1790 the first naturalization act provided that—

"Any alien being a free white person ... may be admitted to become a citizen...." 1 Stat. 103, c. 3.

This was subsequently enlarged to include aliens of African **nativity** and persons of African descent....

In all of the naturalization acts from 1790 to 1906 the privilege of naturalization was confined to white persons (with the addition in 1870 of those of African nativity and descent), although the exact wording of the various statutes was not always the same. If Congress in 1906 desired to alter a rule so well and so long established it may be assumed that its purpose would have been definitely disclosed and its legislation to that end put in unmistakable terms....

It is the duty of this Court to give effect to the intent of Congress. Primarily this intent is **ascertained** by giving the words their natural significance, but if this leads to an unreasonable result plainly **at variance** with the policy of the legislation as a whole, we must examine the matter further. We may then look to the reason of the enactment and inquire into its **antecedent** history and give it effect in accordance with its design and purpose, sacrificing, if necessary, the **literal** meaning in order that the purpose may not fail.... We are asked [by Ozawa's lawyers] to conclude that Congress, without the consideration or recommendation of any committee, without a suggestion as to the effect, or a word of debate as to the desirability, of so fundamental a change, nevertheless, by failing to alter the identifying words of **section 2169**, which section we may assume was continued for some serious purpose, has radically modified a statute always theretofore maintained and considered as of great importance. It is inconceivable that a rule in force from the beginning of the government, a part of our history as well as our law, welded into the structure of our national **polity** by a century of legislative and administrative acts and judicial decisions, would have been deprived of its force in such **dubious** and casual fashion. We

Nativity: Birth.

Ascertained: Determined.

At variance: Differing.

Antecedent: Referring to a preceding event, condition, or cause.

Literal: Referring to accepting the exact meaning of the words of a statement or opinion and allowing no further interpretation.

Section 2169: A sentence in the naturalization law that said naturalization "shall apply to aliens, being free white persons and to aliens of African nativity and to persons of African descent." Ozama's lawyers argued that because this sentence did not explicitly ban Japanese from becoming naturalized citizens, Congress did not intend to bar Japanese from becoming citizens when it passed a naturalization law in 1906.

Polity: Constitution.

Dubious: Questionable.

are, therefore, **constrained** to hold that the act of 1906 is limited by the provisions of section 2169 of the Revised Statutes.

Second. This brings us to inquire whether, under section 2169, the **appellant** is eligible to naturalization. The language of the naturalization laws from 1790 to 1870 had been uniformly such as to deny the privilege of naturalization to an alien unless he came within the description "free white person. By section 7 of the act of July 14, 1870 …, the naturalization laws were "extended to aliens of African nativity and to persons of African descent." Section 2169 of the Revised Statutes, as already pointed out, restricts the privilege to the same classes of persons, **viz.** "to aliens being free white persons, and to aliens of African nativity and to persons of African descent." It is true that in the first edition of the Revised Statutes of 1873 the words in brackets, "being free white persons, and to aliens" were omitted, but this was clearly an error of the compilers and was corrected by the subsequent legislation of 1875…. Is appellant, therefore, a "free white person," within the meaning of that phrase as found in the statute?

On behalf of the appellant it is urged that we should give to this phrase the meaning which it had in the minds of its original framers in 1790 and that it was employed by them for the sole purpose of excluding the black or African race and the **Indians** then inhabiting this country. It may be true that those two races were alone thought of as being excluded, but to say that they were the only ones within the intent of the statute would be to ignore the **affirmative form** of the legislation. The provision is not that **Negroes** and Indians shall be excluded, but it is, in effect, that only free white persons shall be included. The intention was to confer the privilege of citizenship upon that class of persons whom the fathers knew as white, and to deny it to all who could not be so classified. It is not enough to say that the **framers** did not have in mind the brown or yellow races of Asia. It is necessary to go farther and be able to say that had these particular races been suggested the language of the act would have been so varied as to include them within its privileges….

If it be assumed that the opinion of the framers was that the only persons who would fall outside the designation "white" were Negroes and Indians, this would go no farther than to demonstrate their lack of sufficient information to enable them to foresee precisely who would be excluded by that term in the subsequent administration of the statute. It is not important in **construing** their words to consider the extent of their **ethnological** knowledge or whether they thought

Constrained: Forced.

Appellant: A person bringing a lawsuit from a lower court to a higher court for a new hearing.

Viz.: Namely.

Indians: Native Americans.

Affirmative form: The structure of a phrase denoting assent or agreement.

Negroes: African Americans.

Framers: Those who wrote the Constitution.

Construing: Understanding.

Ethnological: Racial; cultural.

that under the statute the only persons who would be denied naturalization would be Negroes and Indians. It is sufficient to ascertain whom they intended to include and having ascertained that it follows, as a necessary **corollary**, that all others are to be excluded.

The question then is: Who are **comprehended** within the phrase "free white persons"? Undoubtedly the word "free" was originally used in recognition of the fact that slavery then existed and that some white persons occupied that status. The word, however, has long since ceased to have any practical significance and may now be disregarded.

We have been furnished with elaborate briefs in which the meaning of the words "white person" is discussed with ability and at length, both from the standpoint of judicial decision and from that of the science of ethnology. It does not seem to us necessary, however, to follow counsel in their extensive researches in these fields. It is sufficient to note the fact that these decisions are, in substance, to the effect that the words **import** a racial and not an individual test, and with this conclusion, fortified as it is by reason and authority, we entirely agree. Manifestly the test afforded by the mere color of the skin of each individual is **impracticable**, as that differs greatly among persons of the same race, even among **Anglo-Saxons**, ranging by **imperceptible gradations** from the fair blond to the **swarthy** brunette, the latter being darker than many of the lighter hued persons of the brown or yellow races. Hence to adopt the color test alone would result in a confused overlapping of races and a gradual merging of one into the other, without any practical line of separation.... Moreover, that conclusion has become so well established by **judicial and executive concurrence** and **legislative acquiescence** that we should not at this late day feel at liberty to disturb it, in the absence of reasons far more **cogent** than any that have been suggested.... The determination that the words "white person" are **synonymous** with the words "a person of the **Caucasian** race" simplifies the problem, although it does not entirely dispose of it. Controversies have arisen and will no doubt arise again in respect of the proper classification of individuals in border line cases. The effect of the conclusion that the words "white person" means a Caucasian is not to establish a sharp line of **demarcation** between those who are entitled and those who are not entitled to naturalization, but rather a zone of more or less debatable ground outside of which, upon the one hand, are those clearly eligible, and outside of which, upon the other hand, are those clearly in-

Corollary: Deduction that needs no proof.

Comprehended: Included.

Import: Signify.

Impracticable: Incapable of being accomplished.

Anglo-Saxons: Descendants of the Germanic peoples who conquered England in the fifth century C.E., in this case referring to white non-Jews.

Imperceptible gradations: Gradual stages barely capable of being seen.

Swarthy: Dark.

Judicial and executive concurrence: Agreement between courts of justice and the executive branch of government.

Legislative acquiescence: Acceptance by those who make laws.

Cogent: Convincing.

Synonymous: Alike in meaning.

Caucasian: Of or relating to the white race.

Demarcation: Separation.

eligible for citizenship. Individual cases falling within this zone must be determined as they arise from time to time by what this court has called, in another connection …, "the gradual process of judicial inclusion and exclusion."

*The appellant, in the case now under consideration, however, is clearly of a race which is not Caucasian and therefore belongs entirely outside the zone on the negative side. A large number of the federal and state courts have so decided and we find no reported case definitely to the contrary. These decisions are **sustained** by numerous scientific authorities, which we do not deem it necessary to review. We think these decisions are right and so hold.*

*The **briefs** filed on behalf of appellant refer in complimentary terms to the culture and enlightenment of the Japanese people, and with this estimate we have no reason to disagree; but these are matters which cannot enter into our consideration of the questions here at issue. We have no function in the matter other than to ascertain the will of Congress and declare it. Of course there is not implied—either in the legislation or in our interpretation of it—any suggestion of individual unworthiness or racial inferiority. These considerations are in no manner involved.…*

Sustained: Upheld.

Briefs: Legal documents outlining the facts and points in a case.

What happened next …

Two years after the *Ozawa* case, the Supreme Court ruled in another case *(United States v. Bhagat Singh Thind)* involving a man described as "a high-caste Hindu, of full Indian blood, born at Amritsar, Punjab, India" who had applied for citizenship, arguing that he was "Caucasian." In the *Ozawa* case, the Court ruled that the word "white" did not really refer to skin color (since many people have lighter or darker skins), but rather to the "Caucasian" race. But in the *Thind* case, the Court took the opposite approach: Thind might be Caucasian, in a scientific sense, but in a popular sense, his skin was too dark to qualify as "white," and therefore he was not eligible to become a citizen, the court ruled. "It may be true," wrote U.S. Supreme Court justice George Sutherland (1862–1942), "that the blond Scandinavian and the brown Hindu have a common ancestor in the dim reaches of antiquity, but the average man knows perfectly well that there are unmistakable and profound differences between them today; and it is not impossible, if that common ancestor could be materialized in the flesh, we should discover that he was himself sufficiently differentiated from both of his descendants to preclude his racial classification with either." In other words, the "average man" knows a "white" person when he sees one, even if lawyers and scientists cannot agree on what the term means. It was a startling admission that the concept of race and skin color, applied to immigration law, had no real meaning beyond what the "average man" might think at any given moment.

In 1924, Congress took another approach to limiting immigration. The Immigration Act of 1924 set permanent limits on the number of immigrants from each country. From 1924 through 1927, the number of immigrants from any one country was set at 2 percent of the number of foreign-born people of that nationality already in the United States in 1890. After July 1, 1927, the limits on each nationality were determined by a more complicated formula calculated by determining what percentage of the total population was represented by each national group, then multiplying that percentage by 150,000. Thus, if nationality "A" represented 1 percent of the U.S. population in 1890, the number of immigrants of nationality "A" admitted each year would equal 1 percent of 150,000, or 1,500 people. The practical effect of the 1924 law was to limit severely the number of immigrants after 1924, especially immigrants from non-European countries. The law also included a provision that barred anyone from immigrating who was not eligible to become a citizen. This provision was specifically aimed at Japanese immigrants and was at least partly based on the *Ozawa* decision of the Supreme Court.

Did you know ...

- The *Ozawa* case was just one of several examples of how racial consciousness played a large role in American politics during the 1920s. The year before the decision was handed down by the Supreme Court, Congress had passed the Emergency Quota Act of 1921, which limited immigration from any single country to a number equal to 3 percent of the number of immigrants of that country who were living in the United States in 1910.

• The Ku Klux Klan was a secret organization that first appeared after the American Civil War (1861–65) as a means of terrorizing newly freed African American slaves and discouraging them from exercising their right to vote. Members of the original Klan wore long, white robes with a tall, peaked hood. They often burned crosses near African American neighborhoods at night as a means of frightening black people. In 1915, a new organization had been formed, using the same name as the Klan and the same costumes. The second version, however, was more open in its membership. Rather than being limited to the southern states, like the first Klan, the reborn Klan found many members in states of the Midwest, particularly Indiana. Although the second Klan still burned crosses, it also took on the form of a social club. Many elected politicians, including future president Harry S. Truman (1884–1972; served 1945–53), admitted to belonging to the Klan for a time. Whereas the first Klan had aimed its attacks at newly freed slaves, the second Klan attracted people opposed not only to racial minorities but also to Catholics, Jews, and immigrants from southern Europe (many of whom were also Catholic). Inside organizations like the Ku Klux Klan, racial prejudice and religious prejudice went hand in hand.

U.S. Supreme Court Justice George Sutherland, the author of the court's opinion in the *Ozawa v. United States* immigration case. *Supreme Court of the United States.*

• George Sutherland, the Supreme Court justice who wrote the opinion in *Ozawa v. United States,* was himself an immigrant. Sutherland was born in Buckinghamshire, England, and brought to the United States as a baby. His family settled in what was then Utah Territory, which became a state in 1896. Sutherland, a Republican, was Utah's sole U.S. representative from 1901 to 1903 and a U.S. senator from 1905 to 1917. He was nominated for the Supreme Court by President Warren Harding (1860–1924; served 1921–24) on September 5, 1922, and confirmed by the Senate on the same day. He had been a Supreme Court justice for just a month when the *Ozawa* case was argued, October 3–4, 1922. The case was decided one month later, on November 13, 1922.

For More Information

Books

Dudley, William, ed. *Asian Americans: Opposing Viewpoints*. San Diego, CA: Greenhaven Press, 1997.

Ichihashi, Yamato. *Japanese in the United States*. Stanford, CA: Stanford University Press, 1932. Reprint, New York: Arno Press, 1969.

Ichioka, Yuji. *The Issei: The World of the First Generation Japanese Immigrants, 1885–1924*. New York: Free Press, 1988.

Periodicals

Tehranian, John. "Performing Whiteness: Naturalization Litigation and the Construction of Racial Identity in America." *Yale Law Journal* (January 2000): p. 817.

Web Sites

"The History of Japanese Immigration." *The Brown Quarterly* (Spring 2000). http://brownvboard.org/brwnqurt/03-4/03-4a.htm (accessed on February 29, 2004).

"In What Ways Did Our Laws Institutionalize Racial Prejudice Against Japanese Americans?" *Densho‾: The Japanese American Legacy Project.* http://www.densho.org/causes/1racism/1institutionalizedracism.asp (accessed on February 29, 2004).

"Takao Ozawa v. U S, 260 U.S. 178 (1922)." *FindLaw.com.* http://caselaw.lp.findlaw.com/scripts/getcase.pl?navby=search&court=US&case=/us/260/178.html (accessed on February 29, 2004).

Immigration Act of 1924

Enacted by U.S. Congress; approved May 26, 1924

Excerpt published in *United States Statutes at Large*, 68th Cong., Sess. I, Chp. 190

An act to limit the migration of aliens into the United States

13

In 1924, the U.S. Congress passed a law to limit immigration into the United States. The law—the Immigration Act of 1924 (also called the National Origins Act) —reflected worries that too many immigrants from southern and eastern Europe were flooding into the country. Many of these immigrants were Roman Catholics. Many Americans worried that the newcomers would change the nature of the population, which had long been made up of Protestants, whose ancestors came from northern Europe. The law brought to an end four decades of almost unlimited mass immigration.

The act required immigrants to obtain permission to come to the United States in advance of leaving their native countries. The law also specified how many immigrants would be allowed to come from each country. The effect of the law was to limit the number of immigrants from southern European countries like Italy, while allowing almost free immigration from northern European countries like Britain or Germany. The law also stopped all immigration from Japan. (Immigration from another Asian country, China, had been barred in 1882.)

"The annual quota of any nationality shall be 2 per centum of the number of foreign-born individuals of such nationality resident in continental United States as determined by the United States census of 1890, but the minimum quota of any nationality shall be 100."

U.S. senator David Reed of Pennsylvania, the coauthor of the Immigration Act of 1924. © Bettmann/Corbis.

U.S. senator David Reed (1880–1953) of Pennsylvania, who helped write the bill, wrote in the *New York Times* in 1925 that "there has come about a general realization of the fact that the races of men who have been coming to us in recent years are wholly dissimilar to the native-born Americans; that they are untrained in self-government—a faculty [ability] that it has taken the Northwestern Europeans many centuries to acquire. America was beginning also to smart [ache] under the irritation of her 'foreign colonies'—those groups of aliens [foreign-born citizens], either in city slums or in country districts, who speak a foreign language and live a foreign life, and who want neither to learn our common speech nor to share our common life. From all this has grown the conviction that it was best for America that our incoming immigrants should hereafter be of the same races as those of us who are already here, so that each year's immigration should so far as possible be a miniature America, resembling in national origins the persons who are already settled in our country."

Reed went on to say: "It is true that 75 per cent of our immigration will hereafter come from Northwestern Europe; but it is fair that it should do so, because 75 per cent of us who are now here owe our origin to immigrants from those same countries."

In order to achieve what Reed called "a miniature America," the 1924 law specified that the number of immigrants from any one country would be limited to the number equal to 2 percent of existing Americans from each country as of 1890. In practice, since most Americans in 1890 had ancestors from northern Europe, the law meant that far more immigrants would be permitted from England and Germany, for example, than from Italy, Greece, or other countries of southern and eastern Europe whose citizens had not come in large numbers before 1890.

Things to remember while reading an excerpt from the Immigration Act of 1924:

- The 1924 Immigration Act limited the total number of immigrants to 165,000 people a year, less than a fifth of the number who had immigrated each year in the years before World War I (1914–18). The total number of quotas, or number of people who may be admitted to a group, for countries of northwestern Europe (Austria, Belgium, Britain, Denmark, Finland, France, Germany, Holland, Iceland, Ireland, Luxembourg, Norway, Sweden, and Switzerland) was 142,483, or 86 percent of the total. By contrast, the total number of quotas for southern and eastern Europe (including Albania, Bulgaria, Czechoslovakia, Estonia, Greece, Hungary, Italy, Latvia, Lithuania, Poland, Portugal, Romania, Russia, Spain, and Yugoslavia) was 18,439, or 11 percent of the total. A third, tiny quota of 3,745 was set aside for people from the entire continent of Africa, the Middle East region, and countries in the Pacific, such as Australia and New Zealand.

- The quota for Italian immigrants under the 1924 law was 3,845. In the period from 1900 through 1910, an average of 200,000 Italians had emigrated to the United States each year.

- The 1924 Act was not the first effort to limit immigration. A 1917 immigration law had barred a broad range of people, including mentally handicapped adults, psychologically impaired individuals, alcoholics, homeless people, individuals with tuberculosis (an often fatal lung disease) or serious contagious diseases, convicted criminals, polygamists (those who have more than one wife at a time), and anarchists (those against a formal government and in favor of small voluntary associations). In 1921, a similar immigration law had limited immigrants from each country to the number equal to 3 percent of the number of people of that nationality living in the United States in 1900. The intent of the 1924 act was to limit immigration even further and, by basing quotas on the number of people living in the United States in 1890, to favor countries of northern Europe even more.

Excerpt from the Immigration Act of 1924

Be it enacted by the Senate and House of Representatives of the United States of America in Congress assembled, That this Act may be cited as the "Immigration Act of 1924."

Section 2.

(a) A **consular officer** upon the application of any immigrant (as defined in section 3) may (under the conditions hereinafter **prescribed** and subject to the limitations prescribed in this Act or regulations made thereunder as to the number of immigration **visas** which may be issued by such officer) issue to such immigrant an immigration visa which shall consist of one copy of the application provided for in section 7, **visaed** by such consular officer. Such visa shall specify (1) the nationality of the immigrant; (2) whether he is a quota immigrant [defined in an unexcerpted passage as, simply, "any immigrant who is not a non-quote immigrant"] ... or a non-quota immigrant (as defined in section 4); (3) the date on which the validity of the immigration visa shall expire; and such additional information necessary to the proper enforcement of the immigration laws and the **naturalization laws** as may be by regulations prescribed.

(b) The immigrant shall furnish two copies of his photograph to the consular officer. One copy shall be permanently attached by the consular officer to the immigration visa and the other copy shall be disposed of as may be by regulations prescribed.

(c) The validity of an immigration visa shall expire at the end of such period, specified in the immigration visa, not exceeding four months, as shall be by regulations prescribed. In the case of an immigrant arriving in the United States by water, or arriving by water in foreign **contiguous** territory on a continuous voyage to the United States, if the **vessel**, before the expiration of the validity of his immigration visa, departed from the last port outside the United States and outside foreign contiguous territory at which the immigrant **embarked**, and if the immigrant proceeds on a continuous voyage to the United States, then, regardless of the time of his arrival in the United States, the validity of his immigration visa shall not be considered to have expired.

(d) If an immigrant is required by any law, or regulations or orders made pursuant to law, to secure the visa of his passport by a consular officer before being permitted to enter the United States, such immigrant shall not be required to secure any other visa of his passport than the immigration visa issued under this Act, but a record of the number and date of his immigration visa shall be noted on his passport without charge therefor. This subdivision shall not apply to an immigrant who is relieved, under subdivision (b) of section 13, from obtaining an immigration visa.

(e) The manifest or list of passengers required by the immigration laws shall contain a place for entering thereon the date, place

Consular officer: A representative of a country, lower in rank than an ambassador, usually for purposes of conducting day-to-day business.

Prescribed: Laid down by the law.

Visas: Documents giving permission to enter a country.

Visaed: Given a visa.

Naturalization laws: Laws dictating how foreign-born individuals become citizens.

Contiguous: Touching.

Vessel: Ship.

Embarked: Boarded a ship.

of issuance, and number of the immigration visa of each immigrant. The immigrant shall surrender his immigration visa to the immigration officer at the port of inspection, who shall at the time of inspection **indorse** on the immigration visa the date, the port of entry, and the name of the vessel, if any, on which the immigrant arrived. The immigration visa shall be transmitted **forthwith** by the immigration officer in charge at the port of inspection to the Department of Labor under regulations prescribed by the Secretary of Labor.

(f) No immigration visa shall be issued to an immigrant if it appears to the consular officer, from statements in the application, or in the papers submitted therewith, that the immigrant is **inadmissible** to the United States under the immigration laws, nor shall such immigration visa be issued if the application fails to comply with the provisions of this Act, nor shall such immigration visa be issued if the consular officer knows or has reason to believe that the immigrant is inadmissible to the United States under the immigration laws.

(g) Nothing in this Act shall be construed to entitle an immigrant, to whom an immigration visa has been issued, to enter the United States, if, upon arrival in the United States, he is found to be inadmissible to the United States under the immigration laws. The substance of this subdivision shall be printed **conspicuously** upon every immigration visa.

(h) A fee of $9 shall be charged for the issuance of each immigration visa, which shall be covered into the Treasury as miscellaneous receipts.

DEFINITION OF IMMIGRANT.

Section 3.

When used in this Act the term "immigrant" means an **alien** departing from any place outside the United States destined for the United States, except (1) a government official, his family, attendants, servants, and employees, (2) an alien visiting the United States temporarily as a tourist or temporarily for business or pleasure, (3) an alien in continuous transit through the United States, (4) an alien lawfully admitted to the United States who later goes in transit from one part of the United States to another through foreign contiguous territory, (5) a **bona fide** alien seaman serving as such on a vessel arriving at a port of the United States and seeking to enter temporarily the United States solely in the pursuit of his calling as a seaman, and (6) an alien entitled to enter the United

Indorse: Endorse; to record officially on a document.

Forthwith: Immediately.

Inadmissible: Not legally permitted.

Conspicuously: Prominently.

Alien: Foreign-born citizen.

Bona fide: Real, genuine.

States solely to carry on trade under and in pursuance of the provisions of a present existing treaty of commerce and navigation.

NON-QUOTA IMMIGRANTS.

Section 4.

When used in this Act the term "non-quota immigrant" means

(a) An immigrant who is the unmarried child under 18 years of age, or the wife, of a citizen of the United States who resides therein at the time of the filing of a petition under section 9;

(b) An immigrant previously lawfully admitted to the United States, who is returning from a temporary visit abroad;

(c) An immigrant who was born in the Dominion of Canada, Newfoundland, the Republic of Mexico, the Republic of Cuba, the Republic of Haiti, the Dominican Republic, the Canal Zone, or an independent country of Central or South America, and his wife, and his unmarried children under 18 years of age, if accompanying or following to join him;

(d) An immigrant who continuously for at least two years immediately preceding the time of his application for admission to the United States has been, and who seeks to enter the United States solely for the purpose of, carrying on the vocation of minister of any religious denomination, or professor of a college, academy, seminary, or university; and his wife, and his unmarried children under 18 years of age, if accompanying or following to join him; or

(e) An immigrant who is a bona fide student at least 15 years of age and who seeks to enter the United States solely for the purpose of study at an **accredited** *school, college, academy, seminary, or university, particularly designated by him and approved by the Secretary of Labor, which shall have agreed to report to the Secretary of Labor the* **termination** *of attendance of each immigrant student, and if any such institution of learning fails to make such reports promptly the approval shall be withdrawn....*

Section 11.

(a) The annual quota of any nationality shall be 2 **per centum** *of the number of foreign-born individuals of such nationality resident in continental United States as determined by the United States census of 1890, but the minimum quota of any nationality shall be 100.*

(b) The annual quota of any nationality for the **fiscal year** *beginning July 1, 1927, and for each fiscal year thereafter, shall be a*

Accredited: Certified in advance.

Termination: End.

Per centum: Per cent, or part of one hundred.

Fiscal year: A twelve-month financial or accounting period.

number which bears the same ratio to 150,000 as the number of inhabitants in continental United States in 1920 having that national origin (**ascertained** as hereinafter provided in this section) bears to the number of inhabitants in continental United States in 1920, but the minimum quota of any nationality shall be 100.

(c) For the purpose of subdivision (b) national origin shall be ascertained by determining as nearly as may be, in respect of each geographical area which under section 12 is to be treated as a separate country (except the geographical areas specified in subdivision (c) of section 4) the number of inhabitants in continental United States in 1920 whose origin by birth or ancestry is attributable to such geographical area. Such determination shall not be made by tracing the ancestors or descendants of particular individuals, but shall be based upon statistics of immigration and emigration, together with rates of increase of population as shown by successive **decennial** United States censuses, and such other data as may be found to be reliable.

(d) For the purpose of subdivisions (b) and (c) the term "inhabitants in continental United States in 1920" does not include (1) immigrants from the geographical areas specified in subdivision (c) of section 4 or their descendants, (2) aliens ineligible to citizenship or their descendants, (3) the descendants of slave immigrants, or (4) the descendants of American **aborigines.**

(e) The determination provided for in subdivision (c) of this section shall be made by the Secretary of State, the Secretary of Commerce, and the Secretary of Labor, jointly. In making such determination such officials may call for information and expert assistance from the Bureau of the Census. Such officials shall, jointly, report to the President the quota of each nationality, determined as provided in subdivision (b), and the President shall proclaim and make known the quotas so reported. Such proclamation shall be made on or before April 1, 1927.

(f) There shall be issued to quota immigrants of any nationality (1) no more immigration visas in any fiscal year than the quota for such nationality, and (2) in any calendar month of any fiscal year no more immigration visas than 10 per centum of the quota for such nationality, except that if such quota is less than 300 the number to be issued in any calendar month shall be prescribed by the Commissioner General, with the approval of the Secretary of Labor, but the total number to be issued during the fiscal year shall not be in excess of the quota for such nationality.

Ascertained: Determined.

Decennial: Once every ten years.

Aborigines: Original inhabitants of a territory, in this case referring to native Americans.

(g) Nothing in this Act shall prevent the issuance (without increasing the total number of immigration visas which may be issued) of an immigration visa to an immigrant as a quota immigrant even though he is a non-quota immigrant.

NATIONALITY.

Section 12.

*(a) For the purposes of this Act nationality shall be determined by country of birth, treating as separate countries the colonies, dependencies, or **self-governing dominions**, for which separate **enumeration** was made in the United States census of 1890; except that (1) the nationality of a child under twenty-one years of age not born in the United States, accompanied by its alien parent not born in the United States, shall be determined by the country of birth of such parent if such parent is entitled to an immigration visa, and the nationality of a child under twenty-one years of age not born in the United States, accompanied by both alien parents not born in the United States, shall be determined by the country of birth of the father if the father is entitled to an immigration visa; and (2) if a wife is of a different nationality from her alien husband and the entire number of immigration visas which may be issued to quota immigrants of her nationality for the calendar month has already been issued, her nationality may be determined by the country of birth of her husband if she is accompanying him and he is entitled to an immigration visa, unless the total number of immigration visas which may be issued to quota immigrants of the nationality of the husband for the calendar month has already been issued. An immigrant born in the United States who has lost his United States citizenship shall be considered as having been born in the country of which he is a citizen or subject, or if he is not a citizen or subject of any country, then in the country from which he comes.*

*(b) The Secretary of State, the Secretary of Commerce, and the Secretary of Labor, jointly, shall, as soon as **feasible** after the enactment of this Act, prepare a statement showing the number of individuals of the various nationalities resident in continental United States as determined by the United States census of 1890, which statement shall be the population basis for the purposes of subdivision (a) of section 11....*

EXCLUSION FROM UNITED STATES.

Section 13.

Self-governing dominions:
Countries, like Canada, which governs itself but is under authority of a foreign monarch.

Enumeration: Counting.

Feasible: Doable.

(a) No immigrant shall be admitted to the United States unless he (1) has an unexpired immigration visa or was born subsequent to the issuance of the immigration visa of the accompanying parent, (2) is of the nationality specified in the visa in the immigration visa [sic], (3) is a non-quota immigrant if specified in the visa in the immigration visa [sic] as such, and (4) is otherwise admissible under the immigration laws.

(b) In such classes of cases and under such conditions as may be by regulations prescribed immigrants who have been legally admitted to the United States and who depart therefrom temporarily may be admitted to the United States without being required to obtain an immigration visa.

(c) No alien ineligible to citizenship shall be admitted to the United States unless such alien (1) is admissible as a non-quota immigrant under the provisions of subdivision (b), (d), or (e) of section 4, or (2) is the wife, or the unmarried child under 18 years of age, of an immigrant admissible under such subdivision (d), and is accompanying or following to join him, or (3) is not an immigrant as defined in section 3.

(d) The Secretary of Labor may admit to the United States any otherwise admissible immigrant not admissible under clause (2) or (3) of subdivision (a) of this section, if satisfied that such inadmissibility was not known to, and could not have been ascertained by the exercise of reasonable **diligence** by, such immigrant prior to the departure of the vessel from the last port outside the United States and outside foreign contiguous territory or, in the case of an immigrant coming from foreign contiguous territory, prior to the application of the immigrant for admission.

(e) No quota immigrant shall be admitted under subdivision (d) if the entire number of immigration visas which may be issued to quota immigrants of the same nationality for the fiscal year has already been issued. If such entire number of immigration visas has not been issued, then the Secretary of State, upon the admission of a quota immigrant under subdivision (d), shall reduce by one the number of immigration visas which may be issued to quota immigrants of the same nationality during the fiscal year in which such immigrant is admitted; but if the Secretary of State finds that it will not be practicable to make such reduction before the end of such fiscal year, then such immigrant shall not be admitted.

(f) Nothing in this section shall authorize the remission or refunding of a fine, liability to which has **accrued** under section 16.

Diligence: Attention and care legally expected or required of a person.

Accrued: Accumulated; increased.

DEPORTATION

Section 14.

Any alien who at any time after entering the United States is found to have been at the time of entry not entitled under this Act to enter the United States, or to have remained therein for a longer time than permitted under this Act or regulations made thereunder, shall be taken into custody and deported in the same manner as provided for in sections 19 and 20 of the Immigration Act of 1917: Provided, That the Secretary of Labor may, under such conditions and restrictions as to support and care as he may deem necessary, permit permanently to remain in the United States, any alien child who, when under sixteen years of age was heretofore temporarily admitted to the United States and who is now within the United States and either of whose parents is a citizen of the United States....

Deportation: The process of sending a foreign-born individual back to his or her native country.

What happened next ...

President Calvin Coolidge (1872–1933; served 1923–29) signed an order implementing the 1924 Act and laying out the specific quotas for each country. The quotas were:

Afghanistan	100
Albania	100
Andorra	100
Arabian peninsula	100
Armenia	124
Australia	121
Austria	785
Belgium	512
Bhutan	100
Bulgaria	100
Cameroon (British)	100
Cameroon (French)	100
China	100
Czechoslovakia	3,073
Danzig, Free City of	228
Denmark	2,789
Egypt	100
Esthonia	124
Ethiopia (Abyssinia)	100

Finland	170
France	3,954
Germany	51,227
Great Britain and Northern Ireland	34,007
Greece	100
Hungary	473
Iceland	100
India	100
Iraq (Mesopotamia)	100
Irish Free State	28,567
Italy	3,845
Japan	100
Latvia	142
Liberia	100
Liechtenstein	100
Lithuania	344
Luxemburg	100
Monaco	100
Morocco	100
Muscat (Oman)	100
Nauru	100
Nepal	100
Netherlands	1,648
New Zealand	100
Norway	6,453
New Guinea	100
Palestine	100
Persia	100
Poland	5,982
Portugal	503
Ruanda and Urundi	100
Rumania	603
Russia, European and Asiatic	2,248
Samoa, Western	100
San Marino	100
Siam	100
South Africa, Union of	100
South West Africa	100
Spain	131
Sweden	9,561
Switzerland	2,081
Syria and The Lebanon	100
Tanganyika	100
Togoland (British)	100
Togoland (French)	100
Turkey	100
Yap	100
Yugoslavia	671

Japanese immigrant farm workers. The Immigration Act of 1924 canceled an informal agreement Japan and the United States had that allowed a limited number of Japanese immigrants into the United States. © *Bettmann/Corbis.*

Did you know ...

- The Immigration Act of 1924 was especially offensive to Japan. The law did not permit anyone who was ineligible to become a citizen to move to the United States. This included anyone from Asia, since the nation's first immigration law, passed in 1790, had limited citizenship to "white" people. Asians had already been found not to be "white" by several court decisions. The government of Japan had voluntarily limited immigration to the United States under an informal "Gentleman's Agreement" in 1907 and felt offended that this agreement was canceled by barring all Japanese immigration without consultation.

For More Information

Books

Hutchinson, Edward Prince. *Legislative History of American Immigration Policy, 1768–1965.* Philadelphia: University of Pennsylvania Press, 1981.

Isbister, John. *The Immigration Debate: Remaking America*. West Hartford, CT: Kumarian Press, 1996.

LeMay, Michael, and Elliot Robert Barkan, eds. *U.S. Immigration and Naturalization Laws and Issues: A Documentary History*. Westport, CT: Greenwood Press, 1999.

United States Statutes at Large. 68th Cong., Sess. I, Chp. 190, pp. 153–69.

Periodicals

Quinn, Peter. "Race Cleansing in America." *American Heritage* (February–March 2003): p. 34.

Sharav, Itzhak. "Who Is Afraid of the Foreign-Born Among Us?" *Midstream* (February 2001): p. 19.

Swerdlow, Joel L. "Changing America." *National Geographic* (September 2001): p. 42.

Web Sites

Immigration Act of 1924. http://nkasd.wiu.k12.pa.us/vhs/discush1924.html (accessed on January 15, 2004).

14

Harry S. Truman

Excerpt from Message to the House of Representatives on the Veto of the Immigration and Nationality Act of 1952
Presented on June 25, 1952

The president vetoes an immigration bill that would limit the number of immigrants from outside northern Europe

> "This idea behind this discriminatory policy was, to put it baldly, that Americans with English or Irish names were better people and better citizens than Americans with Italian or Greek or Polish names.... Such a concept is utterly unworthy of our traditions and our ideals."

In 1952 a debate broke out on the future immigration policy of the United States. On one side were politicians like U.S. senator Patrick McCarran (1876–1954) of Nevada and U.S. representative Francis Walter (1894–1963) of Pennsylvania. McCarran and Walter wanted to continue to impose quotas, or limits, on immigration from different countries in a way that favored immigrants from northern Europe at the expense of immigrants from southern and eastern Europe and Asia. On the other side were those like President Harry S. Truman (1884–1972; served 1945–53), who wanted to admit more immigrants from areas outside northern Europe.

U.S. Congress passed the Immigration and Nationality Act of 1952—also called the McCarran-Walter Act—to replace the Immigration Act of 1924 (see entry). In both cases, the laws restricted the number of immigrants coming from each country to a small fraction of the number of American citizens who traced their backgrounds to each country. The idea behind the quotas, or limits, was to keep the population of the United States roughly the same. From 1880 to 1920, a large number of immigrants had come to the United States from southern and eastern Europe. The number of immigrants from this region changed the character of the population. For example, as a result of the huge flow of immigrants in those four decades, there were many more Catholics and Jews living in the United States. A country that had once been dominated by people of English, Irish, and German heritage now began looking more like the world outside the United States. People with darker skin and different religions had taken their place alongside the mostly light-skinned Protestants of northwestern Europe who had arrived in the period before 1880.

In 1952, the Congress wanted to continue the policy of limiting immigrants in a way that maintained the balance of national backgrounds found in 1920, just as the law of 1924 had tried to maintain the balance of national backgrounds that was present in 1890. President Truman objected to the 1952 law on two grounds. First, it discriminated on the basis of race and religion, in effect telling the rest of the world that America was mostly for light-skinned Europeans. Second, Truman thought that this policy would hurt the image of the United States in the global contest between communism and capitalism. Communism is a political system under which the government owns large factories, transportation (airlines and railroads), and communications systems (such as telephones, radio, and television). It has usually been accompanied by harsh dictatorships. Capitalism is a system under which ownership of businesses is in private hands. It is often, but not always, accompanied by governments ruled by democracy, like the United States.

In 1952, the issue of competition between communism, led by the Union of Soviet Socialist Republics (also known as the Soviet Union or the U.S.S.R.; a country made up of fifteen republics, the largest of which was Russia, that in

U.S. senator Patrick McCarran of Nevada, a supporter of quotas on immigrants.
© Corbis.

President Harry S. Truman at a press conference. Truman was against the Immigration and Nationality Act of 1952. *AP/Wide World Photos.*

1991 became independent states) and capitalism, led by the United States, was foremost in the minds of most American politicians. Around the world, communists accused the United States of racist behavior, that is, of acting with prejudice based on a person's race. Communists often pointed to the treatment of African Americans as evidence of American hypocrisy: The words of the Declaration of Independence (1776) declared "… all men are created equal," but Americans did not behave as if they believed the words. In Truman's opinion, the Immigration and Nationality Act of 1952 would be used as more evidence of America's racist attitudes. The act would allow relatively few immigrants into the United States from Asia, Africa, and southern and eastern Europe, while the number of people allowed to come from England, Ireland, and other northern European countries would be very large.

A second set of issues in the 1952 law involved efforts to bar "undesirable" people from emigrating to America. Such "undesirables" included criminals and people judged insane. The category also included people who were, or were suspected of being, communists. The law included provisions for deportation, or sending people back to their home country. The law made it possible, long after a person had come to the United States, to deport such undesirable individuals, including anyone who had lied on an application for an immigration visa, the document giving permission to enter the United States.

Things to remember while reading an excerpt from President Truman's Message to the House of Representatives on the Veto of the Immigration and Nationality Act of 1952:

- The year in which the immigration law was passed was also a presidential election year. Truman, who was widely unpopular, had decided not to run for reelection. (Illinois governor Adlai E. Stevenson [1900–1965] wound up being the Democratic nominee.) The issues raised in the debate over the Immigration Act of 1952 often separated Democrats.

- The pressure to admit immigrants in 1952 reflected both the upheavals of World War II (1939–45) and also the political changes in Europe brought about by the war. As a result of World War II, many people had been forced out of their homes and whole cities had been destroyed. The eastern part of Europe had been occupied by the Soviet Army, fighting to push German troops back into Germany, and communist governments had been installed in many countries. Europeans who did not wish to live under communism had fled their countries. Many Europeans wanted to come to the United States, which had been untouched by fighting.

- In some European countries, such as Greece and Italy, communist politicians were in a struggle against capitalist politicians to gain power through democratic means. In such countries, the communists were often popular. President Truman worried that the Immigration and Nationality Act of 1952 would present an image of the United States as hostile to inhabitants of southern and eastern European countries which, consequently, could help communist politicians gain power.

• In order for a law passed by Congress to take effect, the president must agree to the act by signing it. If the president vetoes a bill—refuses to sign it into law, as happened in the case of the 1952 Immigration and Nationality Act—the Congress may then vote again on the law. If two-thirds of both the Senate and the House vote to approve the law, it goes into effect without the president's approval. The process is called "overriding a presidential veto."

Excerpt from President Truman's Message to the House of Representatives on the Veto of the Immigration and Nationality Act of 1952

To the House of Representatives:

*I return herewith, without my approval, **H.R. 5678**, the proposed Immigration and Nationality Act.*

In outlining my objections to this bill, I want to make it clear that it contains certain provisions that meet with my approval. This is a long and complex piece of legislation. It has 164 separate sections, some with more than forty subdivisions. It presents a difficult problem of weighing the good against the bad, and arriving at a judgment on the whole.

*H.R. 5678 is an **omnibus** bill which would revise and **codify** all of our laws relating to immigration, **naturalization** and nationality.*

A general revision and modernization of these laws unquestionably is needed and long overdue, particularly with respect to immigration. But this bill would not provide us with an immigration policy adequate for the present world situation.

Indeed, the bill, taking all its provisions together, would be a step backward and not a step forward. In view of the crying need for reform in the field of immigration, I deeply regret that I am unable to approve H.R. 5678.

H.R. 5678: The numerical designation of the Immigration and Nationality Act of 1952, passed by the House of Representatives (H.R.).

Omnibus: All-inclusive.

Codify: Classify.

Naturalization: The process of becoming a citizen of a country to which one has emigrated.

In recent years our immigration policy has become a matter of major national concern. Long **dormant** questions about the effect of our immigration laws now assume first-rate importance. What we do in the field of immigration and naturalization is vital to the continued growth and internal development of the United States—to the economic and social strength of our country—which is the core of the defense of the **free world.**

Our immigration policy is equally, if not more, important to the conduct of our foreign relations and to our responsibilities of moral leadership in the struggle for world peace.

In one respect this bill recognizes the great international significance of our immigration and naturalization policy, and takes a step to improve existing laws. All racial **bars** to naturalization would be removed, and at least some minimum immigration quota would be afforded to each of the free nations of Asia.

But now this most desirable provision comes before me embedded in a mass of legislation which would perpetuate injustices of long standing against many other nations of the world, hamper the efforts we are making to rally the men of East and West alike to the cause of freedom, and intensify the **repressive** and inhumane aspects of our immigration procedures. The price is too high, and in good conscience I cannot agree to pay it.

I want all our residents of Japanese ancestry, and all our friends throughout the Far East, to understand this point clearly. I cannot take the step I would like to take, and strike down the bars that prejudice has erected against them, without, at the same time, establishing new discriminations against the peoples of Asia and approving harsh and repressive measures directed at all who seek a new life within our boundaries....

In addition to removing racial bars to naturalization, the bill would permit American women citizens to bring their **alien** husbands to this country as non-quota immigrants, and enable alien husbands of resident women aliens to come in under the quota in a **preferred status.** These provisions would be a step toward preserving the integrity of the family under our immigration laws, and are clearly desirable....

But these few improvements are heavily outweighed by other provisions of the bill which retain existing defects in our laws, and add many undesirable new features.

The bill would continue, practically without change, the **national origins quota system**, which was enacted into law in 1924, and put

Dormant: Inactive; unasked.

Free world: A term referring to noncommunist nations during the period 1945–1991.

Bars: Barriers.

Repressive: Restricting.

Alien: Foreign; in immigration law, someone who is not a citizen.

Preferred status: A classification that allowed a person to go to the head of the list of possible immigrants to the United States based on a special situation, such as being the relative of someone living in the United States.

National origins quota system: The system in U.S. immigration law first implemented in 1924 of limiting the number of immigrants from a given country on the basis of how many people of that nationality already lived in the United States.

into effect in 1929. This quota system—always based upon assumptions at variance with our American ideals—is long since out of date and more than ever unrealistic in the face of present world conditions.

This system hinders us in dealing with current immigration problems, and is a constant handicap in the conduct of our foreign relations....

The inadequacy of the present quota system has been demonstrated since the end of [World War II], when we were compelled to resort to emergency legislation to admit **displaced persons.** *If the quota system remains unchanged, we shall be compelled to resort to similar emergency legislation again, in order to admit any substantial portion of the* **refugees** *from communism or the victims of overcrowding in Europe.*

With the idea of quotas in general there is no quarrel. Some numerical limitation must be set, so that immigration will be within our capacity to absorb. But the over-all limitation of numbers imposed by the national origins quota system is too small for our needs today, and the country-by-country limitations create a pattern that is insulting to large numbers of our finest citizens, irritating to our Allies abroad, and foreign to our purposes and ideals....

The greatest vice of the present quota system [enacted in 1924], however, is that it discriminates, deliberately and intentionally, against any of the peoples of the world. The purpose behind it was to cut down and virtually eliminate immigration to this country from Southern and Eastern Europe.

A theory was invented to **rationalize** *this objective. The theory was that in order to be readily* **assimilable,** *European immigrants should be admitted in proportion to the numbers of persons of their respective national stocks already here as shown by the census of 1920.*

Since Americans of English, Irish and German descent were most numerous, immigrants of those three nationalities got the **lion's share**— *more than two-thirds of the total quota. The remaining third was divided up among all the other nations given quotas.*

The desired effect was obtained. Immigration from the newer sources of Southern and Eastern Europe was reduced to a trickle. The quotas allotted to England and Ireland remained largely unused, as was intended. Total quota immigration fell to a half or a third—and sometimes even less—of the annual limit of 154,000. People from such countries as Greece, or Spain, or Latvia were virtu-

Displaced persons: People forced to flee from their homelands after World War II.

Refugees: People forced from their homelands by war.

Rationalize: Justify.

Assimilable: Capable of being absorbed into a new culture.

Lion's share: Largest portion.

ally deprived of any opportunity to come here at all simply because Greeks or Spaniards or Latvians had not come here before 1920 in any substantial numbers.

The idea behind this discriminatory policy was, to put it **baldly,** that Americans with English or Irish names were better people and better citizens than Americans with Italian or Greek or Polish names. It was thought that people of West European origin made better citizens than Rumanians or Yugoslavs or Ukrainians or **Balts** or Austrians.

Such a concept is utterly unworthy of our traditions and our ideals. It violates the great political doctrine of the Declaration of Independence that "all men are created equal." It denied the humanitarian creed inscribed beneath the Statue of Liberty proclaiming to all nations:

"Give me your tired, your poor, your huddled masses yearning to breathe free."

It **repudiates** our basic religious concepts, our belief in the brotherhood of man, and in the words of St. Paul that "there is neither Jew nor Greek, there is neither bond nor free … for ye are all one in Christ Jesus."

The basis of this quota system was false and unworthy in 1924. It is even worse now. At the present time this quota system keeps out the very people we want to bring in. It is incredible to me that, in this year of 1952, we should again be enacting into law such a **slur** on the patriotism, the capacity and the decency of a large part of our citizenry.

Today we have entered into an **alliance,** the North Atlantic Treaty, with Italy, Greece and Turkey against one of the most terrible threats mankind has ever faced [communism]. We are asking them to join with us in protecting the peace of the world. We are helping them to build their defenses, and train their men, in the common cause. But through this bill we say to these people:

You are less worthy to come to this country than Englishmen or Irishmen; you Italians, who need to find homes abroad in the hundreds of thousands—you shall have a quota of 5,645; you Greeks, struggling to assist the helpless victims of a Communist civil war— you shall have a quota of 308; and you Turks, you are brave defenders of the Eastern flank, but you shall have a quota of only 225!

Today, we are "protecting" ourselves, as we were in 1924, against being flooded by immigrants from Eastern Europe. This is

Baldly: Plainly.

Balts: People from nations bordering the Baltic Sea, notably Latvians, Lithuanians, and Estonians.

Repudiates: Rejects.

Slur: Shameful mark.

Alliance: A friendship between nations, usually an agreement for joint protection or action.

fantastic. The countries of Eastern Europe have fallen under the Communist yoke—they are silenced, fenced off by barbed wire and mine fields—no one passes their borders but at the risk of his life.

We do not need to be protected against immigrants from these countries—on the contrary we want to stretch out a helping hand, to save those who have managed to flee into Western Europe, to *succor* those who are brave enough to escape from *barbarism*, to welcome and restore them against the day when their countries will, as we hope, be free again....

In no other realm of our national life are we so hampered and *stultified* by the dead hand of the past as we are in this field of immigration. We do not limit our cities to their 1920 boundaries—we do not hold our corporations to their 1920 *capitalizations*—we welcome progress and change to meet changing conditions in every sphere of life, except in the field of immigration.

The time to shake off this dead weight of past mistakes is now. The time to develop a decent policy of immigration—a fitting instrument for our foreign policy and a true reflection of the ideals we stand for, at home and abroad—is now....

The only *consequential* change in the 1924 quota system which the bill would make is to extend a small quota to each of the countries of Asia. But most of the beneficial effects of this gesture are offset by other provisions of the bill. The countries of Asia are told in one breath that they shall have quotas for their nationals, and in the next, that the nationals of the other countries, if their ancestry is as much as 50 per cent Asian, shall be charged to these quotas....

It is only with respect to persons of oriental ancestry that this *invidious* discrimination applies. All other persons are charged to the country of their birth. But persons with Asian ancestry are charged to the countries of Asia, wherever they may have been born, or however long their ancestors have made their home outside the land of their origin. These provisions are without justification....

The bill would make it even more difficult to enter our country. Our resident aliens would be more easily separated from homes and families under ground of deportation, both new and old, which would specifically be made *retroactive*. Admission to our citizenship would be made more difficult; *expulsion* from our citizenship would be made easier. Certain rights of native-born, *first-generation Americans* would be limited....

Fantastic: Unreal; the result of a dream or fantasy.

Succor: Relieve.

Barbarism: Brutality.

Stultified: Hindered.

Capitalizations: The value of companies.

Consequential: Valuable.

Invidious: Unpleasant or objectionable.

Retroactive: Made effective as of a date in the past.

Expulsion: Ejection.

First-generation Americans: People who immigrated to the United States and became citizens.

We have adequate and fair provision in our present law to protect us against the entry of criminals. The changes made by the bill in those provisions would result in empowering minor immigration and **consular officials** to act as prosecutor, judge and jury in determining whether acts constituting a crime have been committed. Worse, we would be compelled to exclude certain people because they have been convicted by "courts" in Communist countries that know no justice.

Under this provision, no matter how construed, it would not be possible for us to admit many of the men and women who have stood up against **totalitarian repression** and have been punished for doing so. I do not approve of substituting totalitarian vengeance for democratic justice. I will not extend full faith and credit to the judgments of the Communist secret police....

We do not want to encourage fraud. But we must recognize that conditions in some parts of the world drive our friends to desperate steps. An exception restricted to cases involving misstatement of country of birth is not sufficient. And to make refugees from oppression forever deportable on such technical grounds is shabby treatment indeed....

I am asked to approve the reenactment of highly objectionable provisions now contained in the Internal Security Act of 1950—a measure passed over my **veto** shortly after the invasion of South Korea [by North Korea, which sparked a war pitting the communist-ruled North against the U.S.-backed South]. Some of these provisions would empower the **Attorney General** to deport any alien who has engaged or has had a purpose to engage in activities "prejudicial to the public interest" or "subversive to the national security."

No standards or definitions are provided to guide **discretion** in the exercise of powers so sweeping. To punish undefined "activities" departs from traditional American insistence on established standards of guilt. To punish an undefined "purpose" is thought control.

These provisions are worse than the infamous Alien Act of 1798, passed in a time of national fear and distrust of foreigners, which gave the President power to deport any alien **deemed** "dangerous to the peace and safety of the United States." Alien residents were thoroughly frightened and citizens much disturbed by that threat to liberty.

Such powers are inconsistent with our Democratic ideals. Conferring powers like that upon the Attorney General is unfair to him

Consular officials: Representatives appointed by a government who live in a foreign country to defend the interests of citizens of the appointing country.

Totalitarian repression: Creation of fear in countries governed by a dictatorship that controls every aspect of life.

Veto: In the U.S. government, the act by a president of refusing to sign a piece of legislation passed by the Congress into law.

Attorney General: The head of the U.S. Justice Department, responsible for enforcing federal laws.

Discretion: Good judgment.

Deemed: Considered.

as well as to our alien residents. Once fully informed of such vast discretionary powers vested in the Attorney General, Americans now would and should be just as alarmed as Americans were in 1798 over less drastic powers vested in the President.

Heretofore, for the most part, deportation and exclusion have rested upon findings of fact made upon evidence. Under this bill, they would rest in many instances upon the "opinion" or "satisfaction" of immigration of **consular employees.** The change from objective findings to subjective feelings is not compatible with our system of justice. The result would be to restrict or eliminate judicial review of unlawful administrative action....

Native-born American citizens who are **dual nationals** would be subjected to loss of citizenship on grounds not applicable to other native-born American citizens. This distinction is a slap at millions of Americans whose fathers were of alien birth....

Should we not undertake a reassessment of our immigration policies and practices in the light of the conditions that face us in the second half of the twentieth century?

The great popular interest which this bill has created, and the criticism which it has stirred up, demand an affirmative answer. I hope the Congress will agree to a careful reexamination of this entire matter....

Harry S. Truman

The White House,

June 25, 1952

Heretofore: Previously.

Consular employees: Low-level employees responsible for day-to-day affairs of diplomacy, such as granting visas, or permission to travel to the United States.

Dual nationals: Citizens of two nations.

What happened next ...

The 1952 law was enacted by Congress despite President Truman's veto. Thirteen years later, in October 1965, Congress repealed the national quotas of the 1952 law. Congress replaced the quotas based on national origin with a new system based on allowing the entry of people with specific, needed job skills and of the relatives of people living in the United States.

A significant result of the 1965 law was to admit many more people from Asia than had been previously allowed. The law was passed at the time of the Vietnam War (1954–75), which had led to many marriages between American soldiers and Vietnamese women. It was also passed by the same Congress that enacted major civil rights legislation designed to eliminate racial discrimination in the United States.

According to government statistics, immigrants from Europe accounted for half of all immigrants in the period 1955 to 1964 but only 10 percent of immigrants in 1988. The percentage of legal immigrants from Asia jumped from 8 percent in the period 1955 to 1964 to 41 percent in 1988.

U.S. president Lyndon B. Johnson (seated at desk) signs the repeal of the 1952 Immigration and Nationality Act in 1965.

Did you know ...

- Despite the argument between President Truman and Senator McCarran, the national quota system was increasingly irrelevant in the 1950s. Fewer than half the immigrants admitted to the United States in that decade came under the national quota system; the others came under special laws enacted to respond to specific crises or situations, or else they came from the Western Hemisphere, where there were no quotas. A year after the 1952 bill became law over Truman's veto, the Refugee Relief Act of 1953, and a set of amendments the next year, authorized admission of 214,000 people who were fleeing their homes in Europe or had escaped from countries ruled by communist governments. About a third of these immigrants were from Italy, Germany, Yugoslavia, and Greece—far more than would have been admitted under the 1952 law. After a 1956 revolt in Hungary against the communist government there, the United States admitted 38,000 Hungarians, far above their national quota.

For More Information

Books

Briggs, Vernon M. *Mass Immigration and the National Interest.* Amonk, NY: M. E. Sharpe, 1992.

Brown, Mary Elizabeth. *Shapers of the Great Debate on Immigration: A Biographical Dictionary.* Westport, CT: Greenwood Press, 1999.

King, Desmond. *Making Americans: Immigration, Race, and the Origins of the Diverse Democracy.* Cambridge, MA: Harvard University Press, 2000.

Ziegler, Benjamin Munn, ed. *Immigration: An American Dilemma.* Boston: D. C. Heath, 1953.

Periodicals

"Good Riddance to a Bad Law." *The Washington Post* (February 12, 1990): p. A10.

Ngai, Mae M. "Legacies of Exclusion: Illegal Chinese Immigration During the Cold War Years." *Journal of American Ethnic History* (Fall 1998): p. 3.

Web Sites

"Immigration and Nationality Act of June 27, 1952." *U.S. Citizenship and Immigration Services.* http://uscis.gov/graphics/shared/aboutus/statistics/LegisHist/511.htm (accessed on March 1, 2004).

Plyler v. Doe

15

Excerpt from U.S. Supreme Court trial of 1982

Opinion written by U.S. Supreme Court justice William J. Brennan on June 15, 1982

The U.S. Supreme Court rules that the children of illegal immigrants had the same rights as everyone else, especially the right to an education

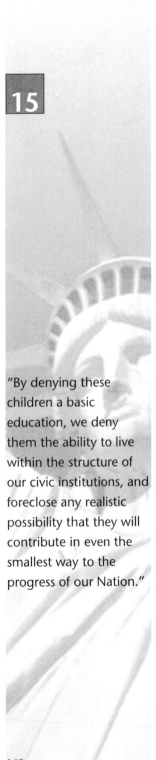

In 1977, children of illegal immigrants were not allowed to attend school in Texas without paying tuition, a fee paid to attend a school. Nearly none could afford the tuition. Five years later, in 1982, the U.S. Supreme Court ruled that Texas could not deny the children of illegal immigrants a public education. The case, called *Plyler v. Doe*, found that depriving children of a basic education would mark them for life, through no fault of their own. They were living in Texas, and that fact gave them the right to an education, just as every other child living in the state had a right to attend public school.

Visas are the government documents that give people the right to enter the United States, usually for a temporary period or for a specific purpose. In the last quarter of the twentieth century, citizens in states bordering Mexico became concerned about the large numbers of immigrants coming across the U.S. border without visas. In Texas, the state enacted a law stating that the children of these "illegal immigrants" were not entitled to attend public schools, a right given to every other child in the state.

"By denying these children a basic education, we deny them the ability to live within the structure of our civic institutions, and foreclose any realistic possibility that they will contribute in even the smallest way to the progress of our Nation."

Mexican emigrants, with children in hand, cross the Rio Grande River.
© Danny Lehman/Corbis.

In Tyler, Texas, parents of immigrant children filed a lawsuit challenging the Texas law. Their legal argument was that the Fourteenth Amendment to the Constitution guaranteed that every person living in the United States would be treated equally; the amendment said nothing about a person's status as a legal immigrant or an illegal immigrant.

The immigrants won their case. The state of Texas appealed to a higher court and, after losing there, appealed the case to the U.S. Supreme Court. There, in 1982, the immigrants won again. In their ruling, the Supreme Court, by a vote of 5 to 4, declared that the children of illegal immigrants were people like everyone else, and had the same rights as everyone else, especially the right to an education. Depriving children of an education could leave them illiterate, or unable to read or write, for life and condemn them to a lifetime of low-paying jobs.

From the standpoint of people migrating to the United States, especially from Mexico and Central America, the rul-

ing had two impacts. First, the ruling meant that the children of immigrants could get a free education in the United States whether or not their parents had legal entry visas. Second, the court recognized that immigrants were people living in the United States, and the provisions of the Constitution applied to them equally as everyone else living in the United States.

The decision in *Plyler v. United States* gave children of illegal immigrants the right to an education in the United States.
© *Mug Shots/Corbis.*

Things to remember while reading an excerpt from *Plyler v. Doe:*

- The case is named after the superintendent of public schools in Tyler, Texas, James Plyler; two unnamed parents who were illegal immigrants, referred to as "J. and R. Doe" to protect their anonymity, or their right in a legal case to not be named; and "Certain named and unnamed undocumented alien [foreign] children." Plyler had enforced the law barring children of illegal immigrants from attending public schools unless they paid tuition.

- The Supreme Court decision agreed that there was no constitutional right to a free public education. Instead, the argument focused on whether children of illegal immigrants had a right, under the U.S. Constitution, to be treated like everyone else, regardless of their parents' legal status in the United States. In Texas, all children did have a right to attend public schools at no cost, and the Supreme Court ruled that children of illegal immigrants had the same right.

- Can people be treated differently depending on whether they are citizens or immigrants, or on whether they are living in the United States legally or not? In some cases, the answer is yes—noncitizens cannot vote, for example, and illegal immigrants can be sent out of the country. But in other cases, the answer is no. *Plyler* addressed the issue of public education. The Fourteenth Amendment has also been applied to many other areas of life, such as giving noncitizens the right to a trial by jury in criminal cases.

Excerpt from Plyler v. Doe

*The question presented by these cases is whether, consistent with the **Equal Protection Clause of the Fourteenth Amendment**, Texas may deny to undocumented school-age children the free public education that it provides to children who are citizens of the United States or legally admitted aliens....*

*Since the late 19th century, the United States has restricted immigration into this country. **Unsanctioned** entry into the United States is a crime ..., and those who have entered unlawfully are subject to **deportation**.... But despite the existence of these legal restrictions, a substantial number of persons have succeeded in unlawfully entering the United States, and now live within various States, including the State of Texas.*

In May 1975, the Texas Legislature revised its education laws to withhold from local school districts any state funds for the education of children who were not "legally admitted" into the United

Equal Protection Clause of the Fourteenth Amendment: Clause that states: "No State shall ... deny to any person within its jurisdiction the equal protection of the laws."

Unsanctioned: Not officially approved.

Deportation: The act of sending a noncitizen out of the country where he or she has been living.

States. The 1975 revision also authorized local school districts to deny enrollment in their public schools to children not "legally admitted" to the country....

[Plyler v. Doe] is a class action, filed in the United States District Court for the Eastern District of Texas in September 1977, on behalf of certain school-age children of Mexican origin residing in Smith County, Tex., who could not establish that they had been legally admitted into the United States. The action complained of the exclusion of plaintiff children from the public schools of the Tyler Independent School District. The Superintendent and members of the Board of Trustees of the School District were named as defendants; the State of Texas intervened as a party-defendant....

The Fourteenth Amendment provides that "no State shall ... deprive any person of life, liberty, or property, without due process of law; nor deny to any person within its jurisdiction the equal protection of the laws." ... **Appellants** argue at the outset that **undocumented aliens**, because of their immigration status, are not "persons within the jurisdiction" of the State of Texas, and that they therefore have no right to the equal protection of Texas law. We reject this argument. Whatever his status under the immigration laws, an alien is surely a "person" in any ordinary sense of that term. Aliens, even aliens whose presence in this country is unlawful, have long been recognized as "persons" guaranteed due process of law by the Fifth and Fourteenth Amendments.... Indeed, we [the Supreme Court] have clearly held that the Fifth Amendment protects aliens whose presence in this country is unlawful from **invidious** discrimination by the Federal Government....

The children who are **plaintiffs** in these cases are special members of this underclass. Persuasive arguments support the view that a State may withhold its **beneficence** from those whose very presence within the United States is the product of their own unlawful

 ## The Fourteenth Amendment

In 1866, the U.S. Congress approved the Fourteenth Amendment to the Constitution. It was ratified, or approved, by the states in July 1868 and became part of the Constitution. The Amendment was one of three that passed after the American Civil War (1861–65), primarily designed to protect the rights of former slaves. The Amendment said: "All persons born or naturalized in the United States, and subject to the jurisdiction [area of authority] thereof, are citizens of the United States and of the State wherein they reside. No State shall make or enforce any law which shall abridge [shorten] the privileges or immunities of citizens of the United States; nor shall any State deprive any person of life, liberty, or property, without due process of law; nor deny to any person within its jurisdiction the equal protection of the laws."

Appellants: People who ask a higher court to review a lower court's decision.

Undocumented aliens: Immigrants who did not enter the United States with a visa.

Invidious: Harmful.

Plaintiffs: Persons who begin a legal proceeding and arrange to bring the case to court.

Beneficence: Kindness.

conduct. These arguments do not apply with the same force to **classifications imposing disabilities on the minor children** of such illegal entrants. At the least, those who elect to enter our territory by **stealth** and in violation of our law should be prepared to bear the consequences, including, but not limited to, deportation. But the children of those illegal entrants are not comparably situated. Their "parents have the ability to conform their conduct to **societal norms**," and presumably the ability to remove themselves from the State's jurisdiction; but the children who are plaintiffs in these cases "can affect neither their parents' conduct nor their own status." ...Even if the State found it **expedient** to control the conduct of adults by acting against their children, legislation directing the **onus** of a parent's misconduct against his children does not **comport** with fundamental conceptions of justice....

Public education is not a "right" granted to individuals by the Constitution.... But neither is it merely some governmental "benefit" indistinguishable from other forms of social welfare legislation. Both the importance of education in maintaining our basic institutions, and the lasting impact of its deprivation on the life of the child, mark the distinction. The "American people have always regarded education and [the] acquisition of knowledge as matters of supreme importance." ...We have recognized "the public schools as a most vital civic institution for the preservation of a democratic system of government" ... and as the primary vehicle for transmitting "the values on which our society rests." ...And these historic "perceptions of the public schools as **inculcating** fundamental values necessary to the maintenance of a democratic political system have been confirmed by the observations of social scientists." ... In addition, education provides the basic tools by which individuals might lead economically productive lives to the benefit of us all. In sum, education has a fundamental role in maintaining the fabric of our society. We cannot ignore the significant social costs borne by our Nation when select groups are denied the means to absorb the values and skills upon which our social order rests.

In addition to the **pivotal** role of education in sustaining our political and cultural heritage, denial of education to some isolated group of children poses an **affront** to one of the goals of the Equal Protection Clause: the **abolition** of governmental barriers presenting unreasonable obstacles to advancement on the basis of individual merit. **Paradoxically,** by depriving the children of any disfavored group of an education, we **foreclose** the means by which that group might raise the level of esteem in which it is held by the majority.

Classifications imposing disabilities on the minor children: Grouping dependent children who are not responsible for their situation in such a way that they suffer a consequence, e.g., not learning to read.

Stealth: Acting in a quiet, secret way to avoid attention.

Societal norms: Acceptable behavior.

Expedient: Suitable for achieving a goal.

Onus: Burden.

Comport: Conform.

Inculcating: Teaching by means of frequent repetition.

Pivotal: Vitally important.

Affront: Offense.

Abolition: Ending.

Paradoxically: In an apparent contradiction.

Foreclose: Shut out in advance.

But more directly, "education prepares individuals to be self-reliant and self-sufficient participants in society." ...Illiteracy is an enduring disability. The inability to read and write will handicap the individual deprived of a basic education each and every day of his life. The **inestimable toll** of that deprivation on the social, economic, intellectual, and psychological well-being of the individual, and the obstacle it poses to individual achievement, make it most difficult to reconcile the cost or the principle of a status-based denial of basic education with the framework of equality....

... More is involved in these cases than the abstract question whether **21.031** discriminates against a suspect class, or whether education is a fundamental right. Section 21.031 imposes a lifetime hardship on a **discrete** class of children not accountable for their disabling status. The **stigma** of illiteracy will mark them for the rest of their lives. By denying these children a basic education, we deny them the ability to live within the structure of our civic institutions, and foreclose any realistic possibility that they will contribute in even the smallest way to the progress of our Nation. In determining the rationality of 21.031, we may appropriately take into account its costs to the Nation and to the innocent children who are its victims. In light of these **countervailing** costs, the discrimination contained in 21.031 can hardly be considered rational unless it furthers some substantial goal of the State....

We are reluctant to impute to Congress the intention to withhold from these children, for so long as they are present in this country through no fault of their own, access to a basic education.... But in the area of special constitutional sensitivity presented by these cases, and in the absence of any contrary indication fairly **discernible** in the present legislative record, we perceive no national policy that supports the State in denying these children an elementary education.

... There is no evidence in the record suggesting that illegal entrants impose any significant burden on the State's economy. To the contrary, the available evidence suggests that illegal aliens underutilize public services, while contributing their labor to the local economy and tax money to the state **fisc**.... The dominant incentive for illegal entry into the State of Texas is the availability of employment; few if any illegal immigrants come to this country, or presumably to the State of Texas, in order to avail themselves of a free education. Thus, even making the doubtful assumption that the net impact of illegal aliens on the economy of the State is negative, we

Inestimable toll: A loss that cannot be calculated.

21.031: The legal description of a section of the Texas law banning use of state funds for the education of children of illegal aliens.

Discrete: Separate; distinct.

Stigma: Scar; brand.

Countervailing: Offsetting.

Discernible: Recognizable.

Fisc: Treasury.

*think it clear that "charging **tuition** to undocumented children con-stitutes a ludicrously ineffectual attempt to stem the tide of illegal immigration," at least when compared with the alternative of pro-hibiting the employment of illegal aliens....*

If the State is to deny a discrete group of innocent children the free public education that it offers to other children residing within its borders, that denial must be justified by a showing that it fur-thers some substantial state interest. No such showing was made here. Accordingly, the judgment of the Court of Appeals in each of these cases is

Affirmed.

Tuition: A fee paid to attend a school.

What happened next ...

The court's decision favoring children of illegal immi-grants led to a new set of restrictions on school districts. The court's ruling that schools could not discriminate against children on the basis of their status as immigrants had impli-cations far beyond whether such children could enroll as stu-dents. Legal experts advised schools that they could not take a role in cooperating with the U.S. Immigration and Natural-ization Service, whose job is to enforce federal immigration laws. For example, schools were banned from asking students about the legal status of their parents, or from letting federal agents interview students while at school. Any actions taken towards a student who was, or might be, the child of an ille-gal immigrant were regarded as discriminatory, and were banned under the court's decision.

Did you know ...

• In 1994, citizens of California voted in favor of a law ti-tled Proposition 184, intended to deprive illegal immi-grants of any benefits paid by the state, such as welfare—and including public schooling for the children of illegal immigrants. (Under California law, citizens can propose laws and vote on them in a general election, a process normally carried out by elected representatives in the state legislature.) Although the voters of California approved the law, federal courts barred the state from carrying out its provisions, in large part because doing so would violate the Constitution as interpreted by the Supreme Court in *Plyler v. Doe.*

For More Information

Books

Dudley, William, ed. *Illegal Immigration: Opposing Viewpoints.* San Diego, CA: Greenhaven Press, 2002.

Irons, Peter, ed. *May It Please the Court: Courts, Kids, and the Constitution.* New York: New Press, 2000.

Mauro, Tony. *Illustrated Great Decisions of the Supreme Court.* Washington, DC: CQ Press, 2000.

Nevins, Joseph. *Operation Gatekeeper: The Rise of the "Illegal Alien" and the Making of the U.S.-Mexican Boundary.* New York: Routledge, 2000.

Periodicals

Briggs, Vernon M., Jr. "Immigrants Out! The New Nativism and the Anti-Immigrant Impulse in the United States" (book review). *Journal of American Ethnic History* (Summer 1998): p. 114.

Unz, Ron. "California and the End of White America." *Commentary* (November 1999): p. 17.

Web Sites

"*Plyler v. Doe*" (full text of the opinion). *FindLaw.com.* http://caselaw.lp.findlaw.com/scripts/getcase.pl?court=US&vol=457&invol=202 (accessed on February 29, 2004).

16

El México and María Medina de Lopez

Excerpts from Mexican Voices, American Dreams: An Oral History of Mexican Immigration to the United States
Published in 1990

Two Mexicans tell their personal stories of the immigration process into the United States

"Yes, little one, I am going to save this sock so that when you're big you can say, 'This is what I wore when I came to the United States.'"

In newspapers and on television, they are illegal "aliens," citizens of one country living in another country. They are denounced in the U.S. Congress and the state legislatures of Texas and California as a problem to be solved. But once in the United States, they pick crops, cut suburban lawns, clean houses, or work in factories—solutions to the different problem of finding people willing to work for very low wages. Most of them come from Mexico or Central America; they speak Spanish. Their voices are seldom heard, their individual stories seldom told. These are immigrants in the twenty-first century, not different from the ancestors of most people living in the United States: people looking for a better life for themselves and their children.

Coming to the United States from Mexico is like playing hide-and-seek. People cross the border hoping to avoid the U.S. immigration officers assigned to catch them. If the immigrants are caught, they are returned to Mexico, to try again. Sometimes, to improve their chances, immigrants hire a "coyote," someone who will help them succeed in crossing the border, for a fee.

Many immigrants crossing into the United States from Mexico without a visa—the difficult-to-obtain official document that allows someone to enter the United States—are not coming to an unknown land of strangers. Often, they have relatives already in the United States. The governments of Mexico and the United States say there is a line, a border, where Mexico ends and the United States begins. For some people, however, the border is an inconvenience at best, a place where a policeman may need to be bribed while traveling to a job or sending a child back to school in the fall.

Following are two unrelated accounts of Mexicans immigrating to America at the end of the twentieth century. They come from Marilyn P. Davis's *Mexican Voices, American Dreams: An Oral History of Mexican Immigration to the United States*. The first story belongs to "El México," a "coyote" who lives in Tijuana, Mexico, just across the border from San Diego, California, who makes a modest living escorting Mexicans into the United States. The other belongs to María Medina de Lopez, a

A worker constructs a fence in El Paso, Texas, at the border of the United States and Mexico. © *Stephanie Maze/Corbis.*

twenty-six-year-old housewife, from Compton, California, formerly of Guadalajara, a favorite American-tourist destination on Mexico's west coast. She was a "chicken," someone who paid a "coyote" to help her join her husband in California.

Things to remember while reading excerpts from *Mexican Voices, American Dreams:*

- On the one hand, the stories of two people coming to the United States without permission may not seem threatening to a large country like the United States. On the other hand, there are estimated to be at least three million Mexican citizens living in the United States without visas— about the same number of people who live in Chicago. The total cost of providing public services to such a large population is substantial. In many cases, immigrants without visas avoid paying some forms of U.S. taxes in order to avoid being discovered by immigration officials.

- The stories told here ended well for the participants, but hundreds of Mexicans have died trying to enter the United States. Trying to cross the border in Arizona during the summer, when temperatures soar past 120°F (49°C), can prove fatal, especially in cases when immigrants get lost and run out of water.

- Mexican emigration to the United States has become a diplomatic issue between the two countries, but despite repeated promises on both sides to address the issue, the flow of migrants across the border continues. Some critics believe that neither country really wants to change the situation: the United States is a source of jobs for unemployed people in Mexico, and Mexicans are a source of inexpensive labor in the United States.

Comments from El México, coyote

I first started bringing people across when I was about twelve or thirteen. At that time I lived on the other side, in San Ysidro [Califor-

nia] with a woman who is like a mother to me. My parents are in Mexico City, and they sent me to live with her when I was young so I could go to school. Our house was right on the border, across from the schoolyard there, and I knew the area with my eyes closed. That's where we played when we were kids. So when I would see people crossing and know that they needed help or they would get caught, I would bring them across. I never charged anything. I guess people got to know me, other guides, and they would ask me to signal for them. That's more or less how it was.

People want to cross with us because they know we are secure and we are serious. They know we are not like those who look for people off the street, or are looking for people to take their money, or those that take people across so they'll have money to drink. We are fathers, we have families to maintain, and our interest is to cross people. When we take someone across and a friend asks them if they know someone, they recommend us. They say, "Oh yes, I know someone secure and responsible."

With those in the street it's no more than an adventure to see if they can make it, and often they're caught or they leave the people with nothing to eat for two or three days. Oh, and there are those who take the people to one side of the fields and leave them when the Immigration isn't around. They tell their clients a vehicle will be by to pick them up, but it never comes.

It's like any other business, if you are a mechanic or an engineer, it takes time to build your **clientele.** When people see you do good work they will look for you. I am very familiar with the **terrain** and the techniques. It's like a game of chess. Each one of us takes one or two, and then we reunite, or if it's **tranquil** we can all go together. Some nights we will have up to twelve people to cross.

Oh, we've been caught. I would say one or two times every six months or maybe four times a year. Each time we give a different name. They want to know your name, where you were born, your father and mother, how old you are, how you entered, and where you entered. You give whatever answer. They put it in a computer, but you answer differently each time.

When I was little in San Ysidro, I was dedicated to passing people, to helping them hide. One time the Immigration saw me and picked me up. The lady who is like my mother didn't know where I was. She thought I was in school, but it was about three or four in the afternoon and they put me in jail in Chula Vista [California].

Clientele: Set of customers.

Terrain: Physical features of the land.

Tranquil: Peaceful and quiet.

Border patrol officers check the area for trespassers at the Mexico/California border. © Greg Smith/Corbis Saba.

Ambiance: Atmosphere.

Fiestas: Spanish term for festivals.

They gave me some slaps and told me that if I would get caught a second time they would put me in juvenile [jail]. I was there a week and then they sent me to the center of California. They were crazy, I was underage, I was maybe fifteen then. They left me without any money. I was going to hitchhike back to San Ysidro. The only thing I was afraid of was Torrance, California. I had heard it was horrible there, and I was afraid they would be going to Torrance. So when I would get a ride I would say, "You aren't going to Torrance, are you?" At one point the police picked me up. I told them I was a Mexican and to send me back to Tijuana. They did, and from there I crossed back over to San Ysidro. My second mother was frantic; she had been looking for me all that time.

My wife is from Tijuana. I was living in San Diego and I would cross to come visit her. When we got married, she didn't want to leave her family. That was when I moved, and I have been here ever since. Now, I'm accustomed to living here and I like it better than the United States. It has a different **ambiance**, much friendlier, not so uptight.

This is how it is. Tonight we will have these two men to take across and there will be three of us. They will pay $50 each, so we'll make about thirty dollars. That's not much, is it? It's what anyone would make in a day, well, not here in Mexico, but on the other side, even more. A professional or skilled person will make about $50 a day, and this is what someone who is unskilled would make, the minimum. There are times when there are more people and we make more money, but then you have to save some of it for when there is no work. This month we had two weeks with no work. The bad months are from September through Christmas. Then it picks up again. In January we have all the people who went to Mexico for the **fiestas**, then in the spring farm workers come over, in the summer we have students, and at the end of summer we have parents crossing to take their kids back to school. The people from several little *pueblos* in Michoacan and Jalisco come to us; the whole pueblo knows us. But we also get people from El Salvador, Guatemala and Peru.

It's $50 to cross to San Ysidro and $300 to go to Los Angeles. But to go to Los Angeles, you first have to arrive at a house. There is a **señora,** she doesn't like to do this, but she has a son who has an **infirmity** where he can't walk. The señora doesn't have a husband. She has other children, and she gets welfare, but it isn't enough to cover the child who is sick. So the señora helps us, taking care of the people. The people she takes in are better off than others, because she does care for them. When we get there, she makes them breakfast, lets them bathe and wash their clothes, for the little bit of money she gets.

Then we have to pay an American with a car. He gets a little more, about one hundred dollars per person. Then arriving in Los Angeles, we have another person we pay to take the people to their houses. Sometimes, when we want to, we go to Los Angeles too, but usually we don't. The person who takes them collects the money when they arrive in Los Angeles. He pays the person who takes them to their houses, and when he returns that night, he pays the señora and us. When someone brings us a client we pay them $5 for making the connection. The person who drives has to get paid well because he has to drive a nice car. If it was one of the little old cars we drive, no, they'd stop us for sure.

Those who make good money are the ones who sell drugs. They make money coming and going. Besides all this, the little that one makes, and then the Mexican police want $100 if they catch you with one or two! We play the game on this side to avoid the police, because when you're caught you have to pay $100 or $200 just so they will leave you alone. And think of it, there are the municipal police, the state police, the **federales,** the governors, and beyond that, those that pass for police. And they all have an interest. What can you do? You have no choice. Sometimes you have to pay them.

Pueblos: Spanish term for villages.

Señora: Spanish term for wife; also used as a title, like Mrs.

Infirmity: Weakness; debility.

Federales: Mexican national police.

Comments from María Medina de Lopez

Where should I begin? My husband, Frederico, called me in Guadalajara [Mexico] from Los Angeles. He asked if I wanted to come. See, I wanted to, but he didn't want me to because it's very dangerous to cross the border. But, I missed him so much, and well, we agreed that I would come.

So, I went to Tijuana [Mexico]. I went with my papa and mama and Freddie, my baby. We took a hotel, and the woman who was going to take us across came to where we were. First she took Freddie. If I knew then, I would have kept him. I told the woman that she was to take Freddie to his father; if not, I wouldn't have her take him. The woman said yes, but she lied to me. She told me that she would cross in a little while.

That day I called Frederico on the phone from Tijuana and he said no, they hadn't brought the baby and the woman who took him hadn't called.

The woman was a friend of Frederico's friend. Well, his friend had **confidence** in her. I thought the woman would be more responsible but she lied to me. I was **mortified** from the beginning because the baby was crying and crying when she took him from me. My mother and father also began to cry. No, now I was very worried.

The next day I called Frederico again. "No," he said, "the woman hasn't brought him." I cried and cried. I wanted to cross however I could, by whatever means. I didn't care about anything but finding my baby. They didn't tell us where they would have him and I didn't know. Aye, yes, I was very afraid because I heard talk about women who cross children and then sell them. They sell them to people who can't have children.

The next day I talked to Frederico again on the telephone. I told him to call the woman and ask her where she had the baby. I told him to go there himself because I was very worried. He said he would.

Then, another coyote came for me. He came to the hotel where we were staying. There were two other women and a young girl. They had been there eight days and couldn't cross. They had been caught and returned, who knows how many times. I felt that by comparison I was in heaven, because here I was and I had my mama and papa and other relatives. If for one reason or another I couldn't pass, they could bring me back my baby and we could return to my pueblo. These poor women didn't have even five **pesos**. They had thrown them down the telephone calling their husbands who were over there. And now, they didn't have any money, not even to call again, nothing.

Confidence: Trust.

Mortified: Extremely embarassed.

Peso: Spanish coinage.

We were told to leave all the things we had brought with us. I said, "Well, I don't have anything of value." And the money, except for a little, I had left with my mother. So I left my bag, a small one.

Then from seven o'clock in the morning, for four hours, we walked. They brought us walking, just walking and walking and walking all through and around Tijuana, around and around. It was pure dust and dirt. We were scratched by scrub and sticks, and we waded through water and mud. The coyote wasn't the woman who had taken Freddie. This was a man. I think the woman was supposed to be waiting for us on the other side and he was to bring us across. So the man told us, "We are going to pass now." Well, I don't know. Surely the man thought he was going to pass us, but he said, "If something happens, remember we are all going together, I'm not taking you across." When we were almost to San Ysidro, they caught us. The immigration arrived. Well, who knows, the coyote had to stay. I think they must have caught him at other times. The man became very nervous.

When they caught us they spoke Spanish and asked where we were coming from and our names. That's all. I told them the truth, what my name was and all. Aye, we passed and now they were going to throw us out! So, they locked us up for an hour and a half, then they threw us back into Tijuana, at the border.

I wasn't afraid or anything. My cousin Nico is on the border; he has a booth there. And then I had a little money so if they threw us back I could get a taxi. I could go to his house. But since we were on the border I found his booth. My cousin just stood there looking at me.

Then he asked, "Well, what happened? Didn't you cross?" I told him, "Well, they caught us."

My father was at Nico's house, so I asked him to take us there. We all went, the two women and the little girl too. They were hungry, and by now they were very thirsty. My cousin gave them water. I told them to come with me and I gave them some money. The two women and the poor little girl. She was about ten years old. The poor thing, I felt so sorry for her—she was so thin—and the women too. Eight days, and they were just eating whatever they could find. They came with us, and we went to get my bag from the hotel. That was the last I saw of the women and the little girl. I never knew what happened to them.

I told my cousin that I was going to call Frederico and tell him that if they are going to have me cross like that, then it's just as well I don't pass. No! Walking that much for nothing, and the woman was supposed to come for me. I thought she was going to pass me in a vehicle. I didn't think I was going like that. Then my cousin told me that he knew a woman. She is a woman who passes people. She is a widow in whom he had confidence. He knows her well. He said, "Let's pass by her house."

Well, by now my father and mother were very afraid. They thought it was very bad, right? But I told them that no, nothing happened, they just caught us, locked us up for a little while and then sent us back again. The only thing was walking for four hours for nothing. Well, then my father calmed down a little.

It was Friday. It wasn't until Friday that I knew—Wednesday, Thursday, Friday—yes. I called Frederico and he said, "Look, I have the baby." The baby was crying and he put the telephone up so I could hear. I could hear him crying and I too began to cry. When he went to get Freddie, he said the baby was—like, drugged—like he was stupid. He was never anything like that. I don't know if he was tired from crying or if they gave him something to make him sleep. I don't know. But when the baby saw Frederico, he put his little hands out as if he knew him. But the baby couldn't have known him; he was only a month old when Frederico left us to come here. It had been three days. It was Wednesday at two in the afternoon when they took him, and it wasn't until Friday that Frederico went to get him. I was so angry at Frederico. I told him that it was his fault. I said, "Look, they probably gave him something because the baby isn't like that. He is always very lively. Probably he was crying the whole time and they gave him something."

I told Frederico that I wouldn't go with that **ratera** now that she wouldn't even show her face. One doesn't know. Me, I didn't trust her. I told him that my cousin was going to get me a coyote, and now he didn't have to do anything. My father told him that this was someone we could trust. I said, "You don't have to do anything, the only thing you have to have is the money. For certain, I will be there tonight."

About 7:30 in the evening, it was the same day, I was bathing because I was covered with mud. Nico arrived from the border. He said, "Get ready, because at 9:00 P.M. you are going to cross." Now I was happy, I felt sure I was going to pass. He told me not to wear high heels because I would be walking for a while. For a minute I thought, "Oh no, not again!"

Another coyote, a man, took me. We went up above on a little hill. I had to jump over the fence, about two meters high, then

Ratera: A Spanish term for a female who exploits illegal immigrants by stealing their money.

down through a ditch along the fence. The man took me. He took me by the hand pulling me, uphill, then down. Awful. I almost fell, more than once; you can believe it. I wore my mother's shoes, they were flat. My high heels were in my bag, and later another man brought it to me in Los Angeles.

Very quickly we arrived on the other side of the border at a café. The man left me there and told me just to ask for a coffee or a soda. He told me not to be nervous. I was going to go in there and buy something. So, I asked for a soda, they gave it to me, and there I was drinking it in the United States. It's right on the border. The coyote had told me that a young man would come shortly with a truck. It would be yellow, he said; "You just go out and he will take you." That's how it was. I didn't even finish the soda. When the truck came I quickly got in. It was very fast, fast. Only five minutes to walk across. It was nothing.

I sat in front just as in any car. The driver began talking to me. Who knows what the man told me; San Juan something ... yes, San Juan Capistrano. This is where we stopped for gasoline and to call Frederico. He told him, in so much time we would be there. He told me we might have to stop someplace overnight. I was very nervous, being alone, and the man was very young. Oh, I was so afraid. He was from Tijuana. I tried not to be nervous. I talked to him, asking him if he was married, and who knows whatnot. So I talked to him and he talked to me, but nevertheless, I got very nervous when he told me that it was possible we would have to stay someplace. I was praying that nothing would happen to me.

But we didn't have to stop at any point. We arrived at twelve or twelve-thirty at night in the center of Los Angeles. Frederico and my brothers were waiting for me.

When I didn't know about Freddie, I thought, "For what am I doing this?" I also sent the birth certificates for him, Frederico, and my brother, and not one of the birth certificates did the woman give us. She said, no, she didn't bring them, that it was another man. Who knows, we went twice to the woman's house, but we couldn't get anything. When I talked with Frederico, he told me that it wasn't how they had told him it would be. It was very different.

It's very dangerous, not only for women, for men too. They charged $300 for me and $200 for Freddie, and this ratera gave him back naked. I sent him with pants, boots, socks, a shirt, and a cute little jacket that I had just bought him because he was going to see his father. And she gave him back naked with just one sock.

*Look here, I still have it. That was it. He was also very sick. I think he had been perspiring and they took him out with nothing on. For a long time he sounded as if he had **asthma**. The next day we took him to the doctor, but he didn't get better. It was just awful.*

No, my mother and father didn't leave Tijuana until they knew that we were safely here. My mama said, "No, daughter, we are going to wait until we know that you are with Frederico, because if we go and then you get thrown back again, oh no."

They stayed another week in Tijuana. At the end they called and talked to Frederico. My father told him, "Now we have brought your wife. We are giving you the responsibility, because we are returning."

They had planned to go to La Paz, but instead they returned directly because my papa was very nervous. He had been drinking from the time we left, all along the way. It was because he was so sad. Not so much for me, but for the baby. The baby lived with them since he was born, and my father took him with him everywhere.

Yes, little one, I am going to save this sock so that when you're big you can say, "This is what I wore when I came to the United States."

What happened next ...

The stories of El México and María Medina de Lopez do not have formal endings. They are both ordinary people who earn a living as best they can. El México lives with his wife and young child in a converted garage in Tijuana. He is a small businessman, a service provider to whom people come for his skill in dodging officials on both sides of the border. María lives in an old house trailer parked in the gritty town of Compton, California. Her life is much like that of any other mother who does not have much money.

To some of her Anglo neighbors in California, María is a threat. In 1994, the voters of California overwhelmingly approved a law, titled Proposition 187 (see entry), that would have prevented her son from attending school. A federal judge stopped the law from taking effect on grounds it would violate the U.S. Supreme Court's ruling titled *Plyler v. Doe* (see

Asthma: A condition that sometimes makes breathing difficult.

entry), guaranteeing that immigrants without visas are treated the same as any other person living in the United States.

Did you know …

- In 2003, the U.S. Census Bureau announced that for the first time, Latinos, people who trace their ancestry to Spanish-speaking inhabitants of the Western hemisphere, were the largest minority in the United States. The Census Bureau estimated there were almost thirty-nine million Hispanics living in the United States, making African Americans the second largest minority. About 40 percent of Latinos living in the United States immigrated, the Census Bureau said.

- One result of the sharp rise in the Latino population has been an increase in their political influence. Increasingly, politicians from states like Texas and California, with large numbers of Latinos, are learning to speak Spanish to appeal for support.

For More Information

Books

Conover, Ted. *Coyotes: A Journey Through the Secret World of America's Illegal Aliens.* New York: Vintage Books, 1987.

Davidson Miriam. *Lives on the Line: Dispatches from the U.S.-Mexico Border.* Tucson: University of Arizona Press, 2000.

Davis, Marilyn P. *Mexican Voices, American Dreams: An Oral History of Mexican Immigration to the United States.* New York: Henry Holt and Co., 1990.

Dudley, William, ed. *Illegal Immigration: Opposing Viewpoints.* San Diego, CA: Greenhaven Press, 2002.

Hayes, Helene. *U.S. Immigration Policy and the Undocumented: Ambivalent Lives, Furtive Lives.* Westport, CT: Praeger, 2001.

Martinez, Ruben. *Crossing Over: A Mexican Family on the Migrant Trail.* New York: Metropolitan Books, 2001.

United States Congress, House Committee on Government Reform. *Federal Law Enforcement at the Borders and Ports of Entry: Challenges and Solutions.* Washington, DC: U.S. Government Printing Office, 2003.

Periodicals

"The Gifts Migrants Bear." *America* (December 28, 1985): p. 454.

"Study Hails Effect of Mexicans on California." *New York Times* (December 10, 1985): p. 10.

Web Sites

Annerino, John. "Photographer Recounts Crossing U.S. Border With Mexican Illegal Immigrants." *National Geographic Adventure Magazine* (January 23, 2003). http://news.nationalgeographic.com/news/2003/01/0123_030123_border.html (accessed on March 1, 2004).

California Proposition 187

Voted into law in 1994 by California voters

Reprinted from *Glenn Spencer's American Patrol Report* (Web site)

California voters approve a law designed to stop immigrants without visas from receiving public benefits from the state

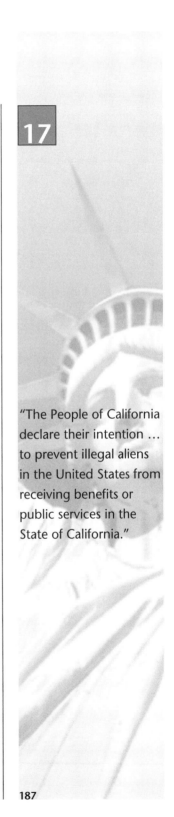

17

In 1994, voters in California approved a law designed to stop immigrants without visas, government documents that grant permission for admission to the country, from receiving public benefits from the state, notably medical care and public education. Voters acted through a provision of California's constitution that allows citizens to propose laws and to vote on them, functions normally carried out by the state legislature. The passage of the law reflected widespread anger in California over the issue of "illegal aliens," or people residing in a country without legal authorization. In California, these illegal immigrants were mostly people from Mexico and Central America who entered the state without federal immigration visas to find work on farms. Those in favor of the law argued that such aliens were collecting benefits without paying taxes.

Proposition 187 was one of several official reactions in the last two decades of the twentieth century to the flow of immigrants from Mexico and Central America. Many of these immigrants entered the United States without a visa. Opposition to the mostly Latino immigrants was most intense in states bordering Mexico, especially California and

"The People of California declare their intention … to prevent illegal aliens in the United States from receiving benefits or public services in the State of California."

Texas, where immigrants entered the country to find work, usually as low-paid farm workers or day laborers. (Day laborers are people who take temporary jobs, for a single day, and are paid by the hour.) The anti-immigrant sentiments of the late twentieth century echoed many of the themes of anti-immigrant feelings a century earlier, which were then directed against immigrants from southern and eastern Europe.

Illegal aliens, as the immigrants were widely known, shared some characteristics of earlier immigrants from countries like Italy: they were mostly Catholics, they did not speak English, and their skin was darker than the dominant northern Europeans. In the late nineteenth and early twentieth centuries, however, immigrants were allowed to enter the United States without documents, while a century later immigration was highly regulated.

Things to remember while reading Proposition 187:

- In the preface to the Proposition, the authors claimed that the people of California had been harmed financially by illegal aliens using state services, such as free medical care and education. Supporters of Proposition 187 claimed that, at the time of the election, there were 1.6 million illegal aliens in California who received services worth about $3 billion a year. The preface to Proposition 187 did not point out, however, the value of contributions by aliens. By working for low wages in agriculture, construction, and other jobs, illegal aliens kept the price of food and other goods low. Few aliens applied for public welfare if they became unemployed, largely because in doing so they would have exposed themselves to deportation, or being forcibly sent back to their native country. Surveys showed that in relation to the general population, illegal aliens used few public services.

- Backers of Proposition 187 realized that some of its provisions had already been found unconstitutional by the U.S. Supreme Court. (In the United States, if a law passed by the legislature violates a provision of the U.S. Constitution, the law cannot be enforced, because the Constitution is the supreme law of the land. Whether laws violate the Constitution is a decision usually made by federal courts, and the U.S. Supreme Court has the final word on whether laws are constitutional.) For example, one provision of Proposition 187 barred the children of illegal aliens from entering public schools. In 1982, the Supreme Court, in a case titled *Plyler v. Doe* (see entry), had ruled that a similar ban on public education for children of illegal aliens in Texas violated the U.S. Constitution and could not be enforced. Supporters of Proposition 187 hoped that this decision would be reconsidered and overruled by the Supreme Court.

California governor Pete Wilson, a strong proponent of Proposition 187. *Getty Images.*

- The campaign for Proposition 187 was highly political. A Republican politician, Pete Wilson (1933–), strongly endorsed the proposition. Wilson was reelected as governor at least in part because he was identified with the anti-immigrant law. Images of immigrants appeared in many campaign ads, and many Californians were led to believe that immigrants were linked to a slowdown in the state's economy.

- The authors of Proposition 187 realized that laws affecting the treatment of immigrants were scattered throughout the entire set of California laws. They therefore combed through the laws, finding specific sections of the law to change in order to achieve their larger purpose: to discourage immigrants from coming to California without visas.

California Proposition 187

*This **initiative** measure is submitted to the people in accordance with the provisions of Article II, Section 8 of the Constitution.*

Initiative: In some states, a law put up for a popular vote as a result of voters signing a petition.

This initiative measure adds sections to various codes; therefore, new provisions proposed to be added are [noted as such].

PROPOSED LAW

SECTION 1. Findings and Declaration.

The People of California find and declare as follows:

That they have suffered and are suffering economic hardship caused by the presence of illegal aliens in this state.

That they have suffered and are suffering personal injury and damage caused by the criminal conduct of illegal aliens in this state.

That they have a right to the protection of their government from any person or persons entering this country unlawfully.

Therefore, the People of California declare their intention to provide for cooperation between their agencies of state and local government with the federal government, and to establish a system of required notification by and between such agencies to prevent illegal aliens in the United States from receiving benefits or public services in the State of California.

SECTION 2. Manufacture, Distribution or Sale of False Citizenship or Resident Alien Documents: Crime and Punishment.

Section 113 is added to the Penal Code, to read:

*113. Any person who manufactures, distributes or sells false documents to conceal the true citizenship or resident alien status of another person is guilty of a **felony**, and shall be punished by imprisonment in the state prison for five years or by a fine of seventy-five thousand dollars ($75,000).*

SECTION 3. Use of False Citizenship or Resident Alien Documents: Crime and Punishment.

Section 114 is added to the Penal Code, to read:

114. Any person who uses false documents to conceal his or her true citizenship or resident alien status is guilty of a felony, and shall be punished by imprisonment in the state prison for five years or by a fine of twenty-five thousand dollars ($25,000).

SECTION 4. Law Enforcement Cooperation with INS.

Section 834b is added to the Penal Code, to read:

834b. (a) Every law enforcement agency in California shall fully cooperate with the United States Immigration and Naturalization

Felony: An especially serious crime, sometimes defined as a crime for which the punishment is one or more years in jail.

Service regarding any person who is arrested if he or she is suspected of being present in the United States in violation of federal immigration laws.

(b) With respect to any such person who is arrested, and suspected of being present in the United States in violation of federal immigration laws, every law enforcement agency shall do the following:

(1) Attempt to verify the legal status of such person as a citizen of the United States, an alien lawfully admitted as a permanent resident, an alien lawfully admitted for a temporary period of time or as an alien who is present in the United States in violation of immigration laws. The verification process may include, but shall not be limited to, questioning the person regarding his or her date and place of birth, and entry into the United States, and demanding documentation to indicate his or her legal status.

(2) Notify the person of his or her apparent status as an alien who is present in the United States in violation of federal immigration laws and inform him or her that, apart from any criminal justice proceedings, he or she must either obtain legal status or leave the United States.

(3) Notify the Attorney General of California and the United States Immigration and Naturalization Service of the apparent illegal status and provide any additional information that may be requested by any other **public entity.**

(c) Any legislative, administrative, or other action by a city, county, or other legally authorized local governmental entity with **jurisdictional boundaries,** or by a law enforcement agency, to prevent or limit the cooperation required by subdivision (a) is expressly prohibited.

SECTION 5. Exclusion of Illegal Aliens from Public Social Services.

Section 10001.5 is added to the Welfare and Institutions Code, to read:

10001.5. (a) In order to carry out the intention of the People of California that only citizens of the United States and aliens lawfully admitted to the United States may receive the benefits of public social services and to ensure that all persons employed in the providing of those services shall diligently protect public funds from misuse, the provisions of this section are adopted.

(b) A person shall not receive any public social services to which he or she may be otherwise entitled until the legal status of that person has been verified as one of the following:

Public entity: A government institution, such as a city, a school district, or a police force.

Jurisdictional boundaries: The boundaries of a government institution, such as a city, a school district, or a county.

(1) A citizen of the United States.

(2) An alien lawfully admitted as a permanent resident.

(3) An alien lawfully admitted for a temporary period of time.

(c) If any public entity in this state to whom a person has applied for public social services determines or reasonably suspects, based upon the information provided to it, that the person is an alien in the United States in violation of federal law, the following procedures shall be followed by the public entity:

(1) The entity shall not provide the person with benefits or services.

(2) The entity shall, in writing, notify the person of his or her apparent illegal immigration status, and that the person must either obtain legal status or leave the United States.

(3) The entity shall also notify the State Director of Social Services, the Attorney General of California, and the United States Immigration and Naturalization Service of the apparent illegal status, and shall provide any additional information that may be requested by any other public entity.

SECTION 6. Exclusion of Illegal Aliens from Publicly Funded Health Care.

Chapter 1.3 (commencing with Section 130) is added to Part 1 of Division 1 of the Health and Safety Code, to read:

Chapter 1.3. Publicly-Funded Health Care Services

130. (a) In order to carry out the intention of the People of California that, excepting emergency medical care as required by federal law, only citizens of the United States and aliens lawfully admitted to the United States may receive the benefits of publicly-funded health care, and to ensure that all persons employed in the providing of those services shall diligently protect public funds from misuse, the provisions of this section are adopted.

(b) A person shall not receive any health care services from a publicly-funded health care facility, to which he or she is otherwise entitled until the legal status of that person has been verified as one of the following:

(1) A citizen of the United States.

(2) An alien lawfully admitted as a permanent resident.

(3) An alien lawfully admitted for a temporary period of time.

(c) If any publicly-funded health care facility in this state from whom a person seeks health care services, other than emergency medical care as required by federal law, determines or reasonably suspects, based upon the information provided to it, that the person is an alien in the United States in violation of federal law, the following procedures shall be followed by the facility:

(1) The facility shall not provide the person with services.

(2) The facility shall, in writing, notify the person of his or her apparent illegal immigration status, and that the person must either obtain legal status or leave the United States.

(3) The facility shall also notify the State Director of Health Services, the Attorney General of California, and the United States Immigration and Naturalization Service of the apparent illegal status, and shall provide any additional information that may be requested by any other public entity.

(d) For purposes of this section "publicly-funded health care facility" shall be defined as specified in Sections 1200 and 1250 of this code as of January 1, 1993.

SECTION 7. Exclusion of Illegal Aliens from Public Elementary and Secondary Schools.

Section 48215 is added to the Education Code, to read:

48215. (a) No public elementary or secondary school shall admit, or permit the attendance of, any child who is not a citizen of the United States, an alien lawfully admitted as a permanent resident, or a person who is otherwise authorized under federal law to be present in the United States.

(b) Commencing January 1, 1995, each school district shall verify the legal status of each child enrolling in the school district for the first time in order to ensure the enrollment or attendance only of citizens, aliens lawfully admitted as permanent residents, or persons who are otherwise authorized to be present in the United States.

(c) By January 1, 1996, each school district shall have verified the legal status of each child already enrolled and in attendance in the school district in order to ensure the enrollment or attendance only of citizens, aliens lawfully admitted as permanent residents, or persons who are otherwise authorized under federal law to be present in the United States.

(d) By January 1, 1996, each school district shall also have verified the legal status of each parent or guardian of each child re-

Students gather on a San Francisco street to show their opposition to Proposition 187. *Getty Images.*

ferred to in subdivisions (b) and (c), to determine whether such parent or guardian is one of the following:

(1) A citizen of the United States.

(2) An alien lawfully admitted as a permanent resident.

(3) An alien admitted lawfully for a temporary period of time.

(e) Each school district shall provide information to the State Superintendent of Public Instruction, the Attorney General of California, and the United States Immigration and Naturalization Service regarding any enrollee or pupil, or parent or guardian, attending a public elementary or secondary school in the school district determined or reasonably suspected to be in violation of federal immigration laws within forty-five days after becoming aware of an apparent violation. The notice shall also be provided to the parent or legal guardian of the enrollee or pupil, and shall state that an existing pupil may not continue to attend the school after ninety calendar days from the date of the notice, unless legal status is established.

(f) For each child who cannot establish legal status in the United States, each school district shall continue to provide education for a period of ninety days from the date of the notice. Such ninety day period shall be utilized to accomplish an orderly transition to a school in the child's country of origin. Each school district shall fully cooperate in this transition effort to ensure that the educational needs of the child are best served for that period of time.

SECTION 8. Exclusion of Illegal Aliens from Public Postsecondary Educational Institutions.

Section 66010.8 is added to the Education Code, to read:

66010.8. (a) No public institution of **postsecondary education** *shall admit, enroll, or permit the attendance of any person who is not a citizen of the United States, an alien lawfully admitted as a permanent resident in the United States, or a person who is otherwise authorized under federal law to be present in the United States.*

(b) Commencing with the first term or semester that begins after January 1, 1995, and at the commencement of each term or semester thereafter, each public postsecondary educational institution shall verify the status of each person enrolled or in attendance at that institution in order to ensure the enrollment or attendance only of United States citizens, aliens lawfully admitted as permanent residents in the United States, and persons who are otherwise authorized under federal law to be present in the United States.

(c) No later than 45 days after the admissions officer of a public postsecondary educational institution becomes aware of the application, enrollment, or attendance of a person determined to be, or who is under reasonable suspicion of being, in the United States in violation of federal immigration laws, that officer shall provide that information to the State Superintendent of Public Instruction, the Attorney General of California, and the United States Immigration and Naturalization Service. The information shall also be provided to the applicant, enrollee, or person admitted.

SECTION 9. Attorney General Cooperation with the INS.

Section 53069.65 is added to the Government Code, to read:

53069.65. Whenever the state or a city, or a county, or any other legally authorized local governmental entity with jurisdictional boundaries reports the presence of a person who is suspected of being present in the United States in violation of federal immigration laws to the Attorney General of California, that report shall be

Postsecondary education: Schooling for students who have finished high school.

transmitted to the United States Immigration and Naturalization Service. The Attorney General shall be responsible for maintaining on-going and accurate records of such reports, and shall provide any additional information that may be requested by any other government entity.

SECTION 10. Amendment and Severability.

The statutory provisions contained in this measure may not be amended by the Legislature except to further its purposes by statute passed in each house by rollcall vote entered in the journal, two-thirds of the membership concurring, or by a statute that becomes effective only when approved by the voters.

Severable: Capable of being cut off; in the law, if part of a law is declared to violate the Constitution, it can be cut off, or severed, from the rest of the law without affecting the other parts that were not found to be unconstitutional.

*In the event that any portion of this act or the application thereof to any person or circumstance is held invalid, that invalidity shall not affect any other provision or application of the act, which can be given effect without the invalid provision or application, and to that end the provisions of this act are **severable.***

What happened next ...

After a majority of voters approved Proposition 187, opponents went to federal court and asked the judge to block the state from putting the proposition into effect. The judge agreed, and the Supreme Court did not revisit its earlier decision.

In 2000, a pair of social scientists, R. Michael Alvarez (1964–) and Tara L. Butterfield, analyzed voting patterns for Proposition 187 and concluded that the underlying issue was the California economy, rather than racial distaste for Latinos or religious prejudice. Writing in the journal *Social Science Quarterly,* Alvarez and Butterfield wrote: "Voters ... blamed illegal immigrants for the state's poor economic condition.... We found that voters who perceive themselves as threatened financially by illegal immigrants are more likely to support the measure and those voters who are racially similar to the immigrants being attacked oppose the measure more than other racial groups.... Specifically, Hispanics strongly opposed the proposition and blacks supported the proposition."

Alvarez and Butterfield's same analysis concluded that "Governor (Pete) Wilson was reelected during bad economic times by focusing his campaign on illegal immigrants and blaming them for the state's drastic financial situation, shifting the focus of the election away from his failure to improve the state's economy. This ... was an important factor in the passage of Proposition 187."

Citizens walk down a street, in protest of Proposition 187. AP/Wide World Photos.

Did you know ...

- Even as Proposition 187 was addressing the problem of illegal aliens in California, the number of people entering the state from Mexico and Central America was actually in decline. A study by the Policy Institute of California in 1996 showed that as the California economy slowed between 1990 and 1993, part of a nationwide decline in economic activity, the number of illegal immigrants entering California fell from around 200,000 a year in the 1980s to around 125,000 a year, and to under 100,000 in 1992. In effect, the national economy had already accomplished what Proposition 187 set out to do.

For More Information

Books

Chiswick, Barry R. *Illegal Aliens: Their Employment and Employers.* Kalamazoo, MI: W. E. Upjohn Institute for Employment Research, 1988.

Haines, David W., and Karen E. Rosenblum, eds. *Illegal Immigration in America: A Reference Handbook.* Westport, CT: Greenwood Press, 1999.

Long, Robert Emmet, ed. *Immigration.* New York: H. W. Wilson Company, 1996.

Nevins, Joseph. *Operation Gatekeeper: The Rise of the "Illegal Alien" and the Making of the U.S.-Mexico Boundary.* New York: Routledge, 2002.

Periodicals

Alvarez, R. Michael, and Tara L. Butterfield. "The Resurgence of Nativism in California?: The Case of Proposition 187 and Illegal Immigration." *Social Science Quarterly* (March 2000): p. 167.

Martis, Nancy H. "Prop 187: Illegal Aliens. Ineligibility for Public Services." *California Journal* (1994).

Web Sites

"Alien Nation?" *Online Newshour.* March 26, 1996 (transcript). http://www.pbs.org/newshour/bb/congress/immigrant_benefits1_3-26.html (accessed on March 1, 2004).

"Proposition 187: Text of Proposed Law." *Glenn Spencer's American Patrol Report.* http://www.americanpatrol.com/REFERENCE/prop187text.html (accessed on March 3, 2004).

"Study: Illegal Immigration to California Ebbing." *Refuse & Resist!* September 24, 1996. http://www.refuseandresist.org/imm/ebb.html (accessed on March 1, 2004).

Patrick J. Buchanan

Excerpt from **The Death of the West**
Published in 2002

*A conservative talk-show host and former presidential candidate
laments the rise in U.S. immigration*

18

In 2000, Patrick Buchanan (1938–) ran for president of the United States as a candidate of the Reform Party. Buchanan was a well-known political figure, having been a television talk-show personality, a speechwriter for President Richard Nixon (1913-1994; served 1969–74), and a champion for conservative causes. In the election, Buchanan received only 448,895 votes, about 0.42 percent of the total cast. Two years later, he published *The Death of the West: How Dying Populations and Immigrant Invasions Imperil Our Country and Civilization,* a book warning that immigration and low birth rates would result in white people being a minority in the United States, where they once constituted an overwhelming majority. In Buchanan's view, such a development was to be dreaded.

The fears expressed by Buchanan in 2002 were echoes of concerns that first arose about 160 years earlier, in the 1840s, among a political group known as the Know Nothings (see entry). The Know Nothings were so-called because when asked about their political activities, their standard response was, "I know nothing." In the 1840s, the sudden arrival of Catholic immigrants from Ireland and Germany sounded

"Uncontrolled immigration threatens to deconstruct the nation we grew up in and convert America into a conglomeration of peoples with almost nothing in common— not history, heroes, language, culture, faith, or ancestors."

Conservative talk show host and former presidential candidate Pat Buchanan.
© *Wally McNamee/Corbis.*

alarms among Protestant Americans. In California, where Chinese immigrants started arriving during the Gold Rush of 1848, similar concerns were raised about the prospect of massive numbers of Asians overwhelming the "white" population that was pouring into California from the East Coast and from Europe. These concerns led to a complete ban on Chinese immigration, adopted in 1882 under pressure from Californians who did not like competing for jobs with Asians. Later laws limited or barred immigration from other Asian countries, including Japan and Korea.

Concern about the impact of immigrants on U.S. society rose again between 1915 and 1925. Large numbers of poor immigrants from southern Italy and other countries around the Mediterranean, as well as of Jews from eastern Europe, raised concerns about an invasion of darker-skinned foreigners who would change the character of the United States. The result then was the Immigration Act of 1924 (see entry), which effectively shut off the flow of immigrants, especially from southern and eastern Europe.

Concerns about immigrants and the possibility that their arrival would change American society have arisen during periods of rapid economic and social change in the United States, change that was related not just to immigration but also to technology, business, and popular culture. The 1840s, for example, were a period of revived interest in religion, with evangelical Protestant groups holding rallies to stir up religious interest in the population. (Evangelical groups emphasize preaching and spreading a belief in personal salvation through Jesus Christ.) The 1840s were also a time of swift technical change, brought about by the development of railroads and the telegraph, a system to transmit messages instantly over long distances by means of coded signals transmitted by electric wire. Continuing industrialization (the building of factories to produce goods that previously had been made by hand) and mechanization of farming (the development of new machines to help plow fields and harvest crops) played a part as well. The sudden arrival of large numbers of immigrants from Ireland (where a massive failure of the potato crop resulted in widespread starvation) and Germany (where crop failures, plus social and political unrest, caused many to leave for a more peaceful, prosperous America) did, in fact, bring about social changes in the United States. Up to this time, the United States had been a country comprised predominantly of people with English, Protestant ancestors and of black slaves who traced their ancestors to Africa.

In the period from about 1890 to 1920, a large wave of immigrants started arriving from southern and eastern Europe, bringing the first large numbers of Jews from Russia and Catholic Italians. The Ku Klux Klan, a secret society that originated after the American Civil War (1861–65) in opposition to political power for freed slaves, was revived in Georgia as a means of protesting against the new wave of immigrants. In 1924, the United States adopted a new immigration law that limited the number of immigrants from any one country to a number that reflected the portion of the U.S. population that had come from that country and were living in the United States in 1890 (see entry). The purpose was to reduce the number of immigrants from countries not well represented before the major wave of immigration that had begun in 1880. (Chinese and Asian immigrants continued to be entirely excluded until 1944.)

In 1965, the United States changed its immigration policy again, and for the first time since 1882 allowed significant numbers of Asians to enter the United States and to become citizens after five years. In 1965, the United States was fighting a war in Vietnam (1954–75) against communist Vietnamese. Because of the war, the United States desired closer ties with Japan and other Asian countries. At a time when the U.S. government was wooing these countries as allies, immigration laws that had obviously discriminated against Asians made it more difficult to gain influence among them.

In addition to the 1965 immigration laws, which greatly expanded the number of immigrants from Asia, during the last two decades of the twentieth century a significant number of workers from Mexico and countries of Central America entered the United States without official permission. These so-called illegal immigrants often took jobs working in agriculture or other low-paid positions.

As a result of changes in U.S. law plus an increase in the flow of illegal immigrants, the portion of the American population represented by immigrants rose to around 11 percent of the population. For Buchanan, this was a cause for alarm, because, as he said in his book, Americans could not be sure whether the newcomers would be loyal to the United States or to the country from which they came.

During the period after 1945, Buchanan also notes, the number of immigrants moving to western Europe has also increased dramatically, especially the number of Muslim immigrants from North Africa and countries of the Middle East. (Muslims are believers in Islam, a religion based on the teachings of the Prophet Muhammad [c. 570–632], as recorded in Islam's holy book, the Koran.) The so-called white population of western Europe had begun to decline as a result of a falling birth rate, or the average number of babies born by women, in many European states. If, on average, women have fewer than two babies each, eventually the total population will decline. (Actually, to maintain the size of a population, women need to have slightly more than two babies, on average, to account for early deaths of people from accidents, disease, or war.) Buchanan expresses concern in his book that the predominant "white" Christian culture of western Europe will be overwhelmed by Islamic immigrants in the next few decades. It is this concern that led to the title of his book, *The Death of the West*.

Things to remember while reading an excerpt from *The Death of the West:*

- Although Buchanan says the inflow of immigrants to the United States is unprecedented, in fact the percentage of Americans who were immigrants was greater between 1870 and 1920 than it was in 2000 (about 13 percent then versus about 11 percent now). Many previous alarms have been raised about the changing nature of the United States. The country's population did change from a predominantly English Protestant base and African slaves to a much more diverse population in 2000. Whether this change is a bad thing depends largely on one's level of comfort with such diversity.

- The United States needs the inflow of immigrants in order to fill jobs that many native-born Americans are unwilling to do. These jobs are often low-paying—in agriculture and in service industries, like restaurants and hotels, for example—that would go unfilled if it were not for immigrants, both legal and illegal.

- In his book, Buchanan often stirs together dissimilar facts and statistics. For example, he writes about a threat to Christianity posed by immigrants, even though in the United States (unlike Europe) many immigrants from Mexico and Central America are Catholics, a Christian religion. Buchanan also writes at length about cultural changes in the United States that started in the 1960s—including different attitudes about sex and nationalism—that had little or nothing to do with immigration. In fact, many immigrants are much more conservative in their social attitudes than many native-born Americans.

Excerpt from The Death of the West

"Pat, we're losing the country we grew up in."

*Again and again in the endless campaign of 2000 I heard that **lament** from men and women across America. But what did they mean by it?*

*Why should sadness or **melancholy**—as though one's father were dying and there were nothing to be done—have crept into the hearts of Americans on the **cusp** of the "Second American Century"? Were these not, as Mr. Clinton [U.S. president Bill Clinton] constantly reminded us, the best of times in America, with the lowest unemployment and **inflation** in thirty years, crime rates falling, and incomes soaring? Are we not, as [U.S. secretary of state] Madeleine Albright never ceased to boast, "the **indispensable** nation"? Was this not, as Mr. Bush [U.S. president George W. Bush] trumpeted,*

Lament: Expression of sorrow.

Melancholy: Sadness.

Cusp: Verge.

Inflation: A general rise in prices.

Indispensable: Necessary.

our time "of unrivaled military power, economic promise, and cultural influence"? We had won the **Cold War.** Our ideas were winning all over the world. What were they talking about? What was their problem?

It is this: America has undergone a cultural and social revolution. We are not the same country that we were in 1970 or even 1980.

We are not the same people. After the 2000 election, pollster William McInturf told the Washington Post: "We have two massive colliding forces. One is rural, Christian, religiously conservative. [The other] is socially tolerant, **pro-choice, secular,** living in New England and the Pacific Coast...."

[British prime minister Benjamin] Disraeli said Victorian England was "two nations," rich and poor. Novelist John Dos Passos wrote after the trial and execution of **Sacco and Vanzetti,** "All right, we are two nations." As I listened to the Inaugural address, a line struck home. President [George W.] Bush seemed to have heard what I had heard and found what I had found. "And sometimes," he said, "our differences run so deep, it seems we share a continent, but not a country."

While the awful events of **September 11** created a national unity unseen since **Pearl Harbor**—behind President Bush and his resolve to punish the **perpetrators** of the massacres of 5,000 Americans—they also exposed a new divide. This **chasm** in our country is not one of income, ideology, or faith, but of ethnicity and loyalty. Suddenly, we awoke to the realization that among our millions of foreign-born, a third are here illegally, tens of thousands are loyal to regimes with which we could be at war, and some are trained terrorists sent here to murder Americans. For the first time since [U.S. general and future president] Andrew Jackson drove the British out of Louisiana in 1815, a foreign enemy is inside the gates, and the American people are at risk in their own country. In those days after September 11, many suddenly saw how the face of America had changed in their own lifetimes.

When [President] Richard Nixon took his oath of office in 1969, there were 9 million foreign-born in the United States. When President [George W.] Bush raised his hand [took office], the number was nearing 30 million. Almost a million immigrants enter every year; half a million illegal aliens come in with them. The adjusted census of 2000 puts the number of illegals in the United States at 9 million. Northeastern University estimates 11 million, as many illegal aliens as there are people in Alabama, Mississippi, and

Louisiana. There are more foreign-born in California—8.4 million—than people in New Jersey, more foreign-born in New York State than people in South Carolina. Even the Great Wave of immigration from 1890 to 1920 was nothing like this.

*"America is God's **Crucible**, the great Melting-Pot where all the races of Europe are melting and reforming," wrote Israel Zangwill, the Russian-Jewish playwright, in his famous 1908 play* The Melting Pot. *But the immigration **tsunami** rolling over America is not coming from "all the races of Europe." The largest population transfer in history is coming from all the races of Asia, Africa, and Latin America, and they are not "melting and reforming."*

*In 1960, only sixteen million Americans did not trace their ancestors to Europe. Today, the number is eighty million. No nation has ever undergone so rapid and radical a transformation. At Portland State [College] in 1998, Mr. Clinton **rhapsodized** to a cheering student audience about a day when Americans of European descent will be a minority: "Today, largely because of immigration, there is no majority race in Hawaii or Houston or New York City. Within five years there will be no majority race in our largest state, California. In a little more than fifty years there will be no majority race in the United States. No other nation in history has gone through demographic change of this magnitude in so short a time."*

*Correction: no nation in history has gone through a demographic change of this magnitude in so short a time, and remained the same nation. Mr. Clinton assured us that it will be a better America when we are all minorities and realize true "diversity." Well, those students are going to find out, for they will spend their **golden years** in a Third World America.*

*Uncontrolled immigration threatens to **deconstruct** the nation we grew up in and convert America into a **conglomeration** of peoples with almost nothing in common—not history, heroes, language, culture, faith, or ancestors. **Balkanization** beckons. "The strongest tendency of the late [twentieth century]," writes Jacques Barzun in his history of the West,* From Dawn to Decadence, *"was **Separatism**.... It affected all forms of unity.... The ideal of **Pluralism** had disintegrated and Separatism took its place; as one partisan of the new goal put it, 'Salad Bowl is better than melting pot.'" The great nations of Europe have begun to break apart. Writes Barzun:*

*"If one surveyed the **Occident** ... one could see that the greatest political creation of the West, the nation-state, was stricken. In*

Crucible: A place or situation in which concentrated forces interact to cause or influence change or development.

Tsunami: A destructive wave caused by an earthquake or a volcano in the ocean.

Rhapsodized: Spoke emotionally.

Golden years: Retirement.

Deconstruct: Break into parts.

Conglomeration: Mixture of unlike parts.

Balkanization: The process of dividing a region or group of people into smaller, quarrelsome units; the name comes from the numerous countries in the Balkan Peninsula.

Separatism: A movement in favor of separation.

Pluralism: A state of society in which people of diverse groups participate in their traditional culture within a common environment.

Occident: The West, as in Europe and the United States, versus the East, as in Asia.

Autonomous: Self-contained.

Bretons, Basques, and Alsatians: People of the regions of Brittany, the western Pyrenées, and Alsace.

Corsica: French island in the Mediterranean Sea.

Transnational elites: Persons and corporations whose power goes beyond national boundaries and interests.

Maastricht: A city in the Netherlands; site of the Maastricht Treaty (1992), which led to the creation of the European Union.

Free-trade zone: A region in which governments set up special arrangements concerning taxes on imports and exports.

Socialist superstate: A country comprised of several smaller ones governed under the principles of socialism, a political philosophy that accepts democratic control over economic affairs.

Visionary: Someone with imagination and creativity.

Interdependent: Dependent on one another.

Elite: Group who uses position or education to yield power or influence.

Recoil: Move back.

Saturated: Filled to capacity.

Hedonistic: Sensuous.

Great Britain the former kingdoms of Scotland and Wales won **autonomous** parliaments; in France the **Bretons, Basques, and Alsatians** cried out for regional power. **Corsica** wanted independence and a language of its own, Italy harbored a League that would cut off the North from the South, and Venice produced a small party wanting their city a separate state.... "

As people return their allegiance to the lands whence they came, **transnational elites** pull us in the opposite direction. The final surrender of national sovereignty to world government is now openly advocated. From [retired CBS news anchor] Walter Cronkite to [American journalist and diplomat] Strobe Talbott, from the World Federalist Association to the UN Millennium Summit, the chorus swells.

At **Maastricht** in 1991, fifteen European nations, including France, Italy, Germany, and Great Britain, decided to begin converting their **free-trade zone** into a political union and transferring their sovereign powers to a **socialist superstate.** In 2000, the president-elect of Mexico [Vicente Fox] came here to propose a North American Union of Canada, Mexico, and the United States. Though the erasure of our borders would mean the end of our nation, Vicente Fox was hailed in the U.S. media as a **visionary,** and President Clinton expressed his regret that he might not be around to see it happen: "I think over the long run, our countries will become more **interdependent** .... It will be the way of the world.... I regret that I won't be around for a lot of it. But I think it's a good thing."

Nor is America immune to the forces of separatism. A sense that America, too, is pulling apart along the seams of ethnicity and race is spreading. Moreover, America has just undergone a cultural revolution, with a new **elite** now occupying the commanding heights. Through its capture of the institutions that shape and transmit ideas, opinions, beliefs, and values—TV, the arts, entertainment, education—this elite is creating a new people. Not only ethnically and racially, but culturally and morally, we are no longer one people or "one nation under God."

Millions have begun to feel like strangers in their own land. They **recoil** from a popular culture that is **saturated** with raw sex and trumpets **hedonistic** values. They see old holidays disappear and old heroes degraded. They see the art and artifacts of a glorious past removed from their museums and replaced by the depressing, the ugly, the abstract, the anti-American. They watch as books

they cherished disappear from the schools they attended, to be re-
placed by authors and titles they never heard of. The moral code
that they were raised to live by has been overthrown. The culture
they grew up with is dying inside the country they grew up in.

In half a lifetime, many Americans have seen their God de-
*throned, their heroes **defiled**, their culture polluted, their values as-*
*saulted, their country invaded, and themselves **demonized** as ex-*
*tremists and **bigots** for holding on to beliefs Americans have held for*
generations. "To make us love our country, our country ought to be
lovely," said [British writer and statesman Edmund] Burke. In too
many ways America is no longer lovely. Though she remains a great
country, many wonder if she is still a good country. Some feel that
she is no longer their country. We did not leave America, they say,
she left us. As [Greek tragic dramatist] Euripides wrote, "There is no
greater sorrow on earth, than the loss of one's native land."

When [British general and statesman Charles] Cornwallis's
army marched out of Yorktown, the fife and drums played "The
World Turned Upside Down." Now our world has been turned up-
side down. What was right and true yesterday is wrong and false
*today. What was immoral and shameful—**promiscuity**, abortion,*
***euthanasia**, suicide—has become progressive and praiseworthy.*
[German philosopher Friedrich] Nietzsche called it the transvalua-
*tion of all values; the old **virtues** become sins, and the old sins be-*
come virtues.

Every few years, a storm erupts when some public figure blurts
out, "America is a Christian nation!" She was once, and a majority
yet call themselves Christians. But our dominant culture should
more accurately be called post-Christian, or anti-Christian, for the
*values it celebrates are the **antithesis** of what it used to mean to be*
a Christian.

"I am the Lord thy God; thou shalt not have strange gods be-
fore me" was the first commandment Moses brought down from
Mount Sinai. But the new culture rejects the God of the Old Testa-
ment and burns its incense at the altars of the global economy.
[British author Rudyard] Kipling's "Gods of the Market Place" have
shouldered aside the God of the Gospels. Sex, fame, money,
power—those are what our new America is all about.

We are two countries, two peoples. An older America is passing
away, and a new America is coming into its own. The new Ameri-
cans who grew up in the 1960s and the years since did not like the

Defiled: Tainted.

Demonized: Cast in the role of a devil.

Bigots: People who are utterly intolerant of any differing creed, belief, or opinion.

Promiscuity: The practice of engaging in sexual relations with a number of partners.

Euthanasia: Mercy killing, as is sometimes practiced on one who is hopelessly sick or injured.

Virtues: Moral purities.

Antithesis: Opposite.

Reactionary: Opposing political or social change.

Repressive: Restraining.

Stodgy: Old-fashioned.

Acolytes: Trainees.

Cultural revolution: The radical social and cultural changes of the 1960s.

Cultural wasteland: A place or a time in history that is intellectually empty.

Moral sewer: Place or situation in which moral standards are judged as extremely low.

Beltway parties: The Beltway is a highway surrounding Washington, D.C.; used to symbolize the activities of political parties.

Bile: Anger.

Florida recount: A reference to the 2000 presidential election in which problems with votes in several Florida counties led to a recount in that state, delaying the final results of the election.

Polarized: Divided into opposites.

Rancorous: Marked by deep-seated ill will.

Desert Storm: The U.S. military operation in 1991 that evicted Iraqi forces from Kuwait.

Fort Sumter: Site of the start of the Civil War.

Seceding: Separating.

*old America. They thought it a bigoted, **reactionary**, **repressive**, **stodgy** country. So they kicked the dust from their heels and set out to build a new America, and they have succeeded. To its **acolytes** the **cultural revolution** has been a glorious revolution. But to millions, they have replaced the good country we grew up in with a **cultural wasteland** and a **moral sewer** that are not worth living in and not worth fighting for—their country, not ours.*

*In the election of 2000, the political differences between the **Beltway parties** were inconsequential. Mr. Bush wanted a larger tax cut than Mr. Gore [Vice President and Democratic presidential nominee Al Gore] who wanted to spend more for prescription drugs. Why then the **bile** and bitterness of the **Florida recount**? Writes Terry Teachout in his postelection assessment of a **polarized** America, "the **rancorous** intensity with which the Bush and Gore camps disputed the outcome of the 2000 election all too clearly reflected the magnitude of their culture differences, and it may be that the tone of that dispute will characterize American politics for the foreseeable future."*

Exactly. The savagery of our politics reflects the depth of the moral divide that separates us as Americans. A hundred times in the campaign of 2000, a voter would come up and say that he or she believed in me and agreed with me, but could not vote for me. These people had to vote for Bush, because only Bush could keep Gore out of the White House, and, "We must stop Gore!" It was not that they disagreed with Clinton and Gore. They detested them. The cultural revolution has poisoned American politics, and we have not begun to see the worst of it.

*In the hours after that awful morning of September 11, Americans did come together again—in grief and sorrow over our terrible losses, in admiration and awe of the heroic firemen who ran into the World Trade Center as others ran out to safety, in our rage and resolution to do justice to those who did this to our countrymen. But by October, that unity had begun to fade. It will not long survive our first victories in the war on terror, anymore than the first President Bush's 90-percent support survived his victory in **Desert Storm**. For our divisions are rooted in our deepest beliefs, and upon those beliefs Americans are almost as divided as we were when [Confederate general Pierre] Beauregard gave the order to fire on **Fort Sumter**.*

*Once again, we are **seceding** from one another; only this time, it is a secession of the heart.*

In one of the more controversial addresses of the twentieth century, I told the 1992 Republican National Convention at Houston: "My friends, this election is about more than who gets what. It is about who we are. It is about what we believe, it is about what we stand for as Americans. There is a religious war going on in our country for the soul of America. It is a cultural war, as critical to the kind of nation we shall one day be as was the Cold War itself. And in that struggle for the soul of America, Clinton and Clinton are on the other side, and George Bush is on our side. And, so, we have to come home—and stand beside him."

The words ignited a firestorm that blazed on through 1992 and has not yet burnt itself out. My words were called divisive and hateful. They were not. They were divisive and truthful. Let others judge, after eight years, whether I spoke the truth about Bill and [then–first lady and future U.S. senator] Hillary Clinton.

But Mr. Clinton was rescued from certain **impeachment** because he personified the other side of that culture war, and his removal [from office] would have **imperiled** the gains of a decade. That not a single Democrat voted to convict Mr. Clinton testifies to the success of the revolution in overthrowing the old moral order and its objective standards of truth, morality, and justice. To the new elite, what advances the revolution is moral, and what threatens it is immoral. Between Senate Democrats and the [retired football player and accused murderer] O. J. [Simpson trial] jury there is a moral equivalence: truth, justice, and morality triumphed in both cases, because our side won and our man got off.

The **Bolshevik Revolution** that began with the storming of the Winter Palace [in St. Petersburg, Russia] in 1917 died with the fall of the **Berlin Wall** in 1989. The dream of its true believers was to create a new socialist man. But police terror, the camps of the **Gulag**, and seventy years of **indoctrinating** children in hatred of the West and the moral superiority of [German philosopher and founder of Marxism Karl] Marx and [Russian revolutionary leader and Soviet premier Vladimir] Lenin did not work. Communism was The God That Failed. When the mighty structure built on a foundation of lies came crashing down, the peoples of Eastern Europe and Russia threw the statues of [Russian leaders Joseph] Stalin and Lenin and the books of Marx and [German socialist Friedrich] Engels onto the landfill of history without looking back.

But where Lenin's revolution failed, the one that erupted on the campuses in the sixties succeeded. It put down roots in society, and

Impeachment: A legislative proceeding formally accusing a public official with misconduct, followed by a trial; in fact, Clinton *was* impeached.

Imperiled: Put at risk.

Bolshevik Revolution: The November 1917 revolution that replaced the king of Russia with a government led by communists.

Berlin Wall: A wall dividing the Soviet-controlled sector of Berlin, Germany, from the three Western-controlled zones, built in an attempt to stem the tide of refugees seeking asylum in the West.

Gulag: A string of prison camps in the former Soviet Union where political enemies were imprisoned.

Indoctrinating: Teaching.

it created a new America. By 2000, the **adversary** culture of the sixties had become our dominant culture, its victory conceded when the political base camp of traditionalism raised a white flag in Philadelphia. On the moral and social issues—the fight for the sanctity of human life and the return of God to the public square of this land we used to call "God's Country"—the Republican party raised its gloves and pleaded, "**No más.**"

In The Death of the West I hope to describe this revolution— what it stands for, where it came from, how it went about dethroning our God, vandalizing our temples, altering our beliefs, and capturing the young, and what its triumph **portends.** For this revolution is not unique to us; it has captured all the nations of the West. A civilization, a culture, a faith, and a moral order rooted in that faith are passing away and are being replaced by a new civilization, culture, faith, and moral order.

But the title of this book is The Death of the West. And though our culture war has divided us, and mass immigration risks the balkanization of America, a graver, more immediate, crisis is at hand.

The West is dying. Its nations have ceased to reproduce, and their populations have stopped growing and begun to shrink. Not since the **Black Death** carried off a third of Europe in the fourteenth century has there been a graver threat to the survival of Western civilization. Today, in seventeen European countries, there are more burials than births, more coffins than cradles. The countries are Belgium, Bulgaria, Croatia, the Czech Republic, Denmark, Estonia, Germany, Hungary, Italy, Latvia, Lithuania, Portugal, Romania, Slovakia, Slovenia, Spain, and Russia. Catholic, Protestant, Orthodox—all the Christian faiths are represented in the great death march of the West.

The new **hedonism** seems unable to give people a reason to go on living. Its earliest fruits appear to be poisonous. Will this new "liberating" culture that our young have so enthusiastically embraced prove the deadliest **carcinogen** of them all? And if the West is in the grip of a "culture of death," as the pope contends and the statistics seem to show, is Western civilization about to follow **Lenin's empire** to the same inglorious end?

A century ago, [French psychologist and sociologist] Gustave Le Bon wrote in his classic The Crowd: "The real cause of the great upheavals which precede changes of civilizations, such as the fall of the **Roman Empire** and the rise of the **Arabian Empire,** is a profound modification in the ideas of the peoples.... The memorable events of history

Adversary: Competitor.

"No más:": Spanish for "no more."

Portends: Indicates for the future.

Black Death: Bubonic plague, a contagious, deadly disease that caused widespread deaths in Europe in the fourteenth century.

Hedonism: The pursuit of pleasure.

Carcinogen: A substance that causes cancer.

Lenin's empire: The Soviet Union, whose founder was Vladimir Lenin.

Roman Empire: The lands and peoples governed by ancient Rome from 27 B.C.E. to 476 C.E.

Arabian Empire: Land occupied in North Africa and the Middle East by Arab peoples in the sixth and seventh centuries C.E., spreading Arab language, knowledge and culture into Europe by the ninth to eleventh centuries.

*are the visible effects of the invisible changes of human thought.… The present **epoch** is one of these critical moments in which the thought of mankind is undergoing a process of transformation."*

Le Bon was speaking of his own time, the end of the nineteenth century, but what he wrote is truer of ours.

*For it is this cultural revolution that has led to just such a "profound modification in the ideas" of peoples. And those ideas have made Western elites apparently indifferent to the death of their civilization. They do not seem to care if the end of the West comes by depopulation, by a surrender of nationhood, or by drowning in waves of Third World immigration. Now that all the Western empires are gone, Western Man, relieved of his duty to civilize and Christianize mankind, reveling in luxury in our age of self-indulgence seems to have lost his will to live and **reconciled** himself to his impending death. Are we in the twilight of the West? Is the Death of the West irreversible? Let us review the pathologist's report.*

Epoch: Era.

Reconciled: Resigned.

What happened next …

Buchanan's book quickly became a best-seller, an indication, perhaps, that he had touched on concerns held by many Americans. In the months following the September 11, 2001, terrorist attacks on the World Trade Center buildings in New York and on the military headquarters in the Pentagon in Washington, D.C., the federal government adopted rules intended to keep closer track of immigrants or visitors from predominantly Muslim nations in the Middle East.

In the wake of the tragic events of September 11, 2001, President Bush quietly stopped pressing for reforms in U.S. immigration law that might affect people from Mexico who wanted to work in the United States, even if they did not plan on immigrating permanently.

Some of the trends that Buchanan mentioned, such as low birthrates, were not things that could be quickly changed. There was no evidence in the first months after Buchanan's book was published that Europeans in particular decided to have more babies in order to counter the population trends

A border patrol worker fingerprints an illegal immigrant. *Library of Congress.*

that Buchanan warned about. Nor did the United States imme-diately adopt drastic measures to make sure that immigrants without visas could not cross the borders separating the United States from Mexico and Canada. The threat of terrorists attacks did result in a higher sense of concern about the possibility that terrorists could enter the United States, and entering the United States became generally more difficult. Immigrants (including temporary visitors, such as students, from foreign countries) came under closer scrutiny for fear they could be terrorists posing as something more innocent.

Did you know ...

- In 1856, another presidential candidate also ran on a platform that objected to immigration. He was former U.S. president Millard Fillmore (1800–1874; served 1850–53), who had previously filled out the term of President Zachary Taylor (1784–1850; served 1849–50), who died in office. Fillmore, denied the nomination of his own Whig Party, ran as the candidate of the American Party, which represented the Know-Nothing movement. Fillmore fared better in his run for the White House than did Buchanan—Fillmore won 21.5 percent of the popular vote, compared to Buchanan's 0.42 percent—but won only one state, Maryland, for a total of eight electoral votes. Like Buchanan, Fillmore had run during a time when immigration threatened to change the nature of the population as a result of a large number of Catholic Irish and German immigrants. The Know-Nothing movement largely faded after 1856, although some of its positions were later adopted by the new Republican Party.

For More Information

Books

Buchanan, Patrick J. *The Death of the West: How Dying Populations and Immigrant Invasions Imperil Our Country and Civilization.* New York: St. Martin's Press, 2002.

Periodicals

Jacoby, Tamar. "Too Many Immigrants?" *Commentary* (April 2002): p. 37.

Klinkner, Philip A. "The Base Camp of Christendom." *The Nation* (March 11, 2002): p. 25.

McNicoll, Geoffrey. "The Death of the West: How Dying Populations and Immigrant Invasions Imperil Our Country and Civilization" (book review). *Population and Development Review* (December 2002): p. 797.

Web Sites

The Official Pat Buchanan for President 2000 Archive. http://www.buchanan.org/ (accessed on March 1, 2004).

Where to Learn More

Books

Adovasio, J. M., with Jake Page. *The First Americans: In Pursuit of Archaeology's Greatest Mystery.* New York: Random House, 2002.

Barrett, Tracy. *Growing Up in Colonial America.* Brookfield, CT: Millbrook Press, 1995.

Brogan, Hugh. *The Longman History of the United States of America.* 2nd ed. London and New York: Addison Wesley Longman, 1999.

Ciongoli, A. Kenneth, and Jay Parini. *Passage to Liberty: The Story of Italian Immigration and the Rebirth of America.* New York: Regan Books, 2002.

Clark, Jayne. *The Greeks in America.* Minneapolis: Lerner Publications, 1990.

Daley, William W. *The Chinese Americans.* New York: Chelsea House, 1996.

Daniels, Roger. *Coming to America: A History of Immigration and Ethnicity in American Life.* New York: HarperCollins, 1990.

Davis, William C. *The American Frontier: Pioneers, Settlers, and Cowboys, 1800–1899.* New York: Smithmark, 1992.

Dezell, Maureen. *Irish America: Coming into Clover.* New York: Doubleday, 2000.

Dolan, Sean. *The Polish Americans.* New York: Chelsea House, 1997.

Dubofsky, Melvyn. *Industrialism and the American Worker, 1865–1920.* 3rd ed. Wheeling, IL: Harlan Davidson, 1996.

Fagan, Brian M. *Kingdoms of Gold, Kingdoms of Jade: The Americas Before Columbus.* London: Thames and Hudson, 1991.

Ferry, Steve. *Russian Americans.* Tarrytown, NY: Benchmark Books, 1996.

Fitzhugh, William W. "Puffins, Ringed Pins, and Runestones: The Viking Passage to America." In *Vikings: The North Atlantic Saga.* Edited by William W. Fitzhugh and Elisabeth I. Ward. Washington and London: Smithsonian Institution Press in association with National Museum of Natural History, 2000.

Fixico, Donald L. *Termination and Relocation: Federal Indian Policy, 1945–1966.* Albuquerque: University of New Mexico Press, 1986.

Freedman, Russell. *In the Days of the Vaqueros: The First True Cowboys.* New York: Clarion Books, 2001.

Frost, Helen. *German Immigrants, 1820–1920.* Mankato, MN: Blue Earth Books, 2002.

Gernand, Renée. *The Cuban Americans.* New York: Chelsea House, 1996.

Gonzalez, Juan. *Harvest of Empire: A History of Latinos in America.* New York: Viking, 2000.

Grossman, James R. *Land of Hope: Chicago, Black Southerners, and the Great Migration.* Chicago: University of Chicago Press, 1989.

Hawke, David Freeman. *Everyday Life in Early America.* New York: Harper & Row, 1988.

Hertzberg, Arthur. *The Jews in America: Four Centuries of an Uneasy Encounter.* New York: Simon and Schuster, 1989.

Hoobler, Dorothy, and Thomas Hoobler. *The Chinese American Family Album.* New York: Oxford University Press, 1994.

Hoobler, Dorothy, and Thomas Hoobler. *The German American Family Album.* New York and Oxford: Oxford University Press, 1996.

Hoobler, Dorothy, and Thomas Hoobler. *The Scandinavian American Family Album.* New York and Oxford: Oxford University Press, 1997.

Howe, Irving. *World of Our Fathers: The Journey of the East European Jews to America and the Life They Found and Made.* New York: Simon and Schuster, 1976.

The Irish in America. Coffey, Michael, ed., with text by Terry Golway. New York: Hyperion, 1997.

Jackson, Robert H., and Edward Castillo. *Indians, Franciscans, and Spanish Colonization: The Impact of the Mission System on California Indians.* Albuquerque: University of New Mexico Press, 1995.

Johnson, Paul. *A History of the Jews.* New York: Harper & Row, 1987.

Kitano, Harry. *The Japanese Americans.* New York: Chelsea House, 1996.

Kitano, Harry H. L., and Roger Daniels. *Asian Americans: Emerging Minorities.* Englewood Cliffs, NJ: Prentice Hall, 1995.

Kraut, Alan M. *The Immigrant in American Society, 1880–1921.* 2nd ed. Wheeling, IL: Harlan Davidson, 2001.

Lavender, David Sievert. *The Rockies*. Rev. ed. New York: HarperCollins, 1975.

Lee, Lauren. *Japanese Americans*. Tarrytown, NY: Marshall Cavendish, 1996.

Lehrer, Brian. *The Korean Americans*. New York: Chelsea House, 1996.

Loewen, James W. *Lies My Teacher Told Me: Everything Your American History Textbook Got Wrong*. New York: Touchstone Books, 1996.

Magocsi, Paul R. *The Russian Americans*. New York: Chelsea House, 1996.

McLynn, Frank. *Wagons West: The Epic Story of America's Overland Trails*. New York: Grove Press, 2002.

Middleton, Richard. *Colonial America: A History, 1565–1776*. 3rd ed. Oxford, UK: Blackwell, 2002.

Monos, Dimitris. *The Greek Americans*. New York: Chelsea House, 1996.

Nabokov, Peter, ed. *Native American Testimony*. New York: Thomas Crowell, 1978.

Odess, Daniel, Stephen Loring, and William W. Fitzhugh. "Skraeling: First Peoples of Helluland, Markland, and Vinland." In *Vikings: The North Atlantic Saga*. Edited by William W. Fitzhugh and Elisabeth I. Ward. Washington and London: Smithsonian Institution Press in association with National Museum of Natural History, 2000.

Olson, Kay Melchisedech. *Norwegian, Swedish, and Danish Immigrants, 1820–1920*. Mankato, MN: Blue Earth Books, 2002.

Palmer, Colin A. *The First Passage: Blacks in the Americas, 1502–1617*. New York: Oxford University Press, 1995.

Petrini, Catherine. *The Italian Americans*. San Diego: Lucent Books, 2002.

Phillips, David, and Steven Ferry. *Greek Americans*. Tarrytown, NY: Benchmark Books, 1996.

Piersen, William D. *From Africa to America: African American History from the Colonial Era to the Early Republic, 1526–1790*. New York: Twayne, 1996.

Pitt, Leonard. *The Decline of the Californios: A Social History of the Spanish-Speaking Californians, 1846–1890*. Berkeley: University of California Press, 1966.

Portes, Alejandro, and Rubén G. Rumbaut. *Immigrant America: A Portrait*. 2nd ed. Berkeley: University of California Press, 1996.

Press, Petra. *Puerto Ricans*. Tarrytown, NY: Benchmark Books, 1996.

Schmidley, A. Dianne. *U.S. Census Bureau, Current Population Reports, Series P23-206, "Profile of the Foreign-Born Population in the United States": 2000*. Washington, DC: U.S. Government Printing Office, 2001.

Scott, John Anthony. *Settlers on the Eastern Shore: The British Colonies in North America, 1607–1750*. New York: Facts on File, 1991.

Shannon, William. *The American Irish*. Amherst: University of Massachusetts Press, 1990.

Stegner, Page. *Winning the Wild West: The Epic Saga of the American Frontier, 1800–1899.* New York: The Free Press, 2002.

Suro, Roberto. *Strangers Among Us: How Latino Immigration Is Transforming America.* New York: Knopf, 1998.

Takaki, Ronald. *Strangers from a Different Shore: A History of Asian Americans.* Boston: Little, Brown, and Company, 1989.

Tonelli, Bill, ed. *The Italian American Reader: A Collection of Outstanding Fiction, Memoirs, Journalism, Essays, and Poetry.* New York: William Morrow, 2003.

Wepman, Dennis. *Immigration: From the Founding of Virginia to the Closing of Ellis Island.* New York: Facts on File, 2002.

Williams, Jean Kinney. *The Mormons: The American Religious Experience.* New York: Franklin Watts, 1996.

Wood, Peter H. *Strange New Land: African Americans, 1617–1776.* New York: Oxford University Press, 1996.

Periodicals

Hogan, Roseann Reinemuth. "Examining the Transatlantic Voyage." Parts I and II. *Ancestry Magazine* (Part 1: November/December 2000): vol. 18, no. 6; (Part II: March/April 2001): vol. 19, no. 2. These articles can be found online at http://www.ancestry.com/library/view/ancmag/3365.asp and http://www.ancestry.com/library/view/ancmag/4130.asp (accessed on April 1, 2004).

Peck, Ira. "How Three Groups Overcame Prejudice." *Scholastic Update* (May 6, 1998): vol. 6, no. 17, p. 12.

Rose, Jonathan. "Organized Crime: An 'Equal-Opportunity' Employer; Every American Ethnic Group Has Had Its Fingers in Organized Crime—a Fact That the Dominance of Italian-American Crime Rings Tends to Mask." *Scholastic Update* (March 21, 1986): vol. 118, p. 12.

Web Sites

"About Jewish Culture." *MyJewishLearning.com.* http://www.myjewishlearning.com/culture/AboutJewishCulture.htm (accessed on April 1, 2004).

"Africa: One Continent, Many Worlds." *Natural History Museum of Los Angeles.* http://www.nhm.org/africa/facts/ (accessed on April 1, 2004).

"The American Presidency State of the Union Messages." *The American Presidency.* http://www.polsci.ucsb.edu/projects/presproject/idgrant/site/state.html (accessed on April 1, 2004).

"American West: Transportation." *World-Wide Web Virtual Library's History Index.* http://www.ku.edu/kansas/west/trans.htm (accessed on April 1, 2004).

"Austrian-Hungarian Immigrants." *Spartacus Educational.* http://www.spartacus.schoolnet.co.uk/USAEah.htm (accessed on April 1, 2004).

Bernard, Kara Tobin, and Shane K. Bernard. *Encyclopedia of Cajun Culture.* http://www.cajunculture.com/ (accessed on April 1, 2004).

"A Brief History of Indian Migration to America." *American Immigration Law Foundation.* http://www.ailf.org/awards/ahp_0203_essay.htm (accessed on April 1, 2004).

Chinese American Data Center. http://members.aol.com/chineseusa/00cen.htm (accessed on April 1, 2004).

"Coming to America Two Years after 9-11." *Migration Policy Institute.* http://www.ilw.com/lawyers/immigdaily/letters/2003,0911-mpi.pdf (accessed on April 1, 2004).

"French Colonization of Louisiana and Louisiana Purchase Map Collection." *Louisiana Digital Library.* http://louisdl.louislibraries.org/LMP/Pages/home.html (accessed on April 1, 2004).

Guzmán, Betsy. "The Hispanic Population: Census 2000 Brief." *U.S. Census Bureau, May 2001.* http://www.census.gov/prod/2001pubs/c2kbr01-3.pdf (accessed on April 1, 2004).

"Haitians in America." *Haiti and the U.S.A.: Linked by History and Community.* http://www.haiti-usa.org/modern/index.php (accessed on April 1, 2004).

"A History of Chinese Americans in California." *National Park Service.* http://www.cr.nps.gov/history/online_books/5views/5views3.htm (accessed on April 1, 2004).

Immigration: The Living Mosaic of People, Culture, and Hope. http://library.thinkquest.org/20619/index.html (accessed on April 1, 2004).

"Landmarks in Immigration History." *Digital History.* http://www.digitalhistory.uh.edu/historyonline/immigration_chron.cfm (accessed on April 1, 2004).

Le, C. N. "The Model Minority Image." *Asian Nation: The Landscape of Asian America.* http://www.asian-nation.org/model-minority.shtml (accessed on April 1, 2004).

Logan, John R., and Glenn Deane. "Black Diversity in Metropolitan America." *Lewis Mumford Center for Comparative Urban and Regional Research, University at Albany.* http://mumford1.dyndns.org/cen2000/BlackWhite/BlackDiversityReport/black-diversity01.htm (accessed on April 1, 2004).

Lovgren, Stefan. "Who Were the First Americans?" *NationalGeographic.com.* http://news.nationalgeographic.com/news/2003/09/0903_03 0903_bajaskull.html (accessed on April 1, 2004).

Mosley-Dozier, Bernette A. "Double Minority: Haitians in America." *Yale–New Haven Teachers Institute.* http://www.yale.edu/ynhti/curriculum/units/1989/1/89.01.08.x.html (accessed on April 1, 2004).

RapidImmigration.com. http://www.rapidimmigration.com/usa/1_eng_immigration_history.html (accessed on April 1, 2004).

The Scottish History Pages. http://www.scotshistoryonline.co.uk/scothist.html (accessed on April 1, 2004).

Simkin, John. "Immigration." *Spartacus Educational.* http://www.spartacus. schoolnet.co.uk/USAimmigration.htm (accessed on April 1, 2004).

Spiegel, Taru. "The Finns in America." *Library of Congress: European Reading Room.* http://www.loc.gov/rr/european/FinnsAmer/finchro.html (accessed on April 1, 2004).

"The Story of Africa: Slavery." *BBC News.* http://www.bbc.co.uk/world service/africa/features/storyofafrica/9chapter9.shtml (accessed on April 1, 2004).

Trinklein, Mike, and Steve Boettcher. *The Oregon Trail.* http://www.isu. edu/%7Etrinmich/Oregontrail.html (accessed on April 1, 2004).

"U.S. Immigration." *Internet Modern History Sourcebook.* http://www. fordham.edu/halsall/mod/modsbook28.html (accessed on April 1, 2004).

Virtual Museum of New France. http://www.civilization.ca/vmnf/vmnfe. asp (accessed on April 1, 2004).

Index

Boldface indicates main entries and their page numbers; illustrations are marked by (ill.).